**Contemporary Ireland**

## Contemporary States and Societies

This series provides lively and accessible introductions to key countries and regions of the world, conceived and designed to meet the needs of today's students. The authors are all experts with specialist knowledge of the country or region concerned and have been chosen also for their ability to communicate clearly to a non-specialist readership. Each text has been specially commissioned for the series and is structured according to a common format.

*Published*

**Contemporary India**
Katharine Adeney
and Andrew Wyatt

**Contemporary Russia** (2ed)
Edwin Bacon with
Matthew Wyman

**Contemporary South Africa** (2ed)
Anthony Butler

**Contemporary France**
Helen Drake

**Contemporary America** (3ed)
Russell Duncan
and Joseph Goddard

**Contemporary China**
Alan Hunter and John Sexton

**Contemporary Japan** (2ed)
Duncan McCargo

**Contemporary Britain** (2ed)
John McCormick

**Contemporary Latin America** (2ed)
Ronaldo Munck

**Contemporary Ireland**
Eoin O'Malley

*Forthcoming*

**Contemporary Spain**
Paul Kennedy

**Contemporary Asia**
John McKay

*Also planned*

**Contemporary Africa**
**Contemporary Europe**
**Contemporary Germany**

Contemporary States and Societies
Series Standing Order
ISBN 978–0–333–75402–3 hardback
ISBN 978–0–333–80319–6 paperback
(*outside North America only*)

You can receive future titles in this series as they are published by placing a standing order. Please contact your bookseller or, in the case of difficulty, write to us at the address below with your name and address, the title of the series and the ISBN quoted above.

Customer Services Department, Palgrave Macmillan Ltd
Houndmills, Basingstoke, Hampshire RG21 6XS, England, UK.

# Contemporary Ireland

Eoin O'Malley

First published 2011 by
PALGRAVE MACMILLAN

Palgrave Macmillan in the UK is an imprint of Macmillan Publishers Limited, registered in England, company number 785998, of Houndmills, Basingstoke, Hampshire RG21 6XS.

Palgrave Macmillan in the US is a division of St Martin's Press LLC, 175 Fifth Avenue, New York, NY 10010.

Palgrave Macmillan is the global academic imprint of the above companies and has companies and representatives throughout the world.

Palgrave® and Macmillan® are registered trademarks in the United States, the United Kingdom, Europe and other countries.

ISBN  978–0–230–51669–4          hardback
ISBN  978–0–230–51670–0          paperback

This book is printed on paper suitable for recycling and made from fully managed and sustained forest sources. Logging, pulping and manufacturing processes are expected to conform to the environmental regulations of the country of origin.

A catalogue record for this book is available from the British Library.

A catalog record for this book is available from the Library of Congress.

10   9   8   7   6   5   4   3   2   1
20  19  18  17  16  15  14  13  12  11

Printed and bound in China

# Contents

# List of Illustrations, Maps, Figures, Tables and Boxes

## Illustrations

## Maps

## Figures

## Tables

## Boxes

# Preface and Acknowledgements

It might be considered unwise for someone who lives in and works in a country to write a book on that country. What is commonplace to the native might be of interest to the outsider; what the natives obsess about may not be so important. Perspective is lost. Having lived and worked outside Ireland before, I think I know what aspects of Irish society are different and interesting. I wrote this book while on sabbatical in Almuñécar (Granada), Spain, which I think gives me some sense of looking at the country from the outside. I'd like to thank Javier Sánchez, the librarian in Almuñécar, for so graciously allowing me work in the library; my Head of School, John Doyle, for allowing me a semester off teaching to work on this and other projects. I have benefited from discussion on Ireland with many of my colleagues, including Francesco Cavatorta, Michael Gallagher, John Garry, Iain McMenamin, Ken McDonagh, Adam McAuley and Garrett O'Boyle. I'd also like to thank Steven Kennedy and Stephen Wenham at Palgrave Macmillan for their forbearance.

But my greatest debt is to my family. My wife, Catherine Lynch, puts up with too much, especially my preference for work over child-care (no one shouts at me in work!). My children, Martha, Pepe and Donogh, who, through their all too regular arrival, have delayed my writing of this book, have also given me a reason to care about the future of Ireland. I hope, when you learn to read, this book helps you understand the country as it was when you were born. I dedicate this book to them.

EOIN O'MALLEY

The author and publishers would like to thank the following who have kindly given permission for the use of copyright material:

Des O'Malley for Illustration 1.2; Houses of the Oireachtas for Illustrations 1.3, 1.4 and 4.2; J.B. Terrins for Illustration 2.2; Library of Congress for Illustrations 2.3 and 8.2; London School of Economics and Political Science for Illustration 4.1; Office of Public Works for Illustration 4.3; Kenneth Benoit and Michael Laver for Figure 5.2, which originally appeared as Figure 7 in 'Mapping the Irish policy space: voter and party spaces in preferential elections', *Economic and Social Review* (2005); Central Bank of Ireland for Illustration 7.1; Zachary Gillman for Illustration 7.2; Julien Behal/ PA Wire for Illustration 8.1 (photo taken 23 June 2008 for Concern Worldwide); Irish Defence Forces for Illustration 8.3.

Every effort has been made to contact all the copyright-holders, but if any have been inadvertently overlooked the publishers will be pleased to make the necessary arrangements at the first opportunity.

# List of Abbreviations

| | |
|---|---|
| BoP | balance of payments |
| CAP | Common Agricultural Policy |
| DUP | Democratic Unionist Party |
| ECB | European Central Bank |
| EEC | European Economic Community |
| EMS | European Monetary System |
| EMU | economic and monetary union |
| ERM | Exchange Rate Mechanism |
| EU | European Union |
| FAI | Football Association of Ireland |
| FDI | foreign direct investment |
| GAA | Gaelic Athletic Association |
| GDP | gross domestic product |
| GFA | Good Friday Agreement |
| GNI | gross national income |
| GNP | gross national product |
| IBEC | Irish Business and Employers Confederation |
| ICTU | Irish Congress of Trades Unions |
| IDA | Industrial Development Authority |
| IFA | Irish Farmers' Association |
| IMF | International Monetary Fund |
| IPP | Irish Parliamentary Party |
| IRA | Irish Republican Army |
| IRB | Irish Republican Brotherhood |
| NICRA | Northern Ireland Civil Rights Association |
| NATO | North Atlantic Treaty Organization |
| OECD | Organisation for Economic Co-operation and Development |
| PDs | Progressive Democrats |
| PR-STV | proportional representation by single transferable vote |
| R&D | research and development |
| SDLP | Social Democratic and Labour Party |

| | |
|---|---|
| UN | United Nations |
| UUP | Ulster Unionist Party |
| UVF | Ulster Volunteer Force |
| WTO | World Trade Organization |
| WVS | World Values Survey |

# Introduction

Ireland was for most of its history a small, rather insignificant island at the edge of Europe, which for most of history meant the outer edge of the known world – *la divisa dal mondo ultima Irlanda* (Beckett, 1981: 14). It had no great natural resources, no political power, an underdeveloped economy, and was sufficiently unattractive that the Romans, who named it Hibernia or 'wintry place', did not try to conquer it. Ireland's underdevelopment in comparison with its wealthy neighbours has been a feature through most of its existence. Not long ago one prominent Irish historian described Ireland as a 'small retarded country' (Lee, 1989: 635). The causes of its backwardness are not clear, but it was not because it was isolated from the outside world. Ireland was the subject of migration, invasion and assimilation of various groups throughout its history. Groups from Ireland even invaded and controlled parts of Scotland and Wales. More recently Ireland's significant emigration meant that it had an impact on other countries and others on it.

But Ireland was never an important country, or even a contented country. Irish politics has rarely been settled for long periods. An English civil servant of the sixteenth century, observing the disturbed nature of Irish affairs, declared that there would never be an end to Ireland's wars (Beckett, 1981: 13), and this instability undoubtedly hampered Ireland's development. Effectively a colony of Britain during the UK's industrial revolution, Ireland suffered a devastating famine and economic stagnation which halved the island's population through starvation and emigration. A resurgent nationalism led to greater instability, and eventually to a messy independence hampered by a civil war. Yet Ireland became a remarkably stable democracy – something that one might expect to have induced economic growth – but failed to succeed economically, leading some in the 1950s to question the viability of the state.

Ireland's discontent seemed to have ended. A recent Economist Intelligence Unit analysis of quality of life put Ireland as the best country in the world to live in. This is probably caused by Ireland's remarkable economic growth, which saw it go from 'the poorest of the rich' to one of the world's wealthiest countries. Despite the economic crisis and the intervention of the IMF, Ireland is still the fifth best place in the world to live according to the 2010 UN Development Index. Ireland remains much wealthier than it was before the advent of the Celtic Tiger phenomenon and there is no expectation that it will return to 1980s or even 1990s levels of wealth. This wealth is matched by political freedoms, reasonably stable family life and strong communities, and Ireland has maintained some of its distinctive culture. A Eurobarometer survey in 2009 showed that 92 per cent of the Irish are satisfied with their quality of life (the EU-27 average is 83 per cent), although it also showed that the Irish are pessimistic about the country's prospects. Other surveys indicate that Ireland is no longer a peripheral and inward-looking country; rather it is one of the most globalized countries in the world. So while Ireland may be stable and wealthy, it is not that Irish society has not undergone remarkable changes – the immigrant population has increased from negligible levels to ten per cent of the population in as many years. Where it was once unusual to see a black person in the capital city, Dublin, now provincial towns have African and South American communities.

This unprecedented transformation is not restricted to the economy and society. Many things seemed to be going right for Ireland – even the ongoing (and, some argue, unsolvable) division in Northern Ireland is largely peaceful. However, Ireland's story is not all good news. Ireland still has high levels of poverty and inequality. Associated social problems such as gangland crime, street violence and under-age drinking appear to be increasing. There is a risk that racial tensions may emerge. The economic crisis has left deep scars on Ireland's social, economic, political and physical landscape. If Ireland was at a crossroads in the 1960s, where it chose the road of modernization, it is now again at a crossroads, being forced to decide how to deal with an economic crisis on a scale not imagined by policy makers or citizens just a few years earlier. Yet it is still surprisingly settled. There is no unrest such as you see in other European countries suffering similar recessions. This book will address this paradox and look at Ireland, its history and influences, and at the operation of the social, political and economic systems. It will study the major changes Ireland is undergoing, their causes and their consequences.

*Table 0.1*   Quick facts about Ireland 2009

| | |
|---|---|
| Official name: | Éire or in English, Ireland (also known as Republic of Ireland). |
| Capital: | Dublin |
| Area: | 70,282 sq. km (The island of Ireland is 84,421 sq. km) |
| Population: | 4.4m |
| Population density: | 63.4 per sq. km |
| Population growth rate per annum: | 1.88% (2005–09) |
| Languages: | English and Irish (Gaelic). Other languages are spoken by immigrants |
| Religion: | Roman Catholic (91%), minority of Protestants (Church of Ireland) and other religions |
| GDP: | €159bn (US$ 210bn) |
| Per capita GDP: | US$ 38,430 |
| GDP at PPP*: | 97.8 (USA=100) |
| Origin of GDP: | Agriculture 4.6%; Industry 46%; Services 49.4% |
| Urban population: | 59.9% |
| Literacy: | 99% |
| Infant mortality: | 3.0 per 1,000 live births (USA 7.0) |
| Human Development Index: | 96.5 |
| Life expectancy: | 79.7 years |
| Government/State type: | Parliamentary democracy/republic. Independent state, comprising 26 counties of the 32 counties on the island of Ireland, since 1922. Formerly British colony. |
| Administration: | Unitary |
| Executive: | Taoiseach (Prime minister) and cabinet |
| Legislature: | Houses of the Oireachtas (parliament). Dáil Éireann directly elected lower house with 166 members) and Seanad Éireann (indirectly elected upper house with 60 members). Have concurrent terms of up to five years. |
| Party structure: | Multiparty with one hitherto dominant party (Fianna Fáil). Coalition government is the norm. |
| Judiciary: | Independent judiciary. The highest court is the Supreme Court |
| Head of State: | President Mary McAleese (1997–2011) |
| Head of government: | Enda Kenny (2011–) |

* Purchasing price parity – a way of estimating level of wealth based on the prices in the country.

*Sources*: Data from Central Statistics Office; Human Development Index Report 2009.

**What is Ireland?**

Ireland, sometimes known as the Republic of Ireland, is a nation-state. That is, a set of sovereign institutions forming a state that identifies itself as ethnically distinct from those outside its borders, and governing a people who regard themselves as part of that ethnic group. However, the Irish state itself is contested. It is not even clear what its name is! Many regard the Irish nation as encompassing the whole island of Ireland, yet the state only extends to 26 of the 32 counties of the island. The other six counties form Northern Ireland, which is a part of the United Kingdom of Great Britain and Northern Ireland. A majority in Northern Ireland regard themselves as British, but a significant and growing minority see themselves as Irish and wish to be governed from Dublin rather than London or even Belfast.

Others, radical Irish and British nationalists, regard the Irish state as illegitimate, but for very different reasons. Some radical Irish nationalists argue that the Irish government had no right to allow the partition of the country, and that only the majority of the whole island can make legitimate decisions. For these, many of whom are associated with the violent campaigns of the Provisional IRA, there is no desire to assimilate the 'six counties', as Northern Ireland is often referred to, into the Republic of Ireland, or the 'Free State' as it is sometime pejoratively known. Rather, they would prefer a revolution which would instigate a 32-county socialist republic. British nationalists challenge the legitimacy of the Irish state on different grounds. Although few British nationalists (normally called unionists or loyalists) would like to see the re-assimilation of the whole island of Ireland into the United Kingdom, they regard Ireland as an aggressor state which (indirectly) supports violence against their state. The nature of the Northern Ireland conflict will be discussed further in Chapters 2 on history and 5 on civil society.

There is also disagreement about what it means to be Irish. For many, Irishness is associated with Gaelic culture – that is, the culture of ancient Ireland and Scotland. Indeed the new state of Ireland from the 1920s embraced this interpretation with alacrity and (successfully) marginalized the significant Anglo-Irish population, (less successfully) attempting to suppress liberal British and European influences on Irish life. For some in the state one's 'Irishness' could be measured, and for them the best measurement was antipathy to the English.

## Why study Ireland?

Given, as I have just argued, that Ireland is a small insignificant country, one might question the need to spend time reading about such a country. Ireland is important for many reasons. In itself it is genuinely interesting. It can be reasonably argued that Ireland is different in terms of almost every social phenomenon – economics, society, culture and politics. Uniquely in Western Europe it has had recent experience as a colony. It also possessed a post-colonial economy – poor, agrarian and dominated by emigration to the former colonizer. The social structure was traditional, and society was domi-nated by a strong institutional Catholic church which still flexed its political muscles. Culturally it seemed more traditional and resistant to the forces of modernization in the rest of Europe. It is one of the few places in Europe where traditional culture is still genuinely popular. The political map is unique in that it contains no major left-wing party. It is seen as a classless society, yet has some of the highest levels of income inequality in the western world. It was involved in one of the few violent territorial disputes in Western Europe. These facts seem incongruous in a stable north-west European democracy. This alone would make it a fascinating country of study. But add to this the rapid change it is undergoing, and Ireland becomes a real-world experiment in social change. Ireland's many differences from the rest of Europe make it a useful comparator for understanding political, economic and social phenomena more generally.

Ireland is also interesting because it is the product of a successful and reasonably recent nationalist revolution. The victors in that revo-lution made a deliberate attempt to fashion a state which rejected the influence of its colonizer, Britain. Yet, as we see below, it is still heavily influenced by Britain. The Irish experience can teach us about post-revolutionary democratic states in central and eastern Europe.

Despite, or perhaps because of its isolation, Ireland has been genuinely influential in the world around it. Politically it is not powerful, yet because of emigration to two of the world's most powerful countries, the UK and USA, Ireland is better known than other countries of its size. Politically the Irish-American lobby is among the most influential ethnic-based sectional groups in the USA. Through religious institutions Ireland has influenced many develop-ing countries. Through the expansion of the British Empire, Irish people became influential in Canada, Australia and New Zealand. Irish names pervade politics and society in some countries one might not have expected. So, for example, Spain had a Prime Minister O'Donnell; important wines and brandies in France bear names like Lynch and Hennessy; Bernardo O'Higgins was the liberator of Chile. Even Che Guevara was of Irish descent. Nowadays the ubiquitous Irish pub is a feature of cities the world over. Irish musicians and writers are important on the world stage, and one does not struggle to name two famous Irish people – which is not the case for some countries. To understand the impact of the Irish on countries such as the USA, it is important to understand Ireland.

## The British influence

There is a bar in Dublin's north inner city, which during the 2010 Six Nations rugby tournament displayed the flags of five of the six nations taking part: France, Ireland, Italy, Scotland and Wales. Probably for political reasons, the English Flag of St. George was not displayed. The same bar advertised on a blackboard below that one could watch Tottenham Hotspur playing Chelsea. This type of situation illustrates the attitude of many Irish to Britain. While there is a deep antipathy to many overtly British or English symbols (the Welsh and Scottish are popular), at the same time most people share interests with and are culturally quite similar to the English, and few see any incongruity in this.

Every aspect of Irish life is indelibly affected by the influence of Britain, Ireland's neighbour and for a long time its ruler. Britain's interest in Ireland was probably in the broader context of European politics – that Ireland could be used as a base from which to invade its more populous and more powerful neighbour. This worked against Ireland's interest, as English and later British rulers, unwilling to allow Ireland to be used as a staging post for invasion, attempted to control the country. Ireland was a 'lordship' of the English crown from the twelfth century, and in the mid-sixteenth century, Henry VIII, the king of England, assumed the title 'King of Ireland'. In 1801, following the Act of Union, Ireland joined with Great Britain to form the United Kingdom of Great Britain and Ireland and was subsumed into the British state. Throughout this period the British, or the English, attempted to impose 'English civility' on an often resistant Ireland. However it is misleading to suggest that Britain's attempts failed and that the Irish on independence reasserted their native, Gaelic ways. Nor is it plausible to suggest that the Irish consistently resisted British influence. In many ways the Irish readily accepted British influences, innovations and institutions, and there has been no successful attempt to revert to Gaelic forms of statehood. To categorize Irish history as a conflict between Gaelic traditions and Anglicized traditions is an inaccurate simplification. In fact, more accurately, we might see four traditions in Ireland: the Gaelic, the Anglo-Norman or Old English, the New English and the non-conformist Ulster-Scots. The Old English became assimilated into Irish life and there are now no discernable divisions between the Old English and the native Irish. The Old English remained faithful to Roman Catholicism following the Protestant Reformation, which gave them shared interests with the native Irish. However, those in the Gaelic tradition practised a Catholicism that was unrecognizable to visitors from continental Europe. And for many centuries the Old English, who were better off, tended to marry within their own group, be educated separately and attend different churches – though one should not overemphasize such divisions. The Old English were distinct from the New English, who were Protestant, and who, rather than assimilate with the Irish, attempted to rule them as a foreign power. The New English successfully took lands from Catholics – in 1641 Catholics held about 60 per cent of land, but by the early 1700s this was just fourteen per cent (Foster, 1988: 115).

The New English attempts to colonize might be considered a failure. The English were rarely comfortable as rulers, continually having to put down nationalist skirmishes. There was successful resistance to most attempts to impose the English established religion (even in Ulster where Protestants form a majority). It was probably the attempt to associate Catholicism with disloyalty to the Crown that united disparate groups against British rule. It is not clear that the Planters, as those who migrated in the seventeenth century can be termed, attempted to convert natives. Many preferred to maintain their elite position as the Protestant 'Ascendancy'. Outside the area around Dublin under full Crown control known as 'the Pale' and the cities, the Irish language remained reasonably strong until the famine in the mid-nineteenth century. Even today, many aspects of Irish culture, such as music and sport, are distinct from England's. Ireland's economy did not follow the British route of industrialization except in a small number of industries – brewing, linen and ship-building – and then only around Belfast. That said, the Irish were not clamouring for independence. Contemporary reports of a royal visit to Dublin in 1911 show a city united in excitement and joy. Andrews

(1979: 9, 45), an Irish republican activist, reported that, at the start of the twentieth century,

> Dublin was a British city and accepted itself as one. Its way of life, its standards and values, its customs were identical with those of say Birmingham or Manchester . . . Ireland was at peace . . . The Union Jack was to be seen everywhere. Irish-Irelanders were looked on as a joke . . . in cricket we followed the fortunes of Surrey and Kent.

However, from the time of the French revolution and the rise in European nationalism in the nineteenth century, there was agreement among representatives of three of the traditions in Ireland that British rule was not in Ireland's interests. Though many 'Home Rule' leaders were Anglo-Irish or New English, the native Irish and the Old English were most vociferous in their desire for a Dublin government. 'Irish Irelanders' looked to a rejection of all things English, favouring the reinstatement of Gaelic values and institutions. The second tradition was the Irish Enlightenment, influenced by ideas such as liberalism and parliamentary democracy. There was an acceptance of the British way of doing things, but an attack on what was seen as the malign British administration of Irish affairs.

The Irish Enlightenment tradition dominated mainstream politics in Ireland for most of the nineteenth century. And had it not been for the outbreak of the First World War, a Home Rule Bill may have been enacted. However the Irish Irelanders were handed the initiative when a small revolt in 1916 provoked a British over-reaction which gave popular support to those looking for independence. Though the revolt was led by Irish Irelanders, the newly independent state retained and even imitated much of the practice of British democracy. Britain's political and legal systems were adopted in the new Irish state. Legislation passed in the UK is still active in Ireland. Irish policy makers tended to look to what Britain had done when problems arose. Ireland's administrative structure is a copy of the British to the extent that secondary schools' final exam results are released on the same day. Ironically after independence English ways are now almost fully accepted in the country. Throughout much of this period there was a rhetorical and often real anti-English sentiment but the influence continued (the phrase 'Burn everything British except their coal' was current in the 1920s and 1930s). But Britain remained the major trading partner and destination for Irish emigrants. Ireland was

**Illustration 0.1   Irish street signs**

Many place and street names show the legacy of British rule. Street signs
were replaced after independence with bilingual ones. The names of some
towns and streets were also changed – Kingstown (outside Dublin)
became Dún Laoghaire. Others, such as Prince of Wales Terrace, remained
unchanged. The old Gaelic Script can also be seen used for translations. It
is also common to see postboxes with the British Monarch's inscription.
These were kept after independence but painted green.

stuck as 'an island behind an island', and when Britain suffered its post-war decline, Ireland's economy was tied to the declining British economy. At a cultural level the availability of British newspapers and radio and television transmissions on the east coast of Ireland may have done more to anglicize independent Ireland than the centuries of political occupation. This availability caused successive governments to introduce and maintain a programme of censorship to prevent the spread of British influence and to protect Irish morals. Throughout independent Ireland's history, it remained in some ways a province of England. Brown (2004: 205) points out that styles and fashion were influenced by English tastes. Success, whether in sport, the arts or academia, was usually measured by success in England, and this remains somewhat true today.

Probably the event which untied Ireland from Britain most was not independence but membership of the European Economic Community (EEC), now the European Union (EU). Here Ireland became a nominally equal player on an international stage. Through the EU, Ireland was forced to make certain changes and voluntarily made others. The EU exposed Ireland and Irish policy makers to new ideas and influences. The Irish currency's parity with sterling ended only in 1979 and the Irish economy has become more internationalized. Ireland is now more confidently independent, but the links with the UK remain strong.

## Recent changes in Ireland

Ireland has undergone rapid social change in the last twenty years in a number of areas. These changes, which are introduced here, will be looked at in more detail throughout the book.

### Demographic

Ireland's population, which had declined for a century, began to turn around in the 1960s. Table 0.2 shows the growth of the population. This growth has accelerated in the last decade, with high immigration combined with a small baby-boom making Ireland the only country in Europe with significant population growth caused by both immigration *and* a natural increase. We also see non-Irish immigrants for the first time, not merely Irish people returning. The immigration is remarkable when one considers that an Irish minister excused the emigration of the 1980s with the breezy exclamation that 'after all, we can't all live on a small island' (*Newsweek,* 19 October 1987). Other major shifts have also occurred in last half-century. The population has shifted eastwards and into cities, with Dublin and its three neighbouring counties now accounting for 40 per cent of the population. Dublin is about eight times bigger than the next biggest city, Cork. Almost two-thirds of the population now lives in urban areas, up from a third in the 1930s.

*Societal*

More significant than the demographic shifts have been the societal changes. While Dublin was always a dominant city in Ireland, for most of the last century Dublin was akin to small provincial towns in other western countries. Ireland was considered one of the most religious countries in Europe, and the Catholic Church appeared to hold great power over politicians. Dublin and Ireland have become more cosmopolitan and more liberal. Irish social attitudes have changed radically, with people becoming less authoritarian in their outlook. The change can be illustrated by the fact in 1991 a music shop was fined £500 for selling condoms and told by the judge that it got off lightly. At the same time the successful presidential candidate, Mary Robinson, a liberal lawyer, deliberately challenged the legitimacy of the law by buying condoms from the shop. By the end of the decade the Irish government was spending money promoting the use of condoms. Films such as Monty Python's *Life of Brian* were banned as recently as the 1980s for offending the Catholic Church. Divorce was banned in Ireland from 1925 until 1996 and then was only legalized following a bitter and closely fought referendum campaign. There are no calls to reinstate the ban. However abortion is still illegal and few politicians have any appetite to start a debate.

The situation of women at work has also changed. Until recently Ireland had a very high proportion of women working in the home. Indeed for many women working in banks or the civil service, getting married meant being forced to leave the workforce. Female labour force participation has risen from seven per cent in 1971 to 33 per cent in 1991 to over 50 per cent two decades later. There has been a huge expansion in education since the 1960s. Whereas a majority of those now over 60 only received primary education, over half of today's school leavers enter tertiary education – though this masks great variation by social class.

*Table 0.2*  Changes in Irish society

|  | 1961–70 | 1971–80 | 1981–90 | 1991–2000 | 2001–09 |
|---|---|---|---|---|---|
| Population | 2.893m | 3.177m | 3.454m | 3.653m | 4.459m |
| Unemployment % | 5.4 | 7.7 | 14.7 | 11.1 | 4.4 |
| Average annual Migration per 1,000 of pop. | -4.7 | 1.8 | -5.9 | 3.7 | 9.2 |
| Urban population | 49.2 | 53.8 | 56.5 | 59.6 | 62.4 |
| % over 15 with 3rd level degree | <0.5 | 2.5 | 4.5 | 8.5 | 12.8 |
| GDP per head (EU-15 =100) | 62.1 | 59.3 | 68.7 | 89.0 | 131.5 |

*Sources*: Data from Central Statistics Office and Eurostat information.

## Economic

The most noted recent change in Ireland has been the economic boom. High growth in the 1990s and 2000s moved Ireland from one of the poor men of Europe to its rising star. Structurally, there has been a move away from agriculture, which has become much less important. Now the service sector accounts for more employment and wealth creation than any other sector. Total employment rose sharply as more people joined the workforce, and unemployment moved from a situation where one in five were unemployed in the 1980s to virtually full employment.

The Irish were not just more likely to find work in Ireland – they are also much richer, with some measures of wealth having put Ireland as the second wealthiest country in Europe, though these should be viewed with some scepticism. Much of this growth was linked to overheating in the property market. Property prices in Ireland rose by 200 per cent from 1997 to 2005. The subsequent collapse of the property market had a major impact on the banking system and the real economy, with emigration resuming and unemployment doubling. Ireland is once again coupled with southern European states.

## Political

Irish politics has been transformed in the last twenty years. Before the late 1980s the party system consisted of two large parties with one,

Fianna Fáil (a nationalist catch-all party), dominating and governing alone. Both were considered centre-right. A small Labour party also existed, which would seem anomalous in a country as poor as Ireland was. It was partly because Ireland was a homogeneous place with no obvious social or ethnic divisions which are usually thought to form the basis of the party system. A raft of new parties formed or became larger in the 1980s and 1990s. Fianna Fáil, which had previously refused to do so, entered coalition. Now coalition government is the norm where single party governments had previously been common. These new small parties have tried to create a left/right policy divide where none previously existed. In the 2011 general election Fianna Fáil's dominance was broken as it fell to just the third largest party in Ireland.

*Artistic*

Ireland, despite being the epitome of a traditional Catholic society, has produced some of the most radical and modern of writers. James Joyce, Oscar Wilde, Samuel Beckett and George Bernard Shaw all exiled themselves from Ireland but were undoubtedly influenced by Ireland. Many of these artists were critical of the new Irish state and what was imposed as 'Irish culture' and some had their works banned. However, there has recently been a revival in the popularity of traditional culture. The success of the show *Riverdance* is an example of this. Contemporary Ireland claims to cherish its artistic community – artists pay less tax on their earnings from artistic endeavours – and the country continues to produce artists and writers of note.

## Causes and consequences

This book is designed to provide the reader with a concise, readable yet sophisticated introduction to contemporary Ireland. The book outlines the structures and forces governing Irish society, politics and the economy without assuming any prior knowledge. It tells a story of Ireland and will reveal Ireland's puzzles and paradoxes. The puzzling aspects of Ireland's performance as a state are brought to the fore and questions posed. The book should stimulate the reader to think and perhaps read more widely about Ireland and the subject of rapid social change.

As well as telling a story, this book also has an argument. The main argument is that Ireland has changed dramatically in the last half-century. This description of a country in flux is not in itself difficult to sustain – throughout the book the reader will see constant and radical change depicted. At a glance, however, one might contest the causes and timing of the changes. The Irish performance in the 1980s was not radically different from that of the 1950s. Ireland still seemed gripped by pre-modern battles: with the church still wielding an influence in the politics of the country and nationalist rhetoric to the fore, violence continued to grip Northern Ireland. Nineteenth- and twentieth-century battles that shaped and modernized Europe seemed to have eluded Ireland. By contrast the changes from the late 1980s to today have been rapid and all-encompassing. It seemed Ireland finally awoke from a slumber it had been in for a century. However it will be shown here that many of the changes we see in contemporary Ireland either began in the 1960s or came about because of decisions taken then. Moreover it will also be shown that Ireland showed some signs of modernism in thought and culture and that its historic battles reflect those in the rest of Europe, but that conservative forces won the political battles.

This book also argues that the radical change we see is caused by political decisions. Politics has been the (not always conscious) driving force behind the changes. The political decision in the 1930s to follow nationalist economic policies increased barriers with its dominant trading partner, Britain. The protectionist policies led to severe economic hardships and stunted Ireland's growth. The decision in the late 1950s to reverse this policy and open up the Irish economy to foreign capital investment arguably led to a mini-boom in the 1960s. Ireland's membership of the EEC, later the EU, forced modernization on a sometimes unwilling political class. The oil crises of the 1970s, in which escalating oil prices caused worldwide recession and increased political competition in Ireland, caused parties to revert to populist economic policies that the country could barely afford. Decisions in 1987 by government and opposition politicians forced the country down a new path of fiscal rectitude or economic cutbacks which led directly to what is now known as the Celtic Tiger. But there was no single decision or even set of decisions that can conclusively be identified. The notable changes that have occurred in the last ten to fifteen years did not occur simply as a result of decisions made during that period. At a general level, though, Ireland moved from being a closed (closed-minded) country to one which allowed and even encouraged outside influence, and this must be considered important to the development of Ireland's economy and Irish society.

These decisions were not made by politicians in a vacuum. Politics was forced or enabled to take bold decisions because of the dire situations Ireland found itself in. So the decision to open up the economy in the late 1950s occurred because of the depression that saw 50,000 people leave Ireland each year. A generation of young post-revolutionary politicians took up this challenge with alacrity. In the late 1980s an equivalent recession enabled politicians to make structural changes to the Irish economy which would soon after lead to the boom Ireland enjoyed.

Ireland again faces a challenge to renew itself. It became comfortable as a European outpost for foreign business, without considering alternatives to that strategy. The recession means that emigration has once again started and the decisions to save parts of the banking industry will, it is estimated, be paid for by future generations of Irish people. There is little confidence in the political system. It remains to be seen whether the Irish can rise once again.

# 1

# The Historical Context

## Introduction: early Ireland

It has been remarked by an historian working on Ireland that the Irish have a more developed sense of history than any other people he knew (Richter, 1986: 41). But if the Irish are keenly aware of history, that history is often manipulated to suit those telling it. Thus the interpretations of history have changed significantly over time. Schoolchildren in Ireland were until quite recently taught a version of history that suited the political leaders of the state, but one that is highly contested by professional historians. A good example of this disjoint between popularly accepted historical interpretation and interpretations established and backed up by evidence relates to Ireland's early settlers.

If countries could have trademarks there is a good chance that Ireland's would be the word 'Celtic'. Most things Irish are ascribed the adjective Celtic to indicate their 'Irishness'. So we have the Celtic Tenors, the Celtic Tiger, the Boston Celtics, Glasgow Celtic and so on. A senior Irish politician recently claimed that Ireland was 'a Celtic and Christian country'. There is broad popular agreement that Ireland is a Celtic island and that the Irish are a Celtic people. Of course reality is always more nuanced. Ireland was not always an island and the Celts are only one of a line of invaders and settlers to occupy the land.

Those who first inhabited Ireland, probably from about 10,000 BCE, were not Celts. They may have been Basque in origin and come via the Atlantic route from what is today Northern Spain. If Ireland was invaded by a Celtic people it would probably have been around 5000 years ago – and not *ca.* 1,000 BCE as is commonly thought.

They too came from Northern Spain along the Atlantic maritime route. But these were just one line of a succession of invaders and the original inhabitants account for more Irish ancestry than the Celts. The fact that the Celts are probably thought to be the influential immigrants is because much of their language, which became Gaelic, and culture was adopted in Ireland. That the Irish now regard themselves as Celtic is as a result of much later nationalist writings. The myth of a once great Celtic civilization barely surviving under the yoke of a more ugly and brutal Anglo-Saxon culture was too useful for nationalists to pass up.

Though the country was not particularly populous, probably covered in forest, over time these people developed a reasonably sophisticated culture with, by 3,000 BCE, sufficient knowledge of astronomy to build impressive passage graves which were linked to the seasons. Ireland was an island at this stage and the closest sea crossing to what is now Britain was from the north-east of the island. The most important centres, including an early capital, were there.

**Illustration 1.1   The passage grave at Newgrange**

The passage grave at Newgrange is about 5,000 years old, predating the pyramids at Giza. It is one of three major prehistoric sites in the Boyne Valley. Measuring 75 metres across, it housed graves for large numbers of people over time rather than a single king. It is interesting not only for its size and age. The stones used to construct the grave came from up to 70 kilometres away. The decoration on the stones is among the best examples of prehistoric art in the world. The inner chamber is flooded with light at sunrise on the winter solstice indicating that the people who built it were learned in astronomy.

The migration of new groups with skills in iron, pottery and bronze probably led to some conflict but over time also to progress, as Ireland would have moved from hunting and gathering to cattle grazing and eventually arable farming. Archaeological evidence shows a highly skilled people capable of fashioning fine jewellery from gold. This evidence indicates that the people had an unusual quantity of disposable income and time to introduce ceremonies not directly linked to immediate survival. Ireland also seems to have had centres of continuous settlement, so the Boyne Valley and Hill of Tara in Co. Meath, were important sites for millennia (Davies, 1999: 32).

## Ireland's Golden Age and the Viking wars

Non-events are important in history and the decision by the Romans not to invade Ireland was probably one which can account for Ireland's peculiarly close attachment to native myth. There were relations with Roman Britain, mainly through trade. As Roman Britain was weakened in the first four centuries of the Christian era, the Irish settlement of Britain could begin with colonies in Wales, Cornwall and Scotland, some of which are reported to have survived until the tenth century (Ó Corráin, 1989: 6). These colonies were not those of a single ruler or even a conspiracy by a set of rulers in Ireland. Ireland, again despite the myth, was still not a unified country – it never had been. These closer relations with Britain through trade, but also through raids and enslavement, meant the Gaels were exposed to Christianity. Myth holds that Patrick came to Ireland and converted the country, but there is evidence of earlier Christian missionaries. Patrick was a Roman from Wales who had been taken as a slave to Ireland. His writings may be unreliable and it is probably not the case that he converted the Irish to Christianity in great numbers, but a myth grew up around Patrick, and it is his feast day that the Irish all over the world celebrate.

A notable feature of Christianity in Ireland is its monasticism. Monasteries became important institutions receiving funding from local kings, and these brought to Ireland an awareness of European culture and enabled the development of writing – though there is evidence that earlier exposure to Roman Britain enabled the development of *Ogham*, the first example of written Irish. Monasteries could be seen as contemporary university cities, although on a much smaller scale, with the provincial king perhaps living there. It was at this time that the great religious manuscripts, such as the Book of Kells, were written. The idea of a High Kingship of Ireland and other myths of national unity emerged at this time, in part from *An Lebor Gabála* (the Book of the Invasions of Ireland) which was written in the eleventh century, making it one of the earlier attempts at national consciousness creation. Irish religious leaders would have had sufficient power and resources to set up missions in other countries – particularly in Northern Europe which at the time was suffering from the chaos caused by the collapse of the Roman Empire. Ireland thus provided a haven for Christianity. The coming of Christianity did not have a major impact on Irish societal structure, which was still organized into a caste system of kings – there may have been over 100 kingdoms (*tuath*) in a country with a population of between half a million and a million people – lords and commons, and below that hereditary slaves, except that the clergy were now afforded legal privilege. Brehon Law, which reflected this strongly inegalitarian societal structure, was developed and codified in this period. This was a thoroughly Christianized law which would also have encompassed earlier Gaelic legal practice, and evidence suggests that it was uniform throughout the country.

The wealth developed in Ireland between the eighth and tenth centuries did not go unnoticed. Norsemen or Vikings (mainly from Norway), who had developed the fine sailing techniques enabling them to 'hit and run', first raided Ireland in the very late eighth century. These raids became more intense and more daring, moving inland by following the rivers. They set up camps to winter in Ireland in the mid-ninth century, and within a few decades had made semi-permanent settlements and set up alliances with Irish kings in internal power struggles. By the mid-tenth century they were fundamental to the founding of the most important Irish cities, Dublin and Limerick, and continued to trade with the native Irish – by this time allowing the monasteries to survive. Indeed they may have been converted to Christianity (or thought it opportune to do so). The different Norse settlers were used by increasingly powerful kings, who could create laws and impose taxes in the eleventh and twelfth centuries in the different parts of Ireland, each in order to further their own power. The Vikings had a major impact on Irish society, founding cities, giving words to the native Irish language and many place names. They introduced the first coins to Ireland, further enhancing trade. Their impact was less obvious as they integrated with the native people.

## The Norman conquests and Gaelic recovery

The wars over the High Kingship of Ireland were central to the next great migration to Ireland, and one which more than any other event would affect Irish society. Dublin, which was possibly a place apart from the rest of Ireland, had become important for achieving the High Kingship of Ireland. As a centre for trade with Britain and as the most powerful city close to Tara, the mythological seat of the High Kings, it became important for any serious pretender to that throne to control Dublin.

One ousted ruler of Dublin, Diarmuid MacMurrogh, invited Anglo-Norman knights based in Wales to assist him retake his throne, offering the leader, Richard de Clare or Strongbow, his daughter Aoife's hand in marriage. Henry II, the king of England who had been granted the Papal right to rule Ireland, approved this venture, though he was uneasy about ceding so much power to these knights. The Normans successfully took Dublin and much of Leinster; the King then granted Strongbow some lands, taking the city of Dublin and the ports on the east coast of Ireland for himself. Many of the Gaelic aristocracy welcomed the English interest in Ireland as a means of controlling the Anglo-Norman knights. Henry then used Ireland to reward his own supporters and strengthen his hold on the kingdom of England. The Irish lords seemed to accept the Anglo-Normans or English invaders without much resistance; they may have felt that in granting them certain lands they could secure their positions. When Henry's son John assumed the throne, he tried to secure his territory by building castles where English rule prevailed, mainly in the east and south. This influence was sometimes welcomed as a rein on the more ambitious elements of the Norman invaders.

In those areas where the Normans were secure, they set about importing tenants from Anglo-Norman Britain. They settled mainly along rivers in the lush valleys and built or added to towns. For the native Irish serfs life would not have changed greatly, but for the aristocracy in those areas of Norman settlement, their status was reduced to that of serfs, so many would have left to resettle outside areas of Norman control. By contrast, all Norman immigrants enjoyed the status of freemen. This also led to the English language taking root in these towns.

John also set about putting in place a governmental system, and a decree was promulgated that the laws and customs of England be observed in Ireland. Common law was thus introduced, though as the

**Illustration 1.2   King John's Castle in Limerick**

The Normans set about securing power in certain parts of Ireland by building great castles in the principal cities. Limerick, which had been founded by the Vikings, was one of the country's most important cities and King John set about protecting it by building a castle and walling the city in the early 13th century. The castle was later important as the scene of the Siege of Limerick in 1691, when King William of Orange King defeated James's forces and effectively forced some Old English and Irish nobility to flee Ireland.

extent of Norman control was limited, there is evidence that Brehon Law was still practised until the seventeenth century. The Anglo-Normans also took control of the church and attempted to ensure that no Gaelic Irish would be promoted to Bishop.

By the thirteenth century the English no longer had clear military superiority, and some revolts took place, particularly in the north and west. These revolts and the use of Irish lands as a resource to support fighting other wars meant that England required local (English) barons for soldiers and taxation, and ceded them more control of Ireland. A reduction in agricultural prices in Europe also meant that the Irish estates were less profitable, and therefore less worth fighting for. The English lost interest in Ireland and the 'English men of Irish birth' (or Old English) were left to run the country, fighting among themselves for control of territories. Within those areas of 'English' control, the Anglo-Norman FitzGeralds eventually dominated and attempted to make the position of King's representative in Ireland an hereditary one. The disruption caused by the aristocratic factionalism appalled many in the Pale (the counties around Dublin which were under complete control of the Old English).

The Irish chieftains also attempted to recover a sense of their own identity by eulogizing early Gaelic achievements. Especially in areas outside the Pale and the cities there was a certain intermingling of the Gaelic Irish and Old English which by the fifteenth and sixteenth centuries would have resulted in some Anglicization of the Gaelic lords and Gaelicization of the Old English (Duffy *et al.*, 2001: 38–9). By the early sixteenth century, outside the Pale and the cities Irish would have been spoken and English control was only nominal.

## The Tudor conquests

Henry VIII ascended the throne of England in 1509, but like his father Henry VII, the first Tudor monarch, his control of the English crown was insecure. The Tudors viewed Ireland as a potential threat because it could be used by the French, Spanish or internal enemies as a staging post for invading England. Elements within Anglo-Irish society had proved unreliable to the English crown, and Henry was left with no practical option except to work with powerful families such as the Butlers and the FitzGeralds in order to secure such frontier as existed with Gaelic Ireland. However this costly arrangement was not ideal for Henry. From 1534 the Pale was brought under closer political control of London and the Kingdom of Ireland was declared in 1541. Conflict ensued, some of it provoked by New English military intent on securing a gift of lands for their services, leading to the proposal that Ireland be colonized with 'Englishmen born in England'.

The problem of the Old English was exacerbated by religious differences. The Reformation took an unusual route in England, arising as it did from Henry's refusal to accept the Pope's authority on the grounds of his personal circumstances. He became supreme head of the Church of England, but the Old English in Ireland maintained their Catholicism even when it would have been opportune to convert. The Old English now found that the crown to which they were loyal rejected the religious head to which they were also loyal. The religious prejudice in England gave further impetus to the need to renew the colonization of Ireland. The Tudors enabled this through

*Table 1.1*   Key dates in Irish history

| | |
|---|---|
| **432** | Traditional date of St. Patrick's arrival |
| **9th–10th century** | Viking raids on Ireland lead to some permanent settlements |
| **1014** | Battle of Clontarf – BrianBorú killed ending the brief unity of Ireland under a single High Kingship |
| **1167** | Diarmait Mac Murchada returns to Ireland with help of Norman forces |
| **1204, 1210** | Dublin Castle established as royal centre for administration of Ireland. Irish kings submit to King John |
| **1607–8** | Ulster kings pronounced traitors. Decision to plant six Ulster counties |
| **1650s** | Cromwellian conquest of Ireland and plantations |
| **1690s** | Williamite forces defeat James II forces in Ireland leading to Penal Laws |
| **1798** | Rising inspired by the French revolution fails |
| **1800** | Act of Union with Britain |
| **1829** | Catholic Emancipation Act permits Catholics sit in parliament |
| **1845–51** | The Irish Famine sees over a million die and more again emigrate. The Irish population halves. |
| **1858** | Irish Republican Brotherhood founded leading to a Fenian rising in 1867 |
| **Late 19th century** | The Church of Ireland is disestablished and Gladstone introduces land reform. Irish Parliamentary Party move for Home Rule. |
| **1914** | Home Rule suspended due to outbreak of War |
| **1916–1923** | Easter Rising in Dublin fails, but leads to War of Independence and Treaty, which is narrowly approved in Dáil. Ireland is partitioned. Civil war ensues. |
| **1937** | New Constitution of Ireland cuts ties with Britain |
| **1969** | Outbreak of 'The Troubles' in Northern Ireland following civil rights marches |
| **1973** | Ireland joins the European Economic Community with the UK and Denmark |
| **1998** | Peace agreement signed in Northern Ireland leading to devolved power-sharing arrangements |
| **2008** | Bank Guarantee Scheme introduced |
| **2010** | EU/IMF financial loans imposed |

the confiscation of lands; most church property was seized. There began a continual series of 'plantations' or colonizations of Protestant English, often in response to military needs. By 1703 three-quarters of the population was Catholic, but they owned just 14 per cent of the land.

The greatest resistance to the Tudor policy occurred in Ulster. The west and north of Ireland had been the least anglicized areas, but a war culminating in the defeat of the Gaelic lords acting with Spanish assistance at the Battle of Kinsale forced them to accept English rule (much of the Gaelic aristocracy fled the country a few years later). The Old English continued in the uncomfortable position of loyalty to a crown that degraded them, removing some lands from those who refused to show loyalty, that is, convert to Protestantism. It was at this time that Ulster was planted (see Box 1.2) with consequences that can still be felt today. From 1641 resistance to the plantations and English rule increased and this was met by Oliver Cromwell's army which successfully put down the insurrection and attempted to systematically de-Catholicize Ireland by retaining lands in three of the four provinces for Protestants only. The transfer of lands at this time meant the Old English were reduced in status and this seems to have driven them into coalition with their co-religionists, the Gaelic Irish. The late seventeenth century was a time of further upheaval when Ireland was the venue for a broader war for the Kingdoms of England and Scotland. James II's taking of that throne was welcomed by the Old English and Gaelic Irish who could at least expect a respite from religious persecution. An army was raised for James's needs, which raised fears among Protestants in England and Ireland who offered the throne to William of Orange. He was able to take the English throne easily, and with the support of the French, James fled to Ireland where William eventually defeated the Jacobite army. The Catholic aristocracy was offered some concessions in the Treaty of Limerick 1691, but many chose to leave the country.

## Protestant Ascendancy

Ireland in the preceding century had set in train laws and institutions which gave a great deal of power to the Protestant population. The term 'Protestant Ascendancy' refers to this group's Ascendancy over Catholics. The new social elite was mainly English with some Scottish settlers. This group, frightened by the ease with which some of these gains were reversed between 1685 and 1690, wished to ensure this could not happen again and so further pursued a state which enabled its hold on power. It introduced more penal laws – discriminatory laws aimed at Catholic clergy and laity – which, among other things, forbade the keeping of weapons, travel overseas for education, running schools and inheriting land. A particularly small-minded restriction was the banning of Catholics from owning horses valued over five pounds. These laws were later presented to Irish schoolchildren and used by nationalists as evidence of the discriminatory state. Had they been strictly enforced, (organized) Catholicism might have been seen to die out, and there was certainly no attempt to convert Catholics. This was possibly because to do so would weaken the Ascendancy of the small but powerful Protestant elite. Recent research suggests that these laws were only partially enforced – certainly there is evidence of fine Catholic churches being built around this time, and over time some of the laws were formally repealed. That Maynooth, a state-funded seminary, was founded in 1795 indicates tolerance towards Catholicism. The London administration and its representatives in Dublin Castle were far less enthused by penal laws, and it is the attitude to London that created the main political divide in Irish Protestant political circles.

The parties represented in parliament were the Whigs and Tories. Though these had the same names as the parties in Westminster, the Irish parties were slightly different. Tories were more patriotic, looking for a greater degree of freedom for the Irish parliament (Whitehall, the seat of government in London, maintained a veto over Irish legislation through Poyning's Law) and for greater control over the administration in Dublin Castle, and suspecting that London would not defend Protestant interests. The Whigs tended to be liberal or radical, tolerant of London, Dublin Castle and dissenters, and more likely to be sympathetic to Catholic opinion.

Ireland during this period went through a form of renaissance. Foreign trade expanded, and the wealth and confidence that this brought is reflected in some of the fine buildings that can be seen in Dublin today: the Parliament House (now Bank of Ireland), Customs House, the Four Courts and Trinity College. Dublin looked like a capital city, and many of its elite would have thought of it as such. Impressive feats of engineering such as the canals linking Dublin to Limerick were also constructed. Ireland was still primarily agricultural, though in the North, the new city of Belfast was becoming a centre due to the production of linen.

The war of independence in America was to have a major impact on Irish politics. For one group, it and the French revolution would provide a model to copy. It also left Ireland more open to attack, as Britain poured its resources into its American difficulty, and further, alerted many in Ireland to the unequal relationship with the United Kingdom. The Protestant Patriots achieved a degree of legislative independence through the repeal of Poyning's Law in 1782, but it was they who would rail against the interest of Catholics or Dissenters. In any case Ireland did not have its own government, and its control of Dublin Castle was questionable. In Ulster, radical Presbyterians were influenced by the ideas of the French revolution, and here the Society of United Irishmen was founded. These were egalitarians, influenced by new democratic ideas. Catholics, also organizing into secret societies of Defenders, allied with the United Irishmen (not always harmoniously as the Defenders were often sectarian Catholics) in a series of rebellions culminating in the landing in 1798 of French forces in the western county of Mayo. These were defeated, but the rebellions cost about 30,000 lives.

## Union with Britain and the rise of nationalism

Catholics had secured some concessions in the later part of the eighteenth century, but the demands from the Catholic middle classes were becoming more difficult to deny. The internal security threat in Ireland and the possibility of its use by France convinced London that a better way to administer Ireland would be to bring it into the United Kingdom. The Act of Union was opposed and supported in some unlikely quarters. The Catholic Church, perhaps fearful of the 1798 rebellion and its similarities to the French revolution, supported the Union. The Church would have also seen Union as a more likely route to Catholic emancipation. The Orange Order, a sectarian Protestant organization, and many Protestant landowners opposed the Union fearing Catholic emancipation (Garvin, 1981: 32). Catholic merchants in Cork and Belfast businessmen supported it on the basis of the promised free trade agreement. Dublin MPs opposed it as it would reduce Dublin's status. The parliament represented the interest of those most opposed to the Union, but it was passed in part through the promise of patronage, economic development and security from Catholic domination.

The Act of Union was something which was supposed to be for all time, yet within a short space of time many complained that it failed to deliver what it had promised. The failure to provide for Catholic emancipation (to allow Catholics to sit in parliament, hold senior government office or be a sheriff, among other posts) proved its primary weakness, and increased mistrust of British government – a government which Irish Catholics had sometimes welcomed as a restraining hand on Irish Protestant action. For nationalists, 'Britain' went from being part of a possible solution to their problems to becoming *the* problem – a dynamic that was to recur in Northern Ireland at the outbreak of the Troubles (see Box 2.5, p. 63). The Protestant elite lost some of its power and position, being reduced to provincials in London, even if it did hold on to its positions in the Irish administration.

The delay in reforms promised by the British offered Catholic campaigners a chance to mobilize the Irish in what became more than a call for Catholic emancipation, but merely preceded the ultimate goal of national emancipation. The Catholic Association, founded by Daniel O'Connell, a brilliant barrister from the Catholic middle class, quickly became a mass movement with branches throughout the country. Elections at that time were often corrupt, with no secret ballot, but the Association organized to ensure the defeat of landlord-backed candidates and used a 'Catholic rent' to support those perse-cuted by their landlords. O'Connell stood in an election in 1828 and won (there was no law against a Catholic standing in election, but Catholics were prohibited from taking a seat in the House of Commons, the British Parliament). These victories forced (a partly willing) British government to introduce Catholic emancipation in 1929, and O'Connell became a national hero. He then turned his attention to a much bigger goal, the repeal of the Union. He followed the same campaigning formula of 'monster meetings', in places of symbolic importance such as Tara and Clontarf, but found more implacable opponents to repeal of the Union in London. O'Connell had given the Irish masses the idea that Irish independence was possi-ble, and a group inspired by him, the Young Irelanders, provided an ideological defence and political strategy for the separatist move-ment. In 1848 this group failed in an insurrection partly inspired by other nationalist insurrections in Europe at the same time. The Great Famine (see Box 1.1) meant that many in the country were dying, leaving or too concerned with survival to think about lofty goals of political independence. It is notable that all the nationalist leaders had tended to come from the upper or middle classes, and that Irish inde-pendence was rarely demanded by the poor. However, they were to

**Box 1.1   The Irish Famine: was it man-made?**

Between 1845 and 1850 one of the worst catastrophes in European history took place. Because of the tradition of sub-division of land on inheritance, Irish peasants had a very small plot on which to subsist and were also almost entirely dependent on the potato for the bulk of their diet. A disease virtually wiped out the crop in 1845 and this continued for another four years, which, coupled with unusually harsh weather, caused about a million people from an estimated population of eight and a half million to die from starvation or disease. This makes it one of the most extensive famines in history. A further million people emigrated from the country (principally to Britain and the USA) to escape its ravages, a trend that was to continue for the next century. That the famine occurred in a part of the United Kingdom, the wealthiest county in the world, adds to the puzzle as to why it happened?

There has been a significant debate as to whether the famine was a man-made or at least a preventable disaster. It seems clear now that there was sufficient food in Ireland or within easy reach to prevent the famine. The Tory government in power at the outbreak of the famine brought in relief schemes but a new Whig government took a less interventionist approach. The response would have been shaped by contemporary religious and ideological beliefs. Religious Protestants would have felt it the work of God, and so not something to be interfered with, and this would have been reinforced by the *laissez-faire* economic orthodoxy of the time. In addition many English thought the Irish Catholic population a savage race, unable to use the land profitably. Ireland at the time was one of the most densely populated places in Europe.

The famine had a major impact in many ways. Memory of the famine and the British response was understandably a powerful tool for later nationalists to use against British rule. Landlordism was also blamed for the disaster. The traditional method of inheritance also changed, ending the sub-division of land. This forced younger children to emigrate. Marriages took place later and often between older men and much younger women. The great emigration to the USA also embedded a deep relationship with that country that continues to this day.

revive the 'Spirit of '98' in yet another group of nationalists with that goal.

The elitist nature of Irish nationalism meant that it had failed to inspire grassroots support. For the average person in Connemara or the Donegal or Kerry peninsulas in the west of Ireland, life in the late nineteenth century was as difficult as it had been before the Union or even further back. Possibly for this reason the question of national independence became merged with the question that affected ordinary Irish people – the Land Question. This coalition could then provide the call for national independence with an issue for which to fight and the backing of large numbers that many of the earlier efforts lacked.

The Land Question was given an organizational personality by the Irish Tenant League, which strove for the 'three Fs' – fair rent, fixity of tenure and freedom for the tenant to sell the interest of his holding. Candidates supporting the Tenant League won many of the Irish seats, but failed to achieve anything, leading some to regard physical force as the route to national freedom (Moody, 2001: 230). The newest nationalists were the Irish Republican Brotherhood (IRB) or Fenians, a group set up simultaneously in Dublin and New York, composed of some involved in the failed 1848 revolt. It was a violent separatist movement, whose attempts at revolts ended equally in failure and popular indifference (Fitzpatrick, 1989: 174). The Land Question did not go away, and the new British Prime Minister Gladstone was unusually troubled by the Irish Question, partly in response to the Fenian revolts. He removed the special status of the Protestant Church of Ireland and introduced a Land Act. Though it was ineffective, his willingness to try marked a change in the relationship between Britain and Ireland.

The extension of the franchise in 1867 enabled the coalition of land reformers and Home Rulers (as those seeking partial independence for Ireland were to become known) to make electoral gains. The Home Rule party, later the Irish Parliamentary Party (IPP), won a majority of the Irish seats in the Commons. The emerging leader of this party, Charles Stewart Parnell, a comfortable Protestant, quickly made a name for himself organizing his party as a disciplined, coherent block, unlike other parties at the time (he could lay claim to have been the inventor of modern political parties), to obstruct the work of the Commons. He and Michael Davitt, a disgruntled Fenian of peasant origin, were to use a crop failure in 1879 to found the Land League. It attracted support from all elements of nationalist opinion, moderate to extreme, and was extremely well organized, serving as a relief agency, depending on remittances from Irish emigrants in the USA. The Land War supported those facing eviction, and the strategy of boycott was introduced when the group ostracized a land agent, Captain Charles Boycott, forcing him to bring in Orangemen to save the crops at huge cost to the taxpayer. The British government clamped down on the leaders of the Land League, including Davitt and Parnell, but also introduced a Bill granting its main aims. The organization's success, however, meant that its expectations had changed. It now wanted peasant proprietorship. Further legislation, introduced principally under Gladstone's administration, further reduced the power of landlords in Ireland. This would have major implications for the eventual new state in Ireland, as the settlement of the Land Question in favour of the middle-class farmer at the expense of the large landlord and smallholder and labourer meant the new state did not have to deal with one of the major social problems Ireland had faced in the previous century.

Parnell had used the Land Question to become the undisputed leader of Irish nationalism, and the election in 1885 was used to push for Home Rule in Ireland. Gladstone recognized the mandate Parnell had and introduced a Home Rule Bill, but this was defeated in the Commons, as it would almost certainly have been in the Lords. The Irish, however, were now closer than ever to achieving their goal, and could do it by constitutional means. Ireland was also being assisted by elements of the British establishment. Efforts to ruin Parnell's reputation using forged letters failed, but the strong moralistic attitudes (in both Ireland and Britain) to his adultery caused a split in his party which only subsided after his death. Splits in the IRB meant that physical force nationalism failed to take advantage of the IPP's weakness.

All of the nationalists from the late eighteenth century spoke in terms of Ireland becoming a nation, implying that Ireland had some of the cultural trappings of a nation. At the time many would have been conscious that it had lost or was losing one of the main manifestations of nationhood, its language. Thomas Davis had argued that 'a people without a language of its own is only half a nation'. While the language was dying out among the general populace, it and Gaelic mysticism had become fashionable among some of the middle classes. An Anglo-Irish literary revival romanticized the life of the Irish peasant and revived interest in Gaelic mythology. This was led by William Butler Yeats, and it was mainly Anglo-Irish Protestants who took part in the revival. Another Protestant, Douglas Hyde, set up Conradh na Gaelige (the Gaelic League) with the purpose of reviving interest in the language, but this was mainly successful in those areas where Irish was already dead (McCartney, 1986: 123). A third group, the Gaelic Athletic Association, had a much greater impact on ordinary Irish people. It sought to organize 'Gaelic' games in order to stop Irish people playing soccer, rugby and cricket.

Together these developments were publicized in an influential newspaper, *The Leader*, which propagated the idea of an Irish Ireland. Though Todd Andrews (1979: 45) would remark that Irish-Irelanders were seen as a joke, the Gaelic League in particular was more important than this suggests as it succeed in changing laws, making Irish language competence effectively compulsory for any Catholic wishing to go to university. Though the League claimed to be non-political, its demonstration that Ireland was a cultural nation was having a political impact, and it shared members with groups such as the IRB. One new political party, Sinn Féin, manifested the split in Irish politics between those who sought a Gaelic Ireland separate from Britain, and those who sought Home Rule through constitutional means. Sinn Féin was an unsuccessful political party which posed no real threat to constitutional nationalism, but it did provide a political instrument for those in the IRB and the Gaelic League. Home Rule remained on the British political agenda in the early years of the twentieth century, but its success depended on there being a Liberal government.

This radicalism belies the fact that Dublin in particular was a comfortable British city, and the vast majority of people would have sought no more than some self-government using a British model. Dublin at the time was a city of contrasts with a large middle class, but also larger areas of extreme poverty. Class relations increasingly became an issue, and in 1913 there was a lockout of workers ensuing from efforts by employers to compel workers to withdraw from trade unions. New political leaders who merged the idea of class and national identity emerged at the time. James Connolly, one of the founders of the Irish Citizens Army and the Irish Labour Party, equated socialism with republicanism.

At this stage Ireland was seeing another split in the country (see Box 1.2). In the north-east of the country, Belfast was becoming an industrial powerhouse, whereas there was minimal industrialization in the rest of Ireland. Shipbuilding helped the expansion of Belfast, which by 1900 was more populous than Dublin. By contrast, southern Ireland was primarily agricultural and dependent on public works such as the Congested Districts Board to provide employment. The provincial towns such as Cork and Limerick went into a decline. The religious landscape of the country was also changing. Protestantism in the north of Ireland became more Evangelical, less liberal and more antagonistic to Catholicism, and sectarian riots became common (Boyd, 1969). Politically it was much more British in char-

---

**Box 1.2    Ulster Unionism and the emergence of Northern Ireland**

It was clear up to the time partition took place that the north of Ireland was different from the rest of the country. Not only did it have far more Protestants, it had a different outlook – these were not just Irish Unionists, desirous of retaining the link with Britain for all of Ireland, these were Ulster Unionists who viewed Ulster as a different entity. The reasons for this go back over four centuries. Although settlements had taken place all over Ireland from the Norman invasion onwards, Ulster, the northern province of Ireland, was among the least settled territories. It was a place where the remaining Gaelic chieftains retained a good deal of political power. In the immediate aftermath of the Scot James VI's assumption of the crown of England and Ireland, Scottish Protestants moved to Antrim and Down in large numbers, largely on a voluntary basis, taking underused lands. The Flight of the Earls (1607) saw Gaelic noblemen flee the country in mysterious circumstances, leaving the Gaelic population leaderless. The administrations in Dublin and London were keen to fill the void. Granting the land in the counties of Ulster that was not already settled to English and Scottish Protestants would enable the remaining significant part of Ireland not under Dublin's control to be 'civilized' and would allow James VI to repay debts and seek new ones from those who helped finance and fight his war to take the crowns of England and Ireland. The planters were predominantly (but not exclusively) Scots and Presbyterian. The people were also more likely to come from all strata of society, so many of the planters did not differ from the native Irish in economic terms.

The Act of Union was opposed by many in the north of Ireland who feared exposure to free trade with England and the possibility of Catholic emancipation. When ethnic nationalism expanded in the south of Ireland in the mid- to late nineteenth century, Ulster nationalism developed in the north of Ireland. Given the likelihood of Home Rule, Ulster Unionists organized and armed, threatening to secede from an independent Ireland. The Great War and the Easter Rising intervened to make Home Rule less likely and Ulster Unionists were powerful enough to ensure that Ireland was partitioned into the Irish Free State and Northern Ireland (encompassing the six counties of Ulster).

---

acter. This led to the Ulster unionists organizing to counter the threat of Home Rule in Ireland which they (rightly) saw as predominantly Catholic and therefore posing the risk of rule from Rome.

This threat became very real in 1912 when the Liberal government was dependent on Irish nationalist MPs under John Redmond for its majority. A third Home Rule Bill was introduced in 1912. The 'Ulster problem' then emerged – Ulster unionists formed the Ulster Volunteer

Force (UVF) in 1913 to resist any Home Rule in Ulster, but no agreement could be made as to how to deal with the problem. In response to the setting up of the UVF, the Irish Volunteers was founded by nationalists to ensure the passage of the Home Rule Bill. This Bill was passed in 1914, despite objections from the Lords, but implementation was postponed due to the outbreak of World War I.

## Revolt, independence and partition

Unlike in Ulster, where rebellion against the proposed Home Rule Bill threatened, Redmond's strategy was to offer good behaviour in the hope that it would be rewarded; thus he campaigned for recruitment to the war effort. The many Irish who served in the British Army in World War I were promised a hero's return and Home Rule, but the Ireland they returned to was very different. The Irish Volunteers split at the outbreak of the war, most moving to Redmond's National Volunteers, while Eóin MacNeill led two to three thousand members (of 160,000) in a radical nationalist group with skeletal organization. This group imported some weapons in 1914, but not enough to be militarily dangerous.

Many in the Irish Volunteers were also members of the Irish Republican Brotherhood, which viewed Britain's position in the war as an opportunity for Ireland to revolt. The IRB planned a military rising from 1915. A small group of Irish Irelanders, many members simultaneously of the Gaelic League, Sinn Féin and the Irish Volunteers, expected to use the IRB, though they kept their plans from MacNeill. James Connolly's Irish Citizens' Army was also to be involved. Militarily it was poorly planned and executed, but it is thought that the leaders, Patrick Pearse in particular, did not expect military success, rather that the sacrifice of their lives would inspire the Irish nation. In this he was spectacularly successful. On Easter Monday 1916, about 1,200 rebels seized the General Post Office and other key sites around Dublin. At the GPO the Proclamation of the Irish Republic was read (see Illustration 1.3). The British were able to defeat the insurgents due to much superior firepower and the limited nature of the Rising, as it came to be known (only 64 insurgents were killed). Though the revolutionaries who declared Ireland a republic in 1916 were easily defeated and initially regarded with scepticism and mild irritation, the immediate execution of most of the leaders led to an outcry against the British and gave the Rising an importance it

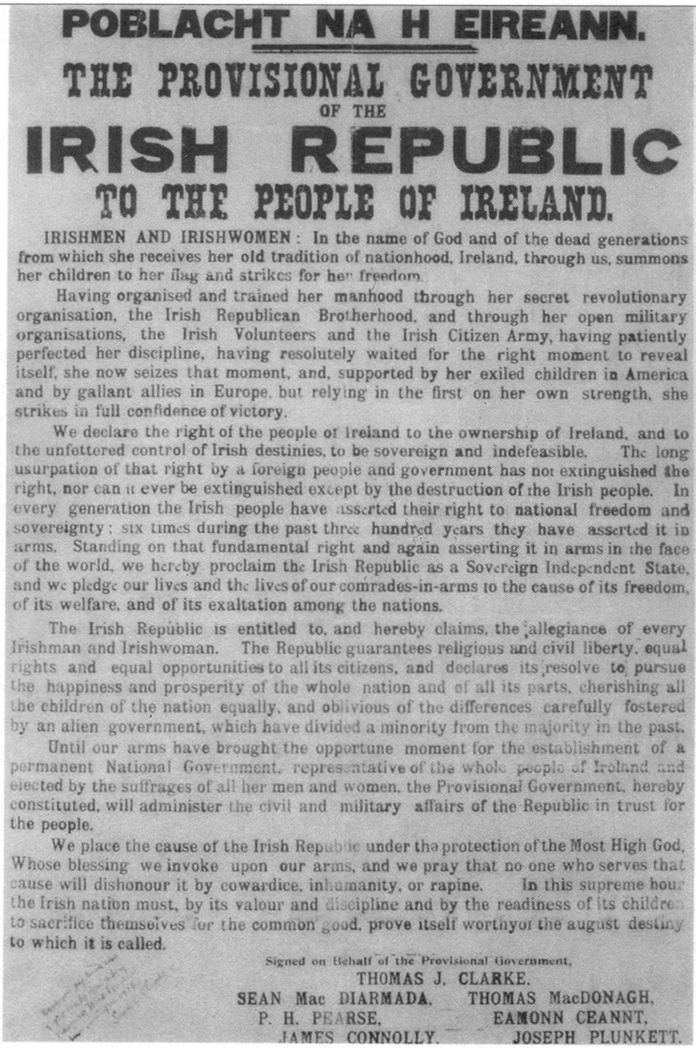

POBLACHT NA H EIREANN.

THE PROVISIONAL GOVERNMENT

OF THE

IRISH REPUBLIC

TO THE PEOPLE OF IRELAND.

IRISHMEN AND IRISHWOMEN: In the name of God and of the dead generations from which she receives her old tradition of nationhood, Ireland, through us, summons her children to her flag and strikes for her freedom.

Having organised and trained her manhood through her secret revolutionary organisation, the Irish Republican Brotherhood, and through her open military organisations, the Irish Volunteers and the Irish Citizen Army, having patiently perfected her discipline, having resolutely waited for the right moment to reveal itself, she now seizes that moment, and, supported by her exiled children in America and by gallant allies in Europe, but relying in the first on her own strength, she strikes in full confidence of victory.

We declare the right of the people of Ireland to the ownership of Ireland, and to the unfettered control of Irish destinies, to be sovereign and indefeasible. The long usurpation of that right by a foreign people and government has not extinguished the right, nor can it ever be extinguished except by the destruction of the Irish people. In every generation the Irish people have asserted their right to national freedom and sovereignty; six times during the past three hundred years they have asserted it in arms. Standing on that fundamental right and again asserting it in arms in the face of the world, we hereby proclaim the Irish Republic as a Sovereign Independent State, and we pledge our lives and the lives of our comrades-in-arms to the cause of its freedom, of its welfare, and of its exaltation among the nations.

The Irish Republic is entitled to, and hereby claims, the allegiance of every Irishman and Irishwoman. The Republic guarantees religious and civil liberty, equal rights and equal opportunities to all its citizens, and declares its resolve to pursue the happiness and prosperity of the whole nation and of all its parts, cherishing all the children of the nation equally, and oblivious of the differences carefully fostered by an alien government, which have divided a minority from the majority in the past.

Until our arms have brought the opportune moment for the establishment of a permanent National Government, representative of the whole people of Ireland and elected by the suffrages of all her men and women, the Provisional Government, hereby constituted, will administer the civil and military affairs of the Republic in trust for the people.

We place the cause of the Irish Republic under the protection of the Most High God, Whose blessing we invoke upon our arms, and we pray that no one who serves that cause will dishonour it by cowardice, inhumanity, or rapine. In this supreme hour the Irish nation must, by its valour and discipline and by the readiness of its children to sacrifice themselves for the common good, prove itself worthy of the august destiny to which it is called.

Signed on Behalf of the Provisional Government,

THOMAS J. CLARKE.

SEAN Mac DIARMADA. THOMAS MacDONAGH.

P. H. PEARSE. EAMONN CEANNT.

JAMES CONNOLLY. JOSEPH PLUNKETT.

**Illustration 1.3 The Proclamation of the Republic, 1916**

The document read at the GPO on Easter Monday 1916 became an important reference point for all subsequent republicans. A major issue on which groups divide has been whether they have been true to the spirit of 1916. The document itself is mainly delusional propaganda with a heavy religious bias.

would not otherwise have had. There was annoyance that the British had destroyed much of central Dublin and that they had declared martial law. The British played into the hands of Sinn Féin, which had little to do with the Rising, by blaming it and imprisoning its members. It was in these prison camps that Ireland's new political elite was formed. The over-reaction by the British led many to question the ability of Britain to govern Ireland competently, let alone fairly.

The efforts by the IPP to prepare for Home Rule came to nothing as focus shifted to Sinn Féin under a new leader, Éamon de Valera. De Valera, despite his senior role in the Rising, was not seen as a radical and he successfully placated the Church, which though vehemently opposed to the physical force tradition may have seen the appeal of Gaelic traditionalism and the inevitability of Sinn Féin's success. De Valera took up the task of canvassing international, particularly US, opinion in favour of independence. The IRB was also organizing under the effective leadership of Michael Collins. By 1918 the IPP had been put under pressure by the British government to accept conscription for Ireland. This unpopular policy further aided Sinn Féin, and so in the election in 1918 (the first with almost universal male suffrage), Sinn Féin won 73 of the 105 seats; unionists won most of their seats in the north of the country. The Irish Parliamentary Party had been virtually wiped out and the policy of Home Rule was no longer sufficient – the mood of the country had changed.

Sinn Féin's policy, worked out by its leader Arthur Griffith, had been that the Act of Union was illegal and therefore sitting in the Commons was unlawful. Its MPs, or TDs as it called them, were to sit in a newly constituted Irish parliament, Dáil Éireann. The Dáil was hardly a functioning chamber, but it tried to demonstrate to the world that it was the democratic organ of a nation. Ulster unionism's growing militancy put southern unionists in a difficult position as the latter group would have to live with Home Rule at a minimum and could not therefore engage in the type of rhetoric seen in the north. At this stage the IRB had effectively begun a war of independence which Collins directed, pioneering guerrilla tactics or 'terrorism' rather than open warfare. As such it was a limited war, but one which wore down the resolve of the British and one which the British again reacted poorly to by importing demobilized soldiers, the Black and Tans, who could hardly claim to be a force for law and order. As the war went on both sides engaged in brutal, sectarian abuses of the general population until the sense of stalemate drove both sides to accept a truce and peace negotiations.

**Illustrations 1.4    De Valera and Collins**

Éamon de Valera (1882–1976) (*left*) and Michael Collins (1890–1922) (*right*) were both legendary Irish revolutionaries whose lives could not have ended more differently. De Valera was saved from execution for his part in the 1916 Rising because of his US citizenship. He went on to be a leader in the Irish War of Independence but opposed the treaty settlement with Britain. His party, Fianna Fáil, later dominated Irish politics and he held the posts of Taoiseach (Prime Minister) and President. Collins became a military leader in the Irish War of Independence, inventing a style of urban guerrilla warfare. He was one of those sent by de Valera to negotiate a settlement with Britain. He accepted the treaty as 'a stepping stone' to a united and free Ireland but was assassinated by anti-treaty forces in the war of Independence aged 32.

The negotiations which would end in the Anglo-Irish Treaty became the subject of intense debate. In the end Ireland achieved self government as a Free State which would remain part of the British Commonwealth with the British monarch as head of state. Northern Ireland, as six of the counties of Ulster had become, effectively achieved self-rule. Northern Ireland quickly set about forming the institutions of a sectarian state. The partition of the island was not a major divisive issue in the south; most accepted it as inevitable if unfortunate – only the northern Catholic population would find this intolerable. The major issue of division in the south was on certain symbolic questions such as an oath of allegiance to be sworn to the King. Collins argued that it would enable Ireland achieve full independence, whereas de Valera (surprisingly) was much more hardline and rejected the treaty. The treaty was put to the Dáil and passed by 64 votes to 57 in January 1922, but anti-treaty Sinn Féin rejected the vote, and a civil war between sides of the Irish Volunteers ensued. The civil war was a bitter dispute and more bloody than the war of independence, but like the war of independence it sometimes degenerated to sectarian murder, robbery and arson. By 1923 it was apparent that anti-treaty forces would not succeed and the war was ended with a new Irish state given the task of rebuilding the country following a decade of upheaval.

## Major events of the twentieth century in Ireland

The immediate task facing the new Irish government was basic but not easy. Faced with civil war, it needed to secure the state. It had a working constitution, largely imposed by Britain, which attempted to maintain the representation of unionist opinion. The new prime minister, W.T. Cosgrave, was far from radical and set about securing the economy, eliciting support from Protestant bankers. Some have argued that given its baptism of fire, the stability of Irish democracy was remarkable. However, Ireland was not comparable with the more unstable democracies of Central Europe. As well as having a culture that accepted parliamentary democracy, Ireland was also a reasonably wealthy place. The speed with which O'Connell Street, the main thoroughfare in Dublin, largely destroyed in the Rising, was rebuilt shows the high level of confidence in the country's prospects in the 1920s. The government of Cumann na nGaedheal, as pro-treaty Sinn Féin became, was one led by middle-class conservative Catholics. It imposed much of its ideology on the state, but this was to make some of the country's laws more conservative. The new state was helped by the fact that most of the civil servants remained, and an unarmed police force (Garda Siochána) was successfully set up which quickly gained the confidence of a population probably relieved at the return to normality. This government was economically conservative, signing a free trade agreement with Britain, but did start some house building programmes designed to clear the tenements in the cities. The Irish Volunteers and IRB formed the basis of a reasonably small army which was subservient to the political actors.

Sinn Féin and the newly constituted Irish Republican Army (IRA) continued to agitate, but the party split on a typically symbolic issue and de Valera formed Fianna Fáil, which entered the Dáil in 1927 (signing the oath but having declared it an empty formula). Thus began reasonably normal party politics – albeit the parties were atypical in a western European context. The Cosgrave government's conservatism, which in historical terms might be seen as its great achievement (treading a delicate line between reform and security) would lead it to unpopularity. Fianna Fáil was able to portray itself as a more radical party, and the true inheritor of 1916 – though the by now tiny Sinn Féin would have contested this.

Fianna Fáil took power in an election in 1932. The transfer of power was crucial, given that one party to a civil war was handing over to the other. Though some claimed they would take guns into the Dáil chamber should the government refuse to hand over office, the new government was appointed normally. Fianna Fáil under de Valera recognized that the Free State institutions had gained acceptance by the general populace and did nothing to upset this. However they did manage to convey the impression that they were more socially-oriented (without being socialist) and activist by extending the house building programme and increasing the retirement pension. Seán Lemass, a particularly activist minister, promoted domestic industry. Fianna Fáil also set about courting the Catholic Church, assuring it that the new government was no group of radicals. Though Cumann na nGaedheal had done much to reduce the influence of the UK, Fianna Fáil abolished the oath and reduced the importance of the Governor-General (the monarch's representative in Ireland). De Valera also started an economic war with Britain on the issue of the payment of land annuities (left over from the Land Acts). The economic war escalated as each side put tariffs on the other's goods. It was consistent with Fianna Fáil's policy of national self-sufficiency and popular with republicans. However de Valera would not allow the IRA a free rein and willingly arrested members when it suited his needs. The 1930s were economically difficult and the economic war and promise of 'frugal sufficiency' did little to assuage the growing numbers forced to emigrate. De Valera recognized this and ended the trade war. He also recognized that his economic policy would not be enough for re-election. In 1937 he drafted a new Constitution which kept most of the institutional structures of the Free State Constitution but added some sectarian and nationalist passages that made it more 'Irish' – for Irish one might read Catholic. It also claimed jurisdiction over Northern Ireland, which itself had become more sectarian as it was freed from the control or interest of either London or Dublin.

De Valera's party became by far the best organized and most electorally successful party. Fine Gael, as Cumann na nGaedheal became, failed to mount a serious challenge to what was becoming a dominant Fianna Fáil. De Valera's next challenge was the Second World War, or 'the Emergency' as it came to be known in Ireland. Ireland remained neutral, which though delivering peace made the prospect of ending partition a more distant prospect. Ireland did well out of the war, agricultural prices increased as a result of British demand, and the workers who emigrated to Britain found jobs easily. Ireland was settling into a cosy Catholicism, not far removed from de Valera's dream of an

Ireland which . . . would be the home of a people who valued material wealth only as the basis of a right living, of a people who were satisfied with frugal comfort and devoted their leisure to the things of the soul. (Radio Éireann broadcast, 17 March 1943)

The 1950s would challenge this stereotype as grinding poverty and economic stagnation once again forced people to leave Ireland. De Valera's policies of self- sufficiency had failed, and it is not clear that, even had his vision been possible, young people would not have found the brighter prospects of the USA and the UK more attractive. Northern Ireland and the newly declared Republic of Ireland continued to grow apart. The war and government investment meant that Northern Ireland remained an, admittedly declining, industrial centre. It also benefited from the social welfare revolution that had taken place in post-war Britain. The south's failure to look beyond its borders was reflected in the growing Catholicization of social life. The censorship of books was just one manifestation of the state-sponsored conservatism that Ireland chose to adopt. An effort to introduce a free health scheme during a coalition government of all parties except Fianna Fáil foundered under opposition from the church.

It was probably the desperation of the 1950s that forced a rethink. Seán Lemass took over from Éamon de Valera as Taoiseach (prime minister) and leader of Fianna Fáil in 1959 and almost immediately more expansionist policies were adopted. These encouraged inward investment and abandoned protectionism. Whether these had a direct effect is debatable, but the economy expanded and the 1960s were a time of optimism in Ireland. Relations with Britain and Northern Ireland also improved. In 1962 the inactive and ineffective IRA called on its members to dump arms as it moved toward class-based politics.

By 1965 Lemass was willing to meet with Terence O'Neill, the North's prime minister, and Ireland signed a free trade agreement with Britain.

Neither Lemass nor O'Neill were to know that Northern Ireland was on the cusp of a bloody civil war that would last over thirty years and claim more than 3,000 lives. The meeting with Lemass sparked an increase in militant Protestant rhetoric and action and events in the next number of years led to the outbreak of the Troubles (see Box 2.5, p. 63). As Northern Ireland descended into widespread inter-communal violence the impact in the Republic was greater for the political parties than for most Irish people. Fianna Fáil, the most nationalistic of the parties, saw a split as some wished to use the Troubles as a means to end partition, whereas the more moderate leadership struggled to contain such rhetoric or activities. Fine Gael and Labour formed a government in 1973, when the Troubles were at their most intense, and supported British attempts to find a solution, but these were rejected by radicals in the unionist population which managed to veto peace proposals. Northern Ireland settled into a 'long war'.

Joining the European Economic Community in 1973 had some immediate impacts (such as the lifting of the ban on married women working in the civil service) and gave the country a renewed sense of confidence on emerging from the UK's shadow. However, Ireland suffered from the oil crises in the 1970s (when the price of oil increased greatly) much as most other countries in the world did. In this context the promises of Fianna Fáil to simultaneously decrease some taxes and increase spending seem profligate. This started an economic recession in Ireland, which, coupled with increased polarization over the hunger strikes in Northern Ireland, left the country in a state of despair. Scandals about the political control of the state and corruption added to this despondency. Ireland had three elections in just two years, as increasingly polarized parties under Garret FitzGerald and Charles Haughey took power alternately. FitzGerald led a more open government which aimed to liberalize some of Ireland's more anachronistic laws (though one of his first acts was to enshrine the ban on abortion in the constitution and other major measures failed to be passed). He also offered a more understanding attitude to unionism – which was not reciprocated – and signed an Anglo-Irish Agreement, which acknowledged the Republic's legitimate interest in the affairs of Northern Ireland. However his governments failed to tackle the rising public debt and saw unemployment continue to rise, as did emigration.

If FitzGerald's government was well-intentioned but ineffectual, it was not expected that Haughey's new government in 1987 would tackle the now critical state of the Irish economy. The new Fine Gael leader, Alan Dukes, offered Haughey's minority government support in cutting spending, and this immediately increased confidence in the economy. Haughey's subsequent coalition with the Progressive Democrats, a small free market party with an agenda to cut taxes and increase competition and inward investment, helped start what was to become a level of sustained economic growth unimaginable just a decade earlier. A new government with Fianna Fáil and Labour continued the agenda of these earlier governments, further eroding any ideological differences among the mainstream parties in the management of the economy.

The Celtic Tiger, as this economic boom was styled, was driven to a great extent by inward investment in the form of European manufacturing bases for US technology companies. Unemployment fell dramatically from a high of 18 per cent in the 1980s to about 4 per cent by the late 1990s. Emigration ended and was reversed, not only as Irish emigrants returned, but new immigrants, mainly from other European countries, chose Ireland as a place to work and live. By 2006 nearly 15 per cent of the population was foreign-born, up from negligible levels in the 1980s. The increased confidence led a construction boom and property price bubble. While many saw this as a sign of a healthy economy it led to an over-reliance on construction which, when the bubble burst, caused widespread problems in the Irish economy, and in turn the whole Euro area. By the end of 2010 an IMF/ EU bailout of Ireland's banks was being negotiated.

The economic growth and modernisztion, in which Ireland rapidly moved from an agricultural country to a post-industrial one, had impacts on Irish society that are still only now being understood. In the mid-1980s Ireland showed signs of a pre-modern country: in 1985 alleged sightings of statues of the Virgin Mary moving, first in Ballinspittle, Co. Cork and then in much of the rest of the country, resulted in mass religious fervour. At that time Ireland rejected, by a comfortable margin, an attempt to legalize divorce. By 1995, divorce was (narrowly) approved by voters in Ireland, homosexuality had been decriminalized, and the church suffered a crisis of trust among Irish people. The Catholic Church was shown to have protected priests who had raped and beaten children, which damaged confidence in the church and its moral authority.

In Northern Ireland from the early 1980s (Provisional) Sinn Féin began to take precedence over the (Provisional) IRA, the main agent for conflict on the nationalist side, and slowly moved towards political methods. Ceasefires in the early 1990s were unstable, but they reflected a genuine desire to move away from war. An agreement among all but one of the main parties led to a power-sharing regime which collapsed as each side demanded more of the other. But by 2007 a government (with powers devolved from London) was formed which included the more extreme elements of both communities. Whether this will lead to a lasting settlement or is just a stage on the way to the united Ireland so desired by Sinn Féin/IRA is unclear. It is, however, a settlement that one might think of as the end of at least a major chapter in the history of Ireland.

# 2

# Land and Peoples

The Republic of Ireland makes up about five-sixths of the island of Ireland, one of the islands of the archipelago known as the British Isles (a term many Irish find offensive) at the north-western edge of the continent of Europe. It is a country characterized by moderation – in size, climate, physical features and people. Ireland is the twentieth largest island in the world, though is still quite small, about the size of South Carolina, or one-sixth the size of Spain. Thus one can easily get from any part of the country to any other part within a day – from Malin Head in Donegal to Mizen Head in Cork is 466 kilometres as the crow flies or about 700 kilometres by road (which gives some indication of the nature of Ireland's road network!). This small size in part accounts for the homogeneity of the people. Except in the north-east of the island, there are few important regional divisions, though the dominance of Dublin over the rest of the country (see Box 2.2) does lead to derogatory references to Dubliners as Jackeens (derived from the assertion that the British flag, the Union Jack, was flown more popularly in Dublin than anywhere else) and anyone outside Dublin, but most particularly rural-based people, as Culchies (derived from the name of a small rural town, Kiltimagh, Co. Mayo).

The mild climate displays few extremes and though there are distinct seasons the seasonal differences in temperature and rainfall (usually high) are not great. The high rainfall and mainly arable land creates a green landscape that earned the country its sobriquet, 'the Emerald Isle'. There is virtually no part of the country that is uninhabitable and nowhere in Ireland is untouched by human habitation. Even in the largely abandoned mountainous regions of the western seaboard, one can make out the remains of stone walls that delineated tiny subsistence plots in the nineteenth century. The climate is suitable for many types of farming and it was the major source of income until relatively recently. The industrial revolution passed Ireland by, in part because it lacked the natural resources to fuel the economic development experienced by Britain. Though the sea is an important physical feature, it plays a surprisingly small part in the Irish economy.

The last century has seen major population shifts from Ireland, to the UK and USA especially, and within Ireland from west to east and particularly into Dublin. The most rural province, Connaught, made up 22 per cent of the population in 1841 but only 12 per cent today. So the west of Ireland, which would have been one of the more densely populated places in Europe in the 1840s, is now one of the most sparsely populated. Ireland is one of the few countries in the world which saw a population decline from the nineteenth century. The trend of emigration and the absence, until recently, of large scale immigration has also maintained the homogeneity of the Irish. Until recently a predominantly rural country, these population shifts mean that today it is largely urban, with 60 per cent living in towns or cities. People have followed the money, through jobs, to cities whose growth has been unplanned.

This chapter looks at the physical and social geography of Ireland. It examines its topography, climate and natural resources. It also looks at the important demographic shifts that have left their mark on the country, including the recent wave of immigration mainly from central and eastern Europe, and the physical and social toll these have taken on the society and the environment.

## Geography

The island of Ireland is mainly made up of flat plain surrounded by elevations at the western edges. The Atlantic Ocean surrounds the island on three sides, over time leaving its mark as a jagged coastline replete with inlets, peninsulas and islands, some of which are still inhabited. Despite its small size Ireland has a rich variety of physical features. The west coast is quite mountainous, though the mountains are comparatively low – Carrantuohill in Co. Kerry in the south-west is just over a thousand metres high (about one-fifth the height of Mont Blanc, western Europe's highest mountain). The Cliffs of Moher in Clare, the highest sea cliffs in Europe, are the spectacular backdrop to The Burren, bare limestone pavements that were once among the

**Box 2.1   What's in a name? Ireland, Éire and the Irish Republic**

When one hears Ireland described in the UK media it sometimes sounds as though a neighbour is awkwardly trying to be polite. It will be called Éire or the Irish Republic, neither of which are technically correct. The Irish Republic does not exist and Éire is sometime incorrectly used to refer to the 26-county area. The official name of the country in English is Ireland. The name Ireland is a mix of the Gaelic (Irish) *Éiru* and the Germanic *Land*. Éiru which became Éire in modern Irish, was named after a migration which possibly took place sometime in the fifth millennium BCE. It may have meant fat or fertile land.

The 26-county area was officially called the Irish Free State from 1921, and Ireland became the official name of the country in 1937 (Éire is its official name in Irish only). Ireland was officially designated a republic in 1949 but though the Republic of Ireland is sometimes used on official documents it is a description of the state rather than the name of the country. Still, a degree of confusion is inevitable when one wants to distinguish between the 26-county state and the whole island.

When speaking about Northern Ireland, what someone chooses to name it often reveals their political opinions. Unionists will often refer to the six-county area as Ulster even though the province of Ulster also contains three other counties in the Republic. Nationalists often refer to the North of Ireland or simply the North. This is because many nationalists did not recognize the legitimacy of Northern Ireland.

Further confusion arises because there is little agreement among the people of Northern Ireland about what to call themselves. Most southern Irish use the term Irish, but even Irish nationalists often use Northern Irish as do many unionists. Before the Troubles many middle-class unionists would have been comfortable with the term Irish, but not any more. Others use Ulsterman/woman or British, which usually indicates whether one is an Ulster loyalist or a British unionist.

more developed and fertile parts of the country but which over-grazing may have laid bare. The narrow body of water that separates Ireland from Britain is the Irish Sea. Ireland and Britain formed a single land mass connected to the European continent even after the end of the last Ice Age, about 15,000 years ago. The eastern seaboard is mainly low sandy dunes with intermittent rocky headlands. The south of the country is made up of rich plains interspersed with slow, winding rivers. This is the best agricultural land in the country and for this reason the south and east were where the initial English colonists settled, creating large ranch-style farms. The north midlands is peppered with small hills (drumlins), lakes, wet marshes and bog lands. The hills were formed from deposits left by the melting ice during an earlier Ice Age. This land was populated by small, less productive farms that offered little beyond subsistence living. The longest river, the Shannon (386 kilometres), is largely navigable, emerging into the Atlantic west of Limerick city. It divides the country between north-west and south-east, with north-west of the Shannon regarded as less developed and more Gaelic than the south and east.

Despite its latitude (between 51°N and 55°N), which makes it at the same level as the Canadian city of Edmonton and the Russian capital Moscow, the Irish climate is temperate with few extremes between winter and summer. This is due to the Mexican Gulf Stream, which pushes warm air and water to the Irish south-west coast and across the country. The average annual temperature is 9°C. The mean summer temperature is 19°C and the average winter one 3°C. Sea temperatures are about 7°C or 8°C warmer than waters at similar latitudes. The coldest months are January and February and the warmest July and August. May and June are the sunniest months, averaging 5 to 6 hours of sunshine each day, but reaching over 7 hours in the south-east. The Gulf Stream's warm moist air falls as rain when it reaches the more mountainous west coast. Rainfall is lowest along the eastern coastal strip. Rain in Ireland is rarely as heavy as in other countries, but the number of wet days is high, ranging from 150 days a year in the east, where the annual average is between 750 mm and 1000 mm, to 225 days in parts of the west (1000 mm–1250 mm). Snow and hail are quite rare and these contribute very little to the annual rainfall totals. Ireland's prevailing wind is south-westerly, from the Gulf Stream. In general Ireland is not particularly windy, but the north and west contain some of the windiest places in Europe. The weather is notoriously changeable, making 'sunny spells and scattered showers' the forecast most favoured by Irish meteorologists. Bright warm sunshine and heavy rain can be experienced within an hour. Despite this the Irish never seem prepared for the weather.

Although Ireland was part of the UK during the industrial revolution of the eighteenth and nineteenth centuries, apart from the north-east of Ireland industrialization largely passed it by. One of the reasons for Ireland's retarded growth was probably the absence of significant natural resources on which to build industry, unlike south Wales and the north of England which had significant coal deposits. The absence of coal, and the almost complete deforestation of the

*Map 2.1*   Physical features of Ireland

country, meant that the Irish came to depend on peat or turf as fuel for heating and cooking. The raised (lowland) and blanket (highland) bogs that make up about 17 per cent of the land in the country can be cut away to reveal a rich brown peat that when dried can be burned as turf. Blanket bogs are formed by carbon deposits from rotting heather over thousands of years. Raised bogs were formed by over-growth in lakes left after the last ice age. These have been exploited industrially and Ireland exports much of its peat as garden fertilizer. Ireland still uses this source to generate about a tenth of its electricity, though there are concerns from environmentalists that it destroys an important landscape and contributes much of Ireland's increasing carbon emissions.

Ireland was one of the first countries in the world to generate electricity through renewable resources when it opened the Shannon Hydro-Electric Scheme in Ardnacrusha (near Limerick) in 1929. Built by the German engineering company Siemens, it uses a large canal to divert the river Shannon to a dam fitted with turbines to generate electricity. It served as a model for later hydro-electric schemes in Europe. Today the challenges of climate change and energy security mean that the state is considering using wind power to generate electricity, and it could probably also harness energy from the strong tidal movements on the Atlantic coast.

Despite considering itself a country devoid of natural resources, from the 1970s on Ireland discovered commercial deposits of natural gas and oil which have been valuable to the Irish economy. A recent discovery off the coast of Co. Mayo in the west thought to contain 30 billion cubic metres of gas has been delayed because of protests at the decision to process the gas on land rather than at sea. The Irish government estimates that there are guaranteed deposits of 10 billion barrels of oil off the Irish coast worth about €500 billion, and there may be as much as 130 billion barrels. If these were exploitable commercially then Ireland would become one of the larger European energy providers. Ireland is Europe's largest producer of zinc, though the mines for it and other base metals have depended on high international metal prices to maintain their viability.

The seas surrounding Ireland provide a natural food resource through fishing. Surprisingly Ireland's fishing industry was never important, though there are some areas that are dependent on fishing. The small size of the fishing community compared to agriculture meant that Irish politicians never did very much to promote or protect fishing. Entry to the EEC in 1973, and particularly Spain's entry in 1986, meant that Irish waters were opened up to larger more productive trawlers. Over-fishing and the quota system introduced by the EU to protect fish stocks mean that Irish waters are no longer a major source of food. Agriculture, on the other hand, has been and continues to be of importance in the Irish economy. Although less than five per cent of the workforce is now employed in farming (it was 20 per cent in the 1980s), a further five per cent works in food processing industries. It is a small but important component of Irish output. About 65 per cent of Irish land is used for agriculture, much higher than the EU average, and there are about 140,000 farm units making Irish farms quite small, on average 31 hectares. There is some variation, however, within the country, with larger farms in the south and east and smaller farms in the north and west. Most farms are family-run and none are industrial producers on the scale seen in North or South America. Land tends to be kept within a family and the pre-Famine trend of subdivision of farms gave the Irish countryside the appearance of a green patchwork.

The warm damp climate makes Irish land most suited to grass, and over 90 per cent of agricultural land is given over to grazing, with just ten per cent for crop cultivation. Ireland is a major source of beef, with over half the farms devoted to beef production. Dairying accounts for a further 20 per cent, and then many smaller farms have a mixture of these. The land devoted to potato production, for a long time the staple diet of the Irish, has fallen to just 12,000 hectares (compared to 656,000 in 1846). Modern farming in Europe means reliance on the Common Agricultural Policy (CAP), which was designed to ensure food security, but which has become a highly bureaucratic and inefficient way of subsidizing farmers and increasing their reliance on non-market payments. Irish farmers have adapted to its system of quotas (where a farmer is allowed to produce a certain amount per year), and strongly resist changes to CAP, which accounts for 40 per cent of the total EU budget. CAP encouraged over-production leading to infamous butter mountains and wine lakes, where unwanted food was put into cold storage. More recent changes mean that farmers receive a single farm payment that is decoupled from production, and instead tied to environmental protection and rural development. The modernization of Irish agriculture meant increased size of farms and the increased use of fertilizers and hormones. These have led to environmental threats, as contaminated waters run into rivers, and food scares about contaminated meat, harming Ireland's traditional image as a clean and unpolluted country.

## The environment

The small-scale nature of Irish agriculture, the use of hedgerows and ditches to separate small fields and the poor road network keeping some (particularly western) parts of the country quite isolated mean that much of the Irish countryside retains a quaint beauty. These hedgerows also mean that the Irish countryside is richer in its biodiversity than other agricultural areas of Europe. But few parts of Ireland are untouched by the effects of humans. Most of the country would have been covered in rich deciduous forest of oak, ash, elm, birch and hawthorn, before settlers started clearing them from about 5,000 BCE to introduce farming. By the seventeenth century Ireland was almost completely deforested. Today just 10 per cent of the land is under forest and much of this is commercially cultivated soft woods not native to Ireland, which appear incongruous in the surrounding countryside. This makes Ireland the least forested country in Europe. Trends in Irish agriculture mean that much of the land is under grass, though wild flowers still grow, particularly in uplands.

Because it is an island and isolated from the rest of Europe, Ireland has less native diversity in flora and fauna. There are just 26 mammal species native to Ireland, including the red fox, hedgehog, the Irish hare, red squirrel and the red deer. A number of other animals are now extinct including the great elk and the wolf. In the coastal waters around Ireland dolphins, whales and sharks are common as well as commercially caught fish. Ireland famously has no native snakes. Legend, of course, has it that St Patrick banished them, but the more likely explanation is that Ireland was an island by the time it was

**Illustration 2.1    The Twelve Bens, Connemara, Co. Galway**

The mountainous west coast shows fewer signs of human occupation, though many Spanish-style villas blight the otherwise beautiful countryside.

warm enough for snakes to have migrated there naturally. Birds, of course, were less affected by Ireland's becoming an island and there are about 200 regularly occurring species. It is the breeding ground for fewer species than most European counties, but is used by many migrating birds.

The urban landscape in Ireland is the product of centuries of building. There is no obvious native architectural style, except perhaps the small, single-storey traditional cottage, with small windows, thick stone walls and a thatch-covered roof. Many of the building designs are imported from the UK, and the influence of the Protestant Ascendancy can be seen especially in the reorientation and reorganization of Dublin, in particular the grand Georgian squares and the classical styles of the Bank of Ireland, the General Post Office and Trinity College. The post-independence style perhaps resembles art deco US buildings. There was little appreciation of the architectural heritage of the English, and from the 1960s much of the scale of the streetscapes in Irish cities was ruined by incongruous glass and steel constructions that had all the flair of the arch-modernist Soviet-style skyscrapers on which they seemed to be modelled.

The recent economic boom increased the price of housing and caused a construction frenzy which has negatively affected the Irish environment. Land on the edges of nearly all cities and towns was sold by farmers and used to build sprawling suburbs. Little of this was centrally planned, and tax breaks introduced to stimulate development were probably retained for too long which eventually led to an oversupply in the market and a property price crash. The Irish planning system is entrepreneurial and reactive. It depends on developers identifying land or buildings for development or redevelopment, and submitting their proposals for local authorities to judge. Only rarely has government become directly involved in the redevelopment of areas by compulsorily purchasing land and overseeing its development. Where it has done so, the results are broadly successful: an example is the Dublin Docklands development which transformed a run-down port area into a thriving and well-designed district which includes retail, office and residential use.

Most Irish building developments, however, are poorly designed, do not fit into the surrounding area and rarely consider the needs of the community. The system allows anyone to use small bits of land for their preferred purpose, which since the 1990s meant putting as many houses or apartments on a site as possible. The annual number of applications had more than doubled since the early 1990s and 90

**Box 2.2    The dominance of Dublin**

It was the least 'Irish' of the parts of Ireland that was chosen as the capital for the new Irish state. Its questionable 'Irishness' is probably because it was the administrative capital for most of British rule. Its strategic location on the east coast allowed it to be used by English military rulers to attempt to control Ireland. For much of this time, their control was limited to Dublin and the surrounding counties (known as the Pale). As well as an administrative and military centre it became an important port for trade in and out of Ireland, making it a commercial centre. During the Protestant Ascendancy of the eighteenth century Dublin further developed and it was then that much of its grander architecture was built. It suffered a decline in the nineteenth century with the loss of its parliament and failure to industrialize. By 1900 Belfast was a larger city than Dublin.

Since independence, however, Dublin has grown. Ireland has a centralized state with little regional autonomy or local government, and all power and major organizations are based in Dublin. Dublin's proximity to the UK meant that it was more affected by UK media and trends, making it the part of Ireland most affected by modernity. It became one of the locations Irish people went to escape the insularity of rural society, though many saw Dublin as insular and moved to London. With a population of 1.2 million it is much larger than the second city in the Republic, Cork (population 190,000). Dublin and surrounding counties make up about 40 per cent of the country's population. Newer industries thus tend to locate in Dublin where there is an available workforce. Dublin's dominance is reflected in the fact that there are few large Irish companies with headquarters anywhere other than Dublin. Nearly all national media outlets are based in Dublin. Irish government and private infrastructural spending has focused on Dublin, escalating the divide with the rest of the country. So, for instance, broadband is more easily available in the east of Ireland than the west. Dublin is wealthier than any other part of Ireland and any major cultural developments tend to be centred on Dublin. A failed attempt to relocate the public sector outside Dublin didn't suggest building a competitor metropolis, but instead for localist political reasons promised to distribute the decentralised workers almost evenly throughout the country, including in the counties which effectively make up Dublin's suburbs.

per cent of applications are granted. The now ubiquitous out-of-town shopping centres and retail parks have also adversely affected parts of town and city centres by driving people out of the centres. We now know that much of the planning system was subject to massive corruption, as local authority decisions could quadruple the value of land overnight. An ongoing tribunal into land rezoning continues to reveal that developers expected to pay politicians large amounts of money to get planning approval.

Ireland presents a 'worst case' for urban development, as the suburbs combine poor transport infrastructure, poor quality housing and an absence of services. Sprawling low-density suburbs mean Dublin covers more space than many more populous cities. Much of the development was outside Dublin, but inhabited by people who work in Dublin, who have no connection to the area and are forced travel by car for many hours each day. This has led to air and traffic pollution as the number of cars in Ireland increased greatly in a short period of time (from 1.2 million in 1998 to 1.7 million in 2007). One of the problems is that the Irish tend to live in houses, and few families with children live in apartments. Apartments are for the poor (when they are called flats), for those in their twenties, or increasingly for retired couples whose children have left home. In the countryside ribbon development is common, with houses built along a road connecting towns. This low-density spread means there is no obvious boundary to towns or villages such as can be seen in many other countries, and because people are increasing living outside towns and villages, they rely increasingly on cars. The tendency to allow people to build houses on their own land also means the loss of flood plains and increased flooding. Added to this is the problem of 'ghost estates'. These are estates built at the height of the boom which are unoccupied; many are incomplete and have been abandoned by the developers who ran out of money. These leave a physical and social scar on the landscape. Many are now owned by the Irish state (see Chapter 6) but there is no plan as to what to do with them.

Visitors to Ireland are usually surprised at the poor quality of Irish roads. Ireland has a relatively underdeveloped road network, with most of the limited motorway routes emanating from or circling Dublin. There are 5,500 kilometres of national routes and twice that in regional roads. Local roads, often known as boreens (an anglicization of the Irish word for road, *bóthar*, with the typical Irish suffix, 'een' to indicate the diminutive) are often of such poor quality that two cars are not able to pass each other. Though it leaves some visitors exasperated, it probably adds to the charm of the Irish countryside. The transport system is largely based on roads. The road network is now expanding rapidly and spending on the road infrastructure is much greater than on other forms of transport. Although Ireland and Dublin had an extensive rail network at the start of the

**Illustration 2.2    Housing estates in Galway**

The 1990s saw a rapid expansion in house building. Much of it, such as this estate in Galway City, was poorly planned and led to car dependency and a degradation of city centres. The people living in these areas have few services such as schools, shops, restaurants or pubs within walking distance. Some more recent developments are known as 'ghost estates' because no one lives in them.

twentieth century, this was gradually eroded as lines were closed. The transport system is largely provided by CIÉ, the state transport holding company which, through Bus Éireann, runs a nationwide bus network (which is subject to competition); Dublin Bus, the capital's main transport system; and Iarnród Éireann, the depleted state rail company. All of these are regarded as poorly run, but there is little political appetite to either reform them or open them up to competition. Though Dublin has introduced a light rail system, it is very limited and its two lines do not even meet! This further encourages car dependency and increases traffic. It has been estimated that Dublin is now, with Athens, the capital city in Europe that takes the longest time to traverse.

Because the country is an island, transport to and from the island is important. Aer Lingus was the national airline until it was recently privatized, though the state retains a major shareholding. It operated

*Figure 2.1* Ireland's physical infrastructure compared

(a) Quality of overall infrastructure, 2008

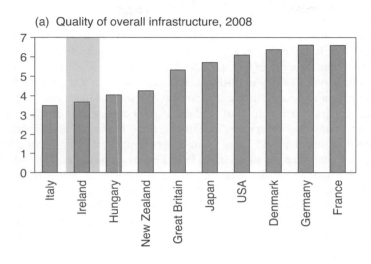

(b) Motorway and main roads, 2007

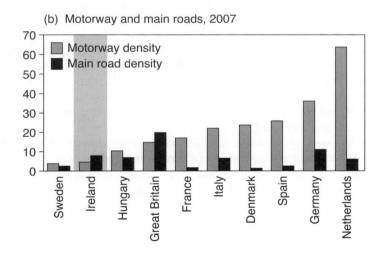

*Note*: General infrastructure in the country is (1 = underdeveloped, 7 = extensive and efficient by international standards).

*Source*: Data from *OECD Economic Survey*, no. 17, *Ireland*, 2009.

an expensive service until deregulation of routes in the late 1980s allowed a small fledgling airline, Ryanair, to compete with Aer Lingus fairly. Prices dropped significantly and emigration became more bearable for many as it was now cheap and easy to fly home for the weekend. Ryanair is now the second largest indigenous Irish company, with routes throughout Europe, and Aer Lingus has copied its low-cost model in order to stay in business. Ryanair's success has made Ireland a much more accessible place, and only the increased security checks and general discomfort of Ireland's publicly-owned airports has allowed passenger ferry services from Ireland to the UK and France to thrive in recent years. There is no longer a national ferry service and the one that purports to be Irish, Irish Ferries, controversially laid off its Irish staff to employ eastern European workers at below Ireland's minimum wage (it was able to do this because the company is registered in the Caribbean). Most of the freight in Ireland comes into the port of Dublin, close to the city centre, which meant freight traffic blocked up the city centre until an expensive tunnel was built connecting the port to the motorway system.

The increased mobility of the Irish has had an impact on the environment. Ireland is governed by strict EU regulations on environmental quality. Though there have been problems of river and sea pollution, Ireland on the whole has clean air and water. Carbon emissions have increased hugely – Ireland's per capita annual carbon footprint is 16 tonnes, higher than the UK, Germany or France, but much lower than the USA. One of the major sources of carbon in Ireland is the large animal population (cows let off steam!), but increased car use and manufacturing is also important. The Irish are reasonably enthusiastic recyclers, and in recent years urban councils have made it easier to recycle. Though household and business waste is continuing to rise, over 36 per cent of it is now recycled. The rest is put into landfill, as the practicality of incineration of waste usually leads to local objections for those close to the proposed site of any incinerator. In 2003 Ireland introduced a charge for plastic bags in shops, which has dramatically reduced the number of bags used each year. This initiative was welcomed by most Irish people, but few other innovations have emerged. Refuse bin charges were introduced which also increased the incentives for green behaviour. Ireland is one of the few countries in Europe with no water charges, which might make sense given the abundance of rain, but it could have an impact on water quality as there is less investment in water treatment than in other countries. However

**Box 2.3    The county system**

The island of Ireland is divided into 32 counties. Of these the Republic is made up of 26 counties. Originally Ireland was divided into about five provinces and 150 *tuath*. Provinces are still used for some sporting events, though there are four now – Ulster, Munster, Leinster and Connaught. The county system was imported by the English based on the English shire. They evolved gradually – Dublin and most of the east and south were 'shired' by 1200. The last county to be formed was Wicklow in 1606. As a result they are very different in terms of size and population. County Cork is the largest, but Dublin now has the highest population. Though an English invention and not based on previous kingdoms in Ireland, counties have assumed great cultural importance. It is the primary way in which people designate where in Ireland they are from. The Gaelic Athletic Association (GAA), the country's largest sporting organization, organizes its competitions on a county basis. They are also still the principal administrative unit for delivery of local services and for electoral constituencies. People's loyalty to these counties appears strong – we know from the analysis of votes in constituencies that traverse two counties, for instance Laois-Offaly, that people from one rarely vote for candidates from the other county.

Ireland's tap water is perfectly drinkable though some object to its fluoridation (adding fluoride to strengthen children's teeth). The unpopularity of bin charges and the protests that followed make governments unwilling to introduce water charges, but a combination of pressure from the EU and the need to diversify government income may force their introduction.

## The peoples of Ireland

Unusually for western Europe, Ireland is less populous today than it was in the mid-nineteenth century. The Great Famine (see Box 1.1, p. 28) reduced Ireland's population through starvation and emigration. Irish emigration continued to be high if cyclical through to the early 1990s, with a net outflow of about 40,000 people per year in the late 1980s. Immigration and the high Irish fertility rate (while it fell dramatically in the 1980s it has since stabilized and remains the highest in Europe) have caused the population to increase significantly, though it remains 2.3 million people lower than in 1841. Most projections expect

Ireland's population to exceed 5 million by 2021. In 1841 Ireland had one of the highest population densities in Europe, but today it is among the lowest, at 59 people per square kilometre compared to 395 in the Netherlands. The density is not uniformly distributed as much of the population has shifted towards Dublin (see Box 2.3). Within Ireland, although the majority live in urban areas (towns or cities), more Irish people still live in rural areas than live in cities.

The populations of most western countries are ageing rapidly. Ireland's population, although ageing, is doing so less quickly. Three components affect population changes. One is the *birth rate*, which, though lower than in the recent past, is still above the replacement rate, where the population maintains itself. This high birth rate means that the population has traditionally been quite young. The average age of an Irish person is 35. In 1986 over 50 per cent of the population was under 25; in 2010 this was about 35 per cent. Another factor is *life expectancy*, which, when rising as it is in Ireland, increases the population. Irish life expectancy has grown as in other parts of Europe, though is slightly below average (76.8 for men and 81.6 for women, up from 71 and 76.7 respectively in 1986). The natural increase in 2008 was 44,600 or about 1 per cent. Ageing populations put pressures on society because the elderly require increased spending on health services; the state's revenues are under pressure as it struggles to cope with increased commitments for pensions. These could increase the divide between old and young, and cause political tensions. In fact because the old are more likely to vote, parties tend to favour supporting the needs of the old over the young, but this does not seem to have caused noticeable tensions in Ireland yet. Figure 2.2 shows the 2006 population and the projected population of Ireland where the fertility rate falls to normal European levels and the net migration rate is zero.

The final factor affecting demographic changes is *rate of migration*. Ireland experienced exceptionally high rates of immigration from the late 1990s, peaking in 2006 when net migration was 71,800. Many of these immigrants were Irish people who were returning due to the job opportunities presented during the economic boom. There are now people from 188 countries living in Ireland, though most are from a small number of countries: Poland, Lithuania, Latvia, the UK, Nigeria and China. By 2009, however, with the collapse of the building industry in which many had worked, some of these immigrants had chosen to return home and Ireland saw a net outflow for the first time since 1995.

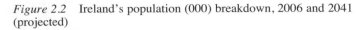

*Figure 2.2* Ireland's population (000) breakdown, 2006 and 2041 (projected)

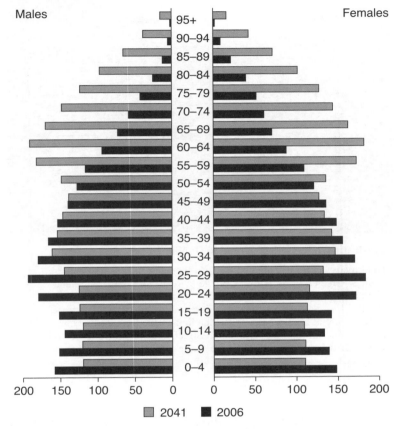

*Source*: Data from Central Statistics Office Population and Labour Force Projections 2011–41.

Ireland is required to allow EU-15 (the 15 EU member states as of 1995) citizens the right to enter and work in the country. In addition, Ireland was one of the few countries among these to place few or no restrictions on citizens from the 2004 EU accession states – mainly central and eastern Europe. The high immigration rates during a very short period of time meant that Ireland moved from being one of the most homogeneous countries in Europe to one of those with the highest rates of foreign nationals living in the country. In 2009 about

**Illustration 2.3   College Green in Dublin**

Dublin city centre is quite compact. At the heart of Ireland's capital, College Green houses Trinity College (shown), the Bank of Ireland (formerly the seat of the Irish Parliament), and nearly every bus route in Dublin! It is close to the Ireland's most fashionable shopping street, Grafton Street, Leinster House (which houses the Irish Parliament) and the city's main thoroughfare, O'Connell Street. This photo from the 1890s shows British army parades and the statue of King William III (now removed).

10 per cent of the Irish population was not Irish, and this does not take account of those born in Ireland of non-Irish parents. This level of immigration is higher than in traditional receptor states such as Germany, France and the UK. There is evidence that Irish people's attitudes to immigrants have become more negative since the late 1990s, particularly among the poor, who are more likely to come into contact with immigrants, and more likely to be competing with them for jobs and public services. There have also been some instances of racial and anti-immigrant abuse, but these have not been widespread. That the immigration happened so quickly and seemingly without the type of tension seen in Germany, France or the UK is quite remarkable. The reasons for this may include:

- Unlike in many European countries, immigrants are not from former colonial territories, which may mean there is an existing tension between the peoples.
- Ireland was a colony and not a colonizer, and a country of emigration, so there may be more understanding of groups migrating for economic reasons.
- Immigrants to Ireland are largely white Europeans and are less easily identifiable as immigrants than in many other countries.
- The immigration took place at a time of virtually full employment, so there was less of a sense that the immigrants were a threat to the native population.

---

**Box 2.4   Pronouncing Irish names**

Because Ireland had so little immigration, it was a remarkably homogeneous place until quite recently. Most people had Irish surnames, and the dominant Irish nationalism meant that many have Irish first names. Many people regularly make mistakes pronouncing Irish names. The pronunciation of some first names such as my own – Eoin – is not obvious from the spelling (Eoin is pronounced like Owen). Many people with Irish names in other countries spell Irish names phonetically in English, so Seán becomes Shaun. Irish surnames are probably the oldest in the world. Although Irish surnames were anglicized, so Ó Broin became Byrne, it is not as easy to change the spelling of surnames and for this reason Irish family names are often mispronounced by non-Irish people. There are three main errors made. One is the pronunciation of vowels in Irish names, a second is misplacing of the emphasis, and the third is how to deal with *gh* in the names.

Irish vowel sounds are softer than in American English. The *a* is pronounced as in mass not as in matrix. So the surname Keohane is pronounced Qyo-HAHN. Irish words and the names that are derived from Irish usually place the emphasis on the first syllable. So Costello should be pronounced COST-ello not Cos-TELL-o as it frequently is in the USA. Similarly Mahoney is MAH-nee not Ma-HONE-ee. Where the names start with O or Mac, which mean from and son of respectively, the emphasis is on the second syllable. So O'Malley is Oh MAH-lee. Unfortunately this is not always the case, as the Keohane example shows. The third problem is the pronunciation of the *g* in Gallagher or Callaghan. Both should be silent but in the UK and Australia are pronounced as GAL-agur and CAL-agan. Sometimes the *gh* is pronounced in Ireland, but oddly not in the USA, as in O'Shaughnessy, which should be Oh SHOCK-nessy and not Oh SHAUN-essy.

The rapid decline in the size of the Irish economy, while prompting some to leave Ireland, may increase tensions between the native and immigrant populations. However, there are some reasons to be optimistic. During the 1980s, a number of black sportsmen played football for Ireland and unlike in England and some other countries this did not cause any adverse reaction. If we can assume that this gives an indication of likely reactions, then perhaps Ireland may avoid such tensions as have been seen in other parts of Europe.

The questions of migration and Irish identity became important in a recent referendum on citizenship. There are two ideal types of citizenship law governing who is entitled to the citizenship of a country: *jus soli,* under which the place of birth is most relevant, and *jus sanguine,* when one's parentage is important. Up to 2004 Ireland had few restrictions and one of the most liberal regimes in Europe, under which people could claim Irish citizenship on either ground. So anyone born on the island of Ireland could claim Irish citizenship, as could anyone with a parent who was an Irish citizen. The rise in immigration caused some elements of one Irish government to voice concerns that the *jus soli* rule was too lenient and one minister claimed that Irish maternity hospitals were exploited by 'citizenship tourism', where heavily pregnant foreign nationals were travelling to Ireland so that their children could gain Irish citizenship. The fact that parents of Irish citizens have the right to residency, to care for the Irish citizen, caused some fears that this would become a major problem. The referendum campaign was quite inflammatory, given the comparatively mild restrictions being proposed (requiring the parents to have lived 'normally' in Ireland for at least three years before the *jus soli* rule would apply). In the end it was easily passed.

Within Ireland there are few ethnic divisions. There is one native ethnic group that is still identifiable – the Travellers. Travellers, of whom there are about 25,000 in Ireland (many more Irish Travellers live in the UK), by and large live a nomadic lifestyle, travelling in caravans. It is unclear how they came to form a separate group, but some suggest that they became nomadic as a result of the famine, while others trace their roots back over 800 years. They speak a dialect, Cant (from the Irish word *caint*, to speak), that is a mixture of Irish (Gaelic) and English, often reversing the order of letters in words. Many had been tin workers, and were generally called Tinkers, but the introduction of plastics killed that trade and they have failed to adapt to modernization. They are the most disadvantaged group in

**Box 2.5    The outbreak of the Troubles**

The Northern Ireland state set up in 1922 was to be a Protestant one, and Catholics were treated in ways that one would today find shocking. The electoral boundaries of Derry City Council were drawn in such a way that a city with a Catholic/nationalist majority could elect a council with a Protestant/unionist majority. There was an exclusively Protestant 'special' police force (in addition to the regular force). Public appointments were much more likely to go to Protestants, as was public housing.

The first victims of the Troubles were Catholics shot dead in random sectarian attacks by the Ulster Volunteer Force. Internationally, civil rights issues were coming to prominence and this may have influenced the Northern Ireland Civil Rights Association (NICRA) to be set up to deal with some of the more blatant inequalities in Northern Ireland. Issues mainly related to the provision of housing for Catholics, an end to gerrymandering and a move to one person, one vote in local elections. NICRA was a coalition of middle-class Catholics, nationalists, socialists and Catholic 'defenders'.

The Northern Ireland government was slow to grant these concessions in the face of increased Protestant militancy, and by the time it did, the nationalists' demands had moved on. Civil rights marches were heavily policed and in 1969 rioting broke out in a number of areas. At this stage the police were no longer able to contain the violence in an impartial manner and the British army was drafted in. Initially it was welcomed by the nationalist community, but the British army's response to problems was security-based rather than political. A breakaway faction in the IRA, the Provisional IRA, with a Belfast-based 'defenderist' leadership (that is, it set itself the task of defending the Catholic community) benefited from the activities of the security forces in imposing curfews, bringing in broad-based internment (detention without trial) and especially Bloody Sunday, when 11 peaceful protesters were shot dead by the British army. These events led to an increase in recruitment to the IRA and an escalation of sectarian violence in Northern Ireland. In 1972 the Stormont government was suspended and direct rule from Whitehall was imposed. Any attempts at political settlements were opposed by extreme nationalists and unionists, and so it would take nearly thirty years of violence before a political agreement could be reached.

Irish society, with life expectancy and infant mortality at levels the rest of the population had in the 1940s. Travellers have become a focus of political protest; few want to have Travellers' halting sites near them, as Travellers are frequently blamed for crime and illegal dumping.

Obviously there is a major ethnic split within Northern Ireland (see Box 2.5), but the vast majority of the people in the Republic are white Irish Catholics. In Chapter 1 we saw that the Irish are descended from Gaelic Irish, Norse, Old and New English as well as some other groups of migrants. But these migrations are long since forgotten and, apart from one of the much depleted number of Protestants of Anglo-Irish stock, it would perhaps be an unusual Irish person who even knew what you were referring to if you asked their ethnic heritage. That few in Ireland would describe themselves as anything other than Irish may be a tribute to the nationalist political project which took hold in the mid-nineteenth century. As this quote from Michael Collins (1922: 98), the nationalist leader, indicates, Irish leaders wanted not just political independence but to be culturally cleansed:

It was not only by the British armed occupation that Ireland was subdued. It was by means of the destruction, after great effort, of our Gaelic civilisation. This destruction brought upon us the loss almost of nationality itself. For the last hundred years or more Ireland has been a nation in little more than in name.

An exclusive image emerged at the start of the twentieth century, where the idealized Irish person was from the west, a devout Catholic who spoke Gaelic, and if male played Gaelic games (see Chapter 7). If a woman, she bore children who would be raised as Catholics and play Gaelic games. They engaged in a traditional culture, one which had been cleansed and approved by the Catholic Church. One of the most important components was anti-Englishness. The realities of Irish history, as we have seen, are very different, but for most of the century the new nationalist state succeeded in framing what Irish meant. This led to intolerance and an authoritarian attitude to difference, which perhaps makes Ireland's seemingly smooth adjustment to immigration all the more remarkable. This conception of Irishness was not without its critics and caused some social divisions, not least for those people who did not fit into this homogeneous ideal type. As we shall see in the next chapter, social divisions do exist and Ireland's responses have not always been appropriate.

# 3

# The Changing Society

Ireland claims to be a republic – a place free from arbitrary rule – and as such its official documents tend to be explicit in terms of the equality of its citizens. The Proclamation of the Republic, the document that, though possessing no legal status, laid the basis for the new Irish state, proclaimed that 'the Republic guarantees religious and civil liberty, equal rights and equal opportunities to all its citizens' (see Illustration 1.3). This claim was no socialist creed: the state later included in its constitution a commitment to the protection of property rights and the market economy. It is arguable that it utterly failed to deliver on its goal of equality of opportunity, because, as we shall see, Ireland suffered from dire poverty and more recently gross inequality that seemed to be based on an individual's childhood circumstances. Many would argue that religious and other civil liberties were only granted to those whose religion and lifestyles were approved by the new state. Given its poverty, Ireland's welfare state developed more slowly than those of other European countries, and it has not yet caught up. The state's social system is controversial, in that many claim that it aggravates existing social divisions. Though a great deal of public money is spent on the public sector, particularly the health and education systems, there is a sense that they are failing. The criminal justice system is liberal and protective of citizens' rights, though the threat to the state from IRA violence caused some restrictions on the rights traditionally enjoyed in common law (Anglo-American) legal systems.

Irish society has changed rapidly since the 1990s when the country was among the wealthiest places in the world. Even after the economic downturn the typical Irish person is middle-class, or at least comparatively wealthy. Whether or not Ireland's (even fleeting) wealth improved Irish society is debatable. Most academic analysts argue that Irish society, as well as having become wealthier, has become happier and more tolerant (Fahey *et al.*, 2007). But there are some misgivings. In 2003, Ireland's then president, Mary McAleese, a prominent cheerleader for Ireland's status as wealthy nation, perhaps reflected the contradictory sentiments of the Irish regarding the rapid changes in their society: 'If the men and women of Ireland's past could choose a time to live, there would be a long queue for this one. It is far from perfect but it is as good as it has ever been' (7 May 2003). Some years later, however, when it was clear that the economic miracle was built on rather shaky ground, she suggested 'that every one of us would have to say with our hands on our hearts that we were all consumed by that same element of consumerism . . . we have paid a very, very big price for that very radical shift. And now the balance presumably is going to swing back the other way and it will be no harm' (14 December 2008).

McAleese and others have spoken in ways that resonate with speeches of early nationalist leaders who condemned consumerism and material wealth as something English and therefore alien to the Irish psyche. But it is clear that the Irish took to wealth and conspicuous consumption with alacrity. This chapter will draw on the demographic shifts highlighted in Chapter 2 to paint a portrait of Irish society in the early twenty-first century. It looks at the frequently ignored issue of social class in Irish society, and how new wealth has changed the way we think about class. With falling fertility rates, families are much smaller than they were, and, as we have seen, with suburbanization many families live in places where they have few social roots and certainly not the extended family living with them or nearby as was common in the past. The recent wholesale move of women into the workforce, and the recent legalization of contraception and divorce have all combined to change the nature of family in modern Ireland. The chapter examines the pressures on the health and social welfare systems brought about by demographic change; the education system, one that is highly regarded by most but might be failing to adapt to the new society, based as it is on a century-old model; and finally, crime and justice. Societal changes in Ireland are conspicuously felt in crime, which many regard as having risen precipitously since the 1990s.

## Social class: a homogeneous society?

As a former colony, on independence Ireland sought to eschew all remnants of the aristocracy associated with British rule. There are still a small number of people who refer to their old British titles, and live in large country estates, but these are treated by most as quaint relics of a long-distant past. There is a sense that all Irish people are from the same stock and just a few generations from subsistence farming. Thus the Irish tend not to think in terms of a class society, and certainly there is not the rigid sense of class that could be observed in Britain until quite recently. A former Taoiseach, Charles Haughey, made a self-serving suggestion that the idea of class distinctions was an 'alien gospel' and 'inherently unIrish' (cited in Munck, 2006: 302). This assumption was supported by the fact that Ireland did not industrialize, and so there were fewer of the urban workers that normally make up the working class. But it would be wrong to say there is no class divide. We saw that Gaelic Ireland was a hierarchical or stratified society, and though many groups lost their status under British occupation, by the end of the nineteenth century there was an identifiable Catholic land-owning middle class. Equally we can see that historically, poor labourers continually struggled and often failed to live off the land. Despite the more fanciful ideas of Irish nationalists, their descendents did not magically become equal on Ireland's achieving independence. The new Irish state was created by a sort of revolution, but it was not accompanied by radical societal upheaval. The guardians of the new state were conservative middle-class Catholics with their own conservative middle-class interests and values.

Societies tend to divide into groups, which are often quite rigid, so movement in and out of groups is difficult. There are a number of social bases on which societies can divide, sometimes referred to as cleavages: class, religion, culture, urban/rural divide. Class is usually thought to be the primary way in which western societies are structured. It is argued that class divisions are important for the maintenance of social order (Saunders, 1990). The class you are born into is important because it can determine the life you will lead. It might be difficult to escape from one's class, and traditionally there was little opportunity for most born poor to achieve entry, for example, to one of the professions. Class is often based on a threefold division between upper, middle and lower class. Even within these there are divisions: the UK upper class sees people with 'old money' (inherited wealth) looking down on people with 'new money' (newly earned wealth). So class is socially constructed or in the minds of the people in the different classes. Class assumes economic wealth is important, but when people refer to other people's class they may also be considering status or power. School teachers may have a higher status than bricklayers, but there is a good chance that bricklayers are far wealthier.

Formal definitions of social class usually depend on the occupation of the head of the household (Goldthorpe, 1987). Here the level of skill and the responsibility of the post matter, with classes that range from company director to long-term unemployed (see Table 3.1). Between 1986 and 2006 the proportion of people in the top two classes has risen from a quarter of the population to a third. Meanwhile the percentage in families led by manual (skilled, semi-skilled and unskilled) workers has fallen from nearly half the population to less than a third. This rise in the middle class does not mean that class differences have ceased to exist. Basing class exclusively on occupation is problematic because it does not take into account new types of work and the general decline in manual labour. Nor does it account for the other ways in which Irish people view and judge each other – accent, education, school attended, sports played, and newspapers read (see Box 3.1). Class certainly exists in Ireland, and particularly in Dublin there are groups who have little in common and tend not to mix in any forum.

*Table 3.1*  Social class in Ireland

---

1. Higher managerial and professional)
   1.1. Managers (company directors); employers (company owners); administrators (senior bureaucrats)
   1.2. Higher professional (lawyers, doctors, architects, university professors, etc.)
2. Lower managerial and professional (nurses, journalists, teachers, computer programmers, etc.)
3. Lower administrative (clerks, secretaries, etc.)
4. Farmers
5. Skilled manual (painters, decorators, electricians, plumbers, etc.)
6. Semi-skilled manual (labourers, drivers, carers, some assembly workers, etc.)
7. Unskilled manual (packers, shop assistants, etc.)
8. Agricultural workers
9. Long-term unemployed

---

*Source*: Based on Goldthorpe (1987).

In an entertaining and probably more apposite take on class and class distinctions in modern Ireland, the economist and commentator David McWilliams (2006) claimed that 'Wonderbra economics' had pushed together and lifted the social classes in Ireland. His adaption of David Brooks' book on the middle class in the USA introduces new stereotypes, such as RoboPaddy, the Irish investor who buys

---

**Box 3.1   Alternative indicators of social class in Ireland**

Social class is normally measured in terms of occupation, which endow groups with varying levels of money, status and power. In the more rigid societies of the past, this may have been appropriate but is less so today. As well as occupation, which is important in conveying status, Irish people use other indicators to classify each other.

- *Dress*   is probably the first thing one notices in another person. We use clothes as uniforms to proclaim which group we belong to. The working classes in Ireland can sometimes be identified by their jewellery, soccer jerseys and tracksuits. The young middle class wear designer clothes with collars turned up.
- *Accent*   is important and for such a small country, Ireland has a huge array of accents. Especially in Dublin there are distinct middle-class and working-class versions of these accents. Many young middle-class people have developed a sort of mid-Atlantic nasal accent with long drawn-out vowels, often referred to as a Dublin 4 (after the postcode) accent. Accent may be one of the major barriers to social mobility in Ireland.
- *School*   Although most people go to free, state-run secondary schools, particularly in and around Dublin many private schools still exist. These convey a certain status, mainly to people who attend them. They are usually religious, sometimes Protestant but often Catholic.
- *Sport*   Children in private schools often play sports such as rugby or hockey. In working-class areas of Dublin soccer is normally played. Outside Dublin the GAA is popular among all classes.
- *Newspapers*   also say something about a person. The *Irish Times* is thought to be a left-leaning liberal paper read by Dublin 4 intellectual types. The more populist and more popular *Irish Independent* is thought to be read by the 'ordinary Irish person'. Tabloids are read by the working classes.

Dublin is probably the most socially divided place in Ireland. The river Liffey which divides the city physically is thought to divide it socially: Northsiders are considered working-class and Southsiders middle-class. In fact some of the wealthiest parts of Dublin are on the Northside and some of the poorest are on the Southside but it is an important symbolic division for many.

property even in countries he's never heard of, Hibernian Cosmopolitans, who are afraid Ireland is losing its cultural soul, the Carrot Juice Contrarians, anti-business, anti-globalization leftists who believe Ireland is on a path to destruction, and Kell's Angels, well-educated, well-travelled, long-distance commuters who live in 'Deckland'. In fact, far from being pushed together, he shows groups are moving further apart in cultural terms. It is just that income is no longer a good predictor of class distinctions. So factors such as the paper you read and the type of car you drive become important in defining class. The *Irish Times*-reading, Irish-speaking cyclist has little or nothing in common with the *Sun*-reading, English soccer-obsessed SUV driver.

McWilliams alludes to some of the values that the different classes might have. Certainly occupational class does not always help us distinguish social values. One type to which the Irish frequently refer, usually pejoratively, is Dublin 4. A Dublin 4 type is a liberal, left-sympathizing, intellectual anti-nationalist, thought to wield huge political power through purported control of media outlets. It is questionable whether this type actually exists at all. The values of the Irish in regard to Europe, nationalism, the economy, religious or moral issues and the environment have changed dramatically over time. A survey from 2002 showed that generational differences and concomitant educational differences (so-called cohort effects), rather than class differences, explain changes in values. So the old are more conservative in relation to the provision of abortion, divorce and gay rights. The young are more liberal on the economy, more tolerant of economic inequality, and less nationalist (Sinnott and Kennedy, 2006).

If generational change is important in terms of values, it is also important for class. Social mobility – the ability to move from one class to another with a change of generation – is important because one would expect in a dynamic society that class origins will not be an important indicator of life chances. Most agree that meritocratic societies are more likely to prosper. Social mobility has increased marginally over time. Although it is difficult to obtain data that can be compared across countries, it appears that Ireland had been one of the more rigid countries in terms of social mobility, but this is easing somewhat. However, much of Ireland's upward mobility is due to the rapid growth in the economy. There has not been an increase in equality of opportunity, so even though those born to a poor household are now more likely to rise out of poverty; those born into wealthy households are yet more advantaged over others (Whelan and Layte, 2007).

For neo-liberals (those committed to a free market economy), inequality of outcome is vital for a dynamic economy and society. For others, on the left and sometimes the European Christian right, poverty and inequality pose dangers to the stability of a society. Ireland's Gini coefficient – a measure of inequality – is around 32, slightly above average for western Europe, though lower than the UK or the USA. Despite the rapid economic growth in Ireland, there is evidence that poverty levels have persisted and that income inequality has grown. This is hardly surprising, given economic polices pursued to free up the economy, but it is worrying if some groups are systematically left behind. Comparatively, Ireland has an above average rate of relative poverty (see Figure 3.1). Relative poverty is

*Figure 3.1* EU-25 'at risk of poverty' rate (60% threshold) including all social transfers, 2006

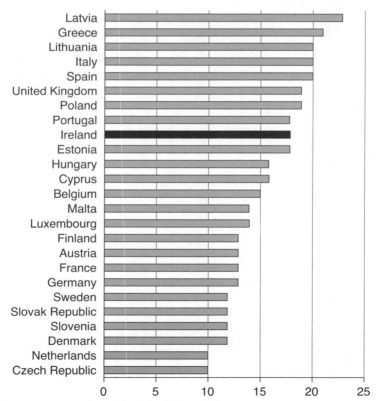

*Source*: Data from Central Statistics Office (2006).

measured in comparison to others within the same society, where relative poverty is defined as having less than 60 per cent of the median (middle) person's income (after social welfare transfers).

While most Irish people's incomes had been rising up to 2007, the rich were getting richer to a greater degree than the poor, increasing the divide between rich and poor. But relative poverty tells us about the distribution of resources, not whether there is real deprivation. Table 3.2 shows that when deprivation is measured, there are very few genuinely poor people in Ireland, though in cities there are some obvious pockets of deprivation. At the same time measures of wealth show that most Irish people are among the most affluent people in the world, with most reporting access to consumer goods such as the internet and household appliances. One of the major factors influencing a person's wealth is their family background and the education of their parents, topics to which we now move.

*Table 3.2*    Percentage of the population at risk of poverty reporting each type of deprivation, 2005–7

| Deprivation Indicators | % of individuals at risk of poverty | | |
| --- | --- | --- | --- |
| | 2005 | 2006 | 2007 |
| Without heating at some stage in the last year | 3.4 | 2.8 | 2.7 |
| Unable to afford a morning, afternoon or evening out in the last fortnight | 5.2 | 4.3 | 3.3 |
| Unable to afford two pairs of strong shoes | 1.8 | 1.6 | 1.9 |
| Unable to afford a roast once a week | 2.0 | 2.3 | 1.8 |
| Unable to afford a meal with meat, chicken or fish every second day | 1.7 | 1.1 | 1.2 |
| Unable to afford new (not second-hand) clothes | 3.0 | 2.9 | 2.5 |
| Unable to afford a warm waterproof coat | 1.4 | 0.7 | 1.4 |
| Unable to afford to keep the home adequately warm | 2.1 | 1.8 | 1.7 |
| Unable to afford to replace any worn out furniture | 5.6 | 5.6 | 4.9 |
| Unable to afford to have family or friends for a drink or meal once a month | 5.6 | 4.8 | 3.8 |
| Unable to afford to buy presents for family or friends at least once a year | 2.8 | 1.6 | 1.7 |

*Source*: Data from Central Statistics Office (2008).

## The welfare state and health policy

One of the ways that inequality and poverty are addressed is through the social welfare system. Unlike the rest of western Europe, Ireland's social welfare was quite limited and late in developing. Traditionally much of the social protection needed for the country was provided by the family and the Church. The few pieces of welfare provisions available in Ireland were ones that the British had introduced, and it is telling that one of the first moves of the independent state was to reduce old-age pensions and unemployment benefit. With no large secular left-wing party, there was little pressure to introduce a comprehensive welfare state. Even the small Labour party tended to defer to the wishes of the Church. Governments rather attempted to alleviate crises with one-off actions. So the housing crisis evident from the 1910s led to the clearance of city centre slums and the building of new housing estates. Attempts to introduce quite mild social assistance measures in the post-war period ran into opposition from the Catholic Church, which preferred itself to be the main outlet for the destitute as a means of controlling the faithful. As a result many of the social services that are normally provided by the state in other countries are offered in Ireland by church-based organizations with financial support from the state. Schools, hospitals and some poverty services are provided by the church. Though there is strong support for the idea of a welfare state, it is widely thought that the Irish one is expensive and inefficient. There have been major increases in spending on social protection and health since the late 1990s, but these have been ad hoc and have not been accompanied by reforms that would make public services better or better value for money. Social protection, and especially the health service, has become politically sensitive and an important issue for voters.

Esping-Andersen (1990) distinguished between types of welfare states: social democratic, corporatist, liberal, and sub-protective, where there is a sliding scale of what is spent by the state on social protection. Placing Ireland in one of these categories is difficult. Ireland's social partnership model is akin to corporatism but the market-oriented welfare provisions resemble the Anglo-Saxon liberal model. The state primarily offers a protection of last resort for those who fail in the marketplace. That much of Ireland's social services is means-tested, rather than citizen-based and available to all, contrasts with the social democratic model which actively tries to ensure a more even redistribution of resources on the basis of guaranteeing certain services.

About 22.5 per cent of Irish gross national income (GNI) was spent on social protection in 2005, a steady increase over the previous ten years. This is slightly below the Organization for Economic Cooperation and Development (OECD) average (24.4 per cent), but in cash terms Ireland spends about the same amount per person on social protection as other wealthy European countries (€7,083 for every man, woman and child in 2005). In real terms this doubled between 1997 and 2005. In 2008 spending on health and social welfare made up nearly 47 per cent of government spending. And given that this was at a time that Ireland experienced high employment, one would expect spending on social protection to be lower than average. If Ireland spends so much money on social protection, why does it seem to be so ineffectual? This is the problem that Irish governments have grappled with in the last decade.

Some state payments in Ireland are quite high: unemployment assistance, or the dole as it is colloquially known, is €204.50 per week for over-20s. This compares with €72 (£64.50) for over-25s in the UK. These comparatively generous rates, coupled with other benefits received by the unemployed, mean that Ireland has a high 'poverty trap' compared to other OECD countries – this is where the incentive for taking up employment is reduced by the potential loss of social welfare benefits. The absence of incentives to retrain and seek employment means that Ireland has a serious problem of long-term unemployment, with a group of people becoming virtually unemployable.

Another aspect of social spending is that much of it actually acts as a subsidy to the middle classes; so more is spent subsidizing private pensions through tax reliefs than on providing the state pension, currently €11,388 per year for a single person over 66. Child Benefit and other family-related allowance given to those with children, untaxed and regardless of income, have increased. Similar issues are at play in the other major component of social spending, healthcare.

The Irish healthcare system is regarded by Irish people as very poor and is below the European average if measured by the length of time it takes for a public patient to be seen. It is the largest component of state spending in Ireland, costing about €13billion annually, and Irish spending is about average for the OECD. A Health Service Executive runs the health service which until recently was regionally divided. Unlike the rest of western Europe, there is no universal right to free healthcare, and even those on low incomes – entitled to a Medical Card – have to pay fees for some services. But neither is it a fully privatized healthcare system such as traditionally existed in the

USA. Most healthcare is provided or funded by the state, but those with private health insurance (the rate of private insurance coverage is about 50 per cent, among the highest in the EU) have better access to state facilities than others with greater medical need. Though a great deal of money is spent on healthcare, the high pay rates for healthcare professionals in Ireland mean that much of that investment is not in direct patient provision compared to other countries with high investment in healthcare (see Figure 3.2).

Recent changes to the system, though increasing efficiency and value for money, also increase the extent to which the public sector subsidizes private healthcare. Examples of this include the tax reliefs given for health insurance and the leasing of hospital lands to build private hospitals. Because private and public patients share services, but private patients are given privileged access, this has led to a two-tier health system. There have been a small number of highly publicized cases where people have died because the public patient waiting times were longer than those for private patients.

That said, most people who actually use the health service find it satisfactory. Furthermore, there has been significant improvement in the health of the Irish measured in terms of life expectancy and death rates. Ireland's smoking rate is low and it became the first country in the world to ban smoking in public places, including, most controversially, pubs. However there have been increases in obesity, stress and sexually transmitted diseases (thought to be aided by increased alcohol consumption), all related to the pressures of economic growth.

**Changing families in Ireland: breaking traditions**

Ireland is unusual in western Europe in that traditional family structures remained unchanged until quite recently. In most countries traditional families mean nuclear families, where parents and children live together. Traditional Irish families, of the type that were still common in the 1950s, saw a number of generations of the same family living together. Ireland was traditionally characterized by late marriage for men (particularly in rural areas where men might only inherit the farm when already in middle age), and consequently large age difference between parents. They tended to have quite large families, with children born at close intervals (the phrase 'Irish twins' refers to siblings born within a year of each other). There could be many years' age difference between the eldest and the youngest child

*Figure 3.2*    Pay for healthcare providers in Ireland and selected
countries

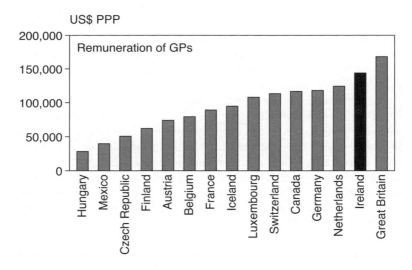

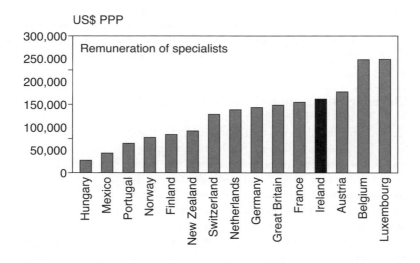

Figures are in US dollars at purchasing price parity.

*Source*: From OECD Health Data 2009.

and it was not uncommon for a nephew to be older than his uncle. The Irish constitution makes significant claims about the importance of the family, by which it meant a traditional family unit of married parents and children living together, so some of the barriers to non-traditional (meaning non-Catholic) living arrangements were legal, but many were social norms that few people were brave enough to challenge.

After a significant fall in the marriage rate from the 1970s to the mid-1990s, marriage rates have since increased (the rate is roughly five per thousand of the population, about the European average). As Table 3.3 shows, far more people are now co-habiting than before, though the rate is still comparatively low. Divorce was only made legal in 1997 following the narrow acceptance by referendum of a change to the constitution, which had explicitly prohibited it. The new regime is quite restrictive; divorce can only be granted after four years of marital breakdown. The divorce rate has risen, but at 0.8 per thousand of the population is well below the EU average (2.0) and far lower than the UK figure (2.6). The fact that the former Taoiseach, Bertie Ahern, was elected despite being separated and in another relationship, demonstrates the extent to which Irish people's attitudes have changed. Just five years earlier his marital status was used against him in a party leadership election.

*Table 3.3*   Type of household and family formation, 1996 and 2006

| Type | 1996 % | 2006 % |
|---|---|---|
| Married without children | 19.2 | 21.4 |
| Co-habiting without children | 2.4 | 7.4 |
| Married with children | 61 | 49 |
| Cohabiting with children | 1.6 | 4.2 |
| Lone parents | 16 | 17.9 |
| Total number of family units | 807,000 | 1,053,000 |
| People living alone as % of all households | 21.5 | 22.5 |
| Non-family units as % of all households (with related and unrelated persons) | 7.2 | 7.3 |
| Total number of households | 1,123,000 | 1,470,000 |

*Note*: Totals do not add to 100 due to rounding.

*Source*: Data from CSO National Census, 1996 and 2006.

Changes have also taken place in relation to the families children are born into. In 1981 just five per cent of births were to unmarried parents. In 2006 almost a third of births were to unmarried parents, half of whom were cohabiting. Two-thirds of births were to married couples. This varies with age, with younger mothers much less likely to be married. Ireland is thus coming close to the European norm for births outside marriage. As we saw in the last chapter, fertility rates have fallen dramatically, halving since the 1970s, and are now steady (1.9) and among the highest in the EU. Until quite recently there were significant restrictions on the ability of Irish people to plan families. In 1991 a music shop was fined for selling condoms, as the legislation at the time only allowed pharmacies and some other outlets to sell contraceptives. A medical prescription is still required for the morning-after pill. Abortion is still illegal (see Box 4.3, p. 108) and is one of the areas where a traditional morality still seems to hold sway. No political party has ever ventured to propose liberalizing the laws on abortion, despite evidence that between 5,000 and 10,000 women travel to Britain to terminate pregnancies there each year. A number of high-profile cases have softened attitudes somewhat, as most are in favour of allowing abortion in some circumstances. In other traditional areas of morality there has been some tentative change. A Civil Partnership Act allows same-sex couples most rights that heterosexuals have in terms of inheritance and pensions, but stops short of calling it marriage and denies the possibility of adoption.

As a result of the changes in Irish society the average size of the household has fallen from 4.0 in 1966, to 3.5 in 1986 and 2.8 in 2006. Just over five per cent of households consist of six or more people compared to a quarter of all households in 1966. For the children in these households, their experience is also changing. As many mothers work, more infants are being cared for by non-family members – about 15 per cent of those under three. As childcare costs in Ireland are prohibitively expensive (up to €1,200 a month in parts of Dublin) and there are no state-funded places, it is hardly surprising that the number in childcare is lower than the OECD average (about 22 per cent), though the Irish figure actually represents a significant increase. There has been a significant weakening of the social pressures on people to get married and have children. In 1988, 83 per cent of survey respondents agreed that 'people who want children ought to get married'; in 2002, 53 per cent agreed with that statement. The smaller family size is in part for practical purposes, and more and more women wish to enter the workforce, thus postponing the age at which they have chil-

---

**Box 3.2   Northern Irish society**

Political cleavages are the structural basis for the divisions between a people in society. These could be class divisions, religious divisions, urban/rural divisions or cultural divisions. If the Republic of Ireland can be treated as an homogeneous society, Northern Ireland provides a classic example of a deep societal cleavage where the divisions tend to be reinforced, so divisions on religion are congruent with divisions on constitutional and cultural issues. These divisions are structural – so the people from different sides of the political divide read different news-papers, go to different schools, and live in different areas. Catholics (Irish nationalists) and Protestants (British or Ulster nationalists) in Northern Ireland read different papers (the *Irish News* and the *Ulster Newsletter*), attend different schools (Catholic and state schools) and live in different areas (segregation is high, West Belfast, for instance, being predominantly Catholic whereas East Belfast is predominantly Protestant). Areas are often physically divided by high 'peace walls' keeping the two sides apart. These cleavage divisions manifest them-selves in political terms as Catholics tend to vote for Sinn Féin or the Social Democratic and Labour Party (SDLP), whereas Protestants vote for the Democratic Unionist Party and the Ulster Unionist Party. Indeed people's social characteristics often provide an indication of how they will vote, so a middle-class, middle-aged, church-going Catholic woman is most likely to vote for the SDLP. It is among working-class people that the divisions are greatest and among whom tensions tend to be highest.

---

dren. Just eight per cent of married women were working outside the home in 1971; by 2007 over 60 per cent of women between 15 and 64 worked outside the home. Despite this women still carry out most household tasks, such as cooking and cleaning. There has also been a weakening of the strength of the Catholic Church, and the values of the younger generations have changed as a result of exposure to media and culture from the UK and the USA in particular. Another factor that is probably important in determining the changing family structures is the increasing levels of educational attainment that younger Irish people have compared to their parents.

## Education in Ireland

Education has traditionally been important in Irish society, and for many was seen as the main route to escape from poverty. They were probably right, as both Irish and international research shows that education is related to health, wealth and happiness. The Irish like to think that they have one of the best education systems in the world, and politicians continually speak about Ireland having a young well-educated workforce and the importance of the 'knowledge economy'. It was often cited as one of the causes of the Celtic Tiger economy (see Chapter 6). However it is arguable that the education system even today is quite archaic and differs only marginally from that delivered by the Catholic Church 100 years earlier. The education system is highly centralized and effectively controlled by a government department widely thought to be highly conservative. It still puts an emphasis on an academically-oriented classical education.

Education is one of the most important aspects of society because it is through it and in the family that socialization takes place and values are formed. It is also one of the main ways others use to judge and select people for employment and other opportunities. That the focus is on academic education probably reflects a middle-class culture that alienates many students and effectively leaves them outside the education system. That said, retention rates in Ireland are quite high, lower than in Scandinavia but above the EU average.

The Irish education system is divided into three levels. There is primary education for children aged between 4 and 12, delivered in state-funded schools. One of the most distinctive characteristics of the Irish education system is that education is predominantly controlled by churches. Over 90 per cent of primary schools are managed by the Catholic Church, which imbues the school day with religion even outside formal religious classes. The school day is highly structured around classes that last about 40 minutes and the ethos of Irish schools is hierarchical, with students having little input into what is taught or how. Another unusual feature of the education system at both primary and secondary level is the prevalence of single-sex schools and the fact that most schools insist that students wear uniforms. Entry to primary schools is usually based on location, so children tend to go to their local schools. In urban areas where there is greater class segregation, this means that in some schools in disadvantaged areas, it is hard for students to keep up with others in more affluent areas where parents are likely to be more supportive of and familiar with education.

From the age of 12 to about 18 students go to secondary schools (the ages of compulsory education are between 5 and 16). Selection for these schools is devolved to the schools, but living in a catchment area or whether one has siblings at the school are important. There are no formal entry exams. Again the influence of the Church is still present though not as widespread, with just over half of students in church-run schools. The major change the education system has seen is the introduction of free secondary-level education in the late 1960s. Before then, bright children who could not otherwise afford it were educated by the Christian Brothers, in what we now know was a pretty brutal fashion – mental and physical abuse, including even rape, were widespread. Private schools existed for the middle classes, nearly all run by religious orders, be they Catholic or Protestant and these would produce the gentlemen expected to reach the top of society.

The introduction of free education entailed the expansion of the network of state schools, as opposed to state-funded religious schools, and these tended to offer some non-academic, vocational education as well as academic subjects. That said, there continued to be a strong emphasis on academic subjects delivered in a hierarchical and didactic manner. The writer John McGahern, as a school teacher in the 1960s, calculated that over half the school day was devoted to teaching Irish and religious instruction. The main exams are now the Junior Certificate, taken when students are about 15, and the Leaving Certificate taken at about 18. Students take between five and ten subjects, usually about seven, of which Irish (Gaelic Language), English and Mathematics are compulsory. One aspect of the Irish education system is that it is almost completely geared towards preparation for these examinations, which may detract from the quality of education as students become practised in learning by rote rather than independent thought. More recently there have been changes to the curriculum and attempts to direct the attention of students away from individual exams into more active learning with continuous assessment, but only a minority of students take these courses. The impact of free education is easy to see, as only about 20 per cent of schoolchildren completed secondary school in the early 1960s, rising to nearly 50 per cent by the end of the 1970s. Retention rates for Irish students have grown even higher. Almost 90 per cent of 20- to 24-year-olds in 2008 had completed secondary school, well above the EU average of 78 per cent.

Control of schools by religious institutions is contested as many parents who no longer want their children to be educated within religious schools have few other options. A number of grassroots initiatives have provided some alternatives, though usually against

**Illustration 3.1    St Vincent de Paul National School, Marino, Dublin**

Like many primary schools in Ireland this one, managed by the Catholic Church, segregates boys and girls who are also required to wear uniforms. The school day in Ireland lasts from about 9 am to 3 pm for primary school, and 9 am to 4 pm for secondary school students. The school year is shorter than in most other countries. According to the OECD secondary schools are open for about 167 days, much lower than the average (185). Primary schools open for 183 days, slightly below the OECD average (187).

significant opposition from the Department of Education, so Gaelscoileanna (Irish-speaking schools) and Educate Together (non-denominational) schools have grown in number, but there is some pressure on the Catholic Church in particular to give control of the running of schools back to the state. There are also controversies about the remaining private schools whose teachers are paid for by the state making private education comparatively cheap – certainly cheaper than sending a child to a crèche. These schools, which are still too expensive for most families, tend to do better if quality is measured on propensity to send students to university.

Entry to tertiary education depends on points calculated from the results in the Leaving Certificate exams. The points system is very fair and not open to bias or abuse, but it does not help identify aptitude for particular areas and push students towards those areas, or away from others. It works on a market basis, with the points for particular courses depending on the number of places on offer and the demand for those places. So high demand courses, in areas such as medicine and law, will have high points requirements and only students with top marks will enter, regardless of what subjects those results were in. There are two types of higher education institution, universities (of which there are seven) and regional Institutes of Technology. The IT sector is less prestigious and tends to give students more practical training. Of the universities, Trinity College, which dates from the sixteenth century, is the oldest and best known. It is (or at least was) a Protestant institution from which Catholics were barred (most recently by their own church). University College, Dublin which is part of the National University of Ireland, was founded as a Catholic University, though the church has little control today. This would have educated the Irish nationalist elite who ran Ireland for the last century. There has been a huge expansion in tertiary education. What had been an exclusive club for the elite (in 1949, just over 1,100 people received undergraduate degrees) is now available to all. In 2007 there were almost 150,000 people enrolled in higher education courses, compared to just over 20,000 in 1966. By 2007 32 per cent of 25- to 65-year-olds had a higher education. There are fears, however, that this might have come at the expense of quality. Since the mid-1990s EU students have been exempt from paying university fees. This was gradually eroded by an ever-rising 'registration fee'. By 2011, the financial crisis had caused such a significant increase in fees that it could no longer be claimed that Ireland had free university fees.

Public expenditure on education is reasonably high. It is about average if it is measured as a percentage of GDP and above the EU average as a percentage of GNI (see Box 6.1, p. 142). Education at all levels, including since 1996 third level, is free, so one might expect that educational attainment would be less affected by class. In fact the development of free education came at a cost for the universities, for whom the rise in revenue failed to keep pace with the increasing number of students. There is no evidence that it increased participation rates from those from poorer backgrounds, who were already struggling in primary and secondary school. In fact it represented a massive subsidy to middle-class parents, an electorally important group. Although there has been increased spending at the primary level, pupil-teacher ratios are among the highest in the EU at 19:1. Comparative measures of educational attainment are problematic because different countries examine students differently, but by most measures of reading, mathematical and scientific literacy, Irish school leavers perform above the average of OECD or EU countries.

## Crime and punishment in Ireland

As perhaps with most countries there is a feeling in Ireland that a crime wave has hit the country and many hark back to an earlier age when discipline and respect were allegedly commonplace. Since 1996 when a drug gang shot dead a journalist, Veronica Guerin, who was writing about crime gangs in Dublin, there has been a feeling that criminal gangs can act with impunity. Since 2000 there has certainly been an increase in the number of murders, and even though these rarely affect people not already involved in crime, they add to a sense of a crime pandemic. Many also fear that the rise in alcohol consumption (see Chapter 7) makes city centres unsafe. Crime has also become a political issue, as opposition politicians tend to argue that the government is doing nothing about crime, or that it has lost control. This sometimes leads to over-reaction and inappropriate reactions.

The Irish police force, the Garda Siochána, was one of the triumphs of the new Irish state. Although Ireland was born into a civil war, it successfully created a broadly accepted police force which remained relatively apolitical and is still unarmed – making it one of the few unarmed police forces in the world. Trust in the Gardaí or Guards remains high, consistently above 80 per cent, despite a number of cases of Garda corruption where Gardaí were found to have victimized certain people, fabricating evidence that led to their conviction. Gardaí have also been accused of brutality at anti-globalization marches. But this is not the first time the Gardaí have been accused of breaking the law. The main threat the Gardaí faced from the 1970s was IRA violence and crime, to which apparently with political approval, they reacted with 'more direct' 'heavy gang' methods to combat IRA crime. At the same time, as we shall see in the next chapter, the criminal justice system was changed to allow trials without juries, and the length of time a person could be detained without charge was extended. The reduction in the threat from Republican terrorism has given way to an apparent increase in gangland activity and drug dealing – and there are suggestions that some in the IRA moved into ordinary crime as they became idle following IRA ceasefires.

Comparing crime levels across countries and over time is difficult. Often the data come from the police forces themselves, who have an

**Illustration 3.2   Ballymun, Dublin**

This housing scheme is typical of many built in the 1960s which moved families from city centres to supposedly modern accommodation. Often these were the most deprived people with extraordinarily high rates of unemployment. These areas became run-down and effectively controlled by drugs gangs. Ballymun, like many others, has since undergone major redevelopment.

interest in manipulating the data downward. Governments and police forces often change the way in which crimes are recorded to avoid criticisms of rising crime rates. There are differences in the way certain behaviours are regarded in different countries and by different people, so how can we compare the incidence of motorcyclists not wearing helmets in Sweden and in Spain? And we also have the problem that Swedes are more likely to report crimes than Spaniards, making any analysis of reported crimes figures problematic. We usually look at serious crimes, indictable offences. In Ireland the rate has fluctuated: crime rose in the mid-1990s, then fell in the late 1990s, and rose again in 2002. Since then rates have been steady, though with public order offences and homicide rates rising. If we take recorded crime at face value, then Ireland has one of the lowest crime rates in the EU, with the UK having one of the highest.

Other measures of crime tell a different story. Victimization surveys, which ask people whether and what crimes they were victims of in the last 12 months, show that almost 22 per cent claim to have been the victims of a crime. This figure is the highest of the OECD countries, higher than Mexico or the USA, which are normally perceived as more dangerous countries. That New Zealand is second highest in this list might make one question the validity of using these types of data. Other questions about how safe people feel show that 73 per cent of Irish people feel safe on the streets after dark. Oddly Spain, Portugal and Greece, all with low victimization rates, have among the highest rates of fear. The prison population has risen steadily, from under 2,000 in 1989 to just over 3,000 in 2009 (including those on trial or on remand). These are usually measured by number of prisoners per 100,000 of the population, and on this measure Ireland (71) has one of the lowest prison populations in the world. This compares with 98 in Germany, the UK's 141, and over 700 in the USA.

A feature of this prison population is that, as in other countries, it is overwhelmingly male and working-class. The prison system does little to rehabilitate prisoners and many regard prisons as dangerous places where any criminal tendencies are likely to be hardened. The criminal justice system might be designed merely to make the middle classes feel safer by imprisoning 'undesirables' for relatively minor offences. At the same time there was a case of a middle-class architect who, driving while drunk, killed a pedestrian. He was released in bizarre circumstances having just served a year of his four year sentence which showed that the judicial and political system regarded him differently. White-collar crime through corruption and tax evasion costs far more to society, yet there have been few cases where white-collar crimes have been brought to trial and resulted in prison sentences.

Ireland is a relatively safe and remarkably cohesive society, and on most measures a pleasant place to live. However, there is a sense that when the Irish economy was booming, large amounts of money were effectively thrown at problems in the hope that the existing institutions and systems would solve them. But progress was not made on outcomes – so investment in education, social welfare, health and policing did not seem to make the Irish better educated, more equal, healthier, more secure or safer. That they did not has emphasized the need for reform of those systems, something that has been controversial and exposes some of the defects of the Irish political system.

# 4

# Government and Policy Making

Though independence promised to rid Ireland of 'a base imperialism that has brought naught but evil' (Sinn Féin manifesto, 1918), the Irish Free State architecture was based heavily on the existing British institutions. Although there was what some call a revolution between 1916 and 1921, the institutions and personnel of the state remained broadly the same (incorrectly, as regime change occurred within the then existing constitutional framework). For instance, much of the personnel in the Irish civil service before independence was Irish and remained in position after independence. Some Irish Irelanders spoke of returning Ireland to a system of Chieftains and Brehon Law (the ancient Irish legal system), but few took this seriously. Given the close links with the USA of many of the political leaders in the new state, it may seem surprising that Ireland did not adopt a Presidential system. Even if they had wanted to, the Irish were forced into accepting the constitutional framework imposed by the British as a result of the Anglo-Irish Treaty which laid down the state structures. The basis for these was changed in 1937 when a new constitution was adopted, but the institutional changes were more symbolic than real.

Ireland is a parliamentary democracy, which means that there is no formal or real separation of powers. The government is formally responsible to the legislature. It is similar in many ways to a classic Westminster model of government although there are some important differences. The principal features of the Irish state are:

1 A unitary state with little power devolved to regions and a local democracy in name only.

2  A strong government which dominates the two-chambered legislature (Dáil and Seanad).
3  A symbolic though directly elected head of state (president) and a
powerful head of government (Taoiseach).
4  An executive (cabinet) consisting of ministers who are career
legislators which is collectively responsible to the parliament.
5  A rigid constitution upheld by a strong, independent judiciary
which is politically appointed, but can impose significant restrictions on policy makers.
6  A permanent, non-partisan, civil service.
7  An unusual preferential voting system (proportional representation by single transferable vote).
8  A multi-party system with (until recently) a dominant party
(Fianna Fáil), strong internal party discipline and a comparatively
large number of non-party legislators.
9  A high degree of corporatism in policy making giving certain
interest groups privileged access to policy making.
10 An influential supra-national body, the European Union, which
dictates policy in a large number of areas.

Some of these topics will be dealt with in Chapter 5 on politics and
civil society. This chapter looks at the governing institutions in
Ireland, beginning with the constitution and the major political actors:
the president, the Houses of the Oireachtas (parliament) and the
Taoiseach (prime minister) and cabinet. The operation of policy
through the bureaucracy and the courts is also explored. Although the
political system has been remarkably stable, especially in the aftermath of the property bubble and the banking crisis, there have been
repeated calls for its reform. Many focus on Ireland's electoral system
which, its critics say, encourages 'excessive localism', but there is
also concern that the Dáil and the Seanad have failed to maintain
proper oversight of the government. There is also anger about the
apparent lack of capacity of the regulatory system and the civil
service, which some claim lack the expertise to deal with complex
issues in a modern economy.

## The constitutional make-up

Constitutions are important documents which lay down the 'rules of
the game' for the operation of government and policy in a country.

These will usually include the nation-state's self-image and the rules governing interactions between the relevant political actors. The current Irish constitution dates from 1937 when Éamon de Valera rewrote what was seen as a British-imposed Free State constitution. There were some offending articles in the Constitution of the Irish Free State (Bunreacht na Saorstát Éireann), such as the requirement in Article 17 that members of the Oireachtas (parliament) must swear an oath to King George V, his heirs and successors, and the fact that the Free State constitution was legally inferior to the treaty between Great Britain and Ireland. The 1937 constitution (Bunreacht na hÉireann) made the southern part of Ireland legally independent of London for the first time in many centuries.

As well as laying down the institutional architecture of the state, the constitution sets out the type of state that Ireland is and the rights of the citizens of the state. The constitution makes clear that Ireland is a Christian state, which gives special recognition to the position of the Catholic Church. The influence of Catholic social thought is obvious in many areas. There is an emphasis on social justice, the rights of the family and the place of women in the home. The right of private property is also emphasized. This was typical of the political thought in much of southern Europe in the 1930s, and although the section on women is hopelessly out of date, the constitution should be considered in the context of its time. The question that arises, of course, is: why is modern Ireland tied to such an old-fashioned document?

The answer is that it is not. First, the constitution has proved remarkably resilient and over seventy years after its adoption the document functions well. Only once, in the late 1980s, was the introduction of a new constitution seriously suggested, and this failed to win any support. Second, the Irish people have changed the constitution to suit the changing needs of the country. There have been a large number of amendments to the constitution, mostly concerning EU membership or religious and social issues. EU treaties must be referred to the people in a referendum before they can be ratified, as they are regarded as amending the constitution. The reason social issues go to referendum is partly because the original Constitution was so conservative, but also because politicians have been reluctant to legislate on issues such as divorce and abortion, preferring to 'insulate' party politics from these issues by offering them directly to the people by referendum. As a result Ireland is a country which sees comparatively large numbers of national referendums. Changing the constitution is possible through a referendum where only a simple

majority of voters is required. There is no facility for popular amendments, that is, suggestions for changes by ordinary people. Proposals
for referendum need to be passed by the Oireachtas, which in effect
means that the government controls what amendments are made.
Although it has been durable and remains broadly popular, a review
in the 1990s suggested that the constitution could be 'cleaned up',
removing sexist language and other outdated provisions (Constitution
Review Group, 1996).

In addition, since the 1960s the constitution has become a much
more flexible document. Since then, and at the urgings of the then
Taoiseach, judges have become much more activist in the tradition of
US legal interpretation; for example, judges have invoked rights,
such as 'bodily integrity', which are not explicitly mentioned in the
constitution. This has meant that the executive needs to consider
much more carefully the likely reaction of the Supreme Court to any
legislation it proposes. This too raises questions for the nature of
democracy in Ireland, for if the Supreme Court does not base its decisions on explicitly stated principles, then on what does it base its
decisions? There is a concern that judges impose their own (distinctive) world view on the citizens of Ireland through their own interpretations (see in particular Morgan, 2001).

## The presidency

The Oireachtas is the collective name for those institutions whose
assent is required for legislation to be passed. It is made up of the
House of the Oireachtas and the president. As a directly elected head
of state, the President of Ireland is an important political figure. She,
or he, is the first citizen. The president is required to appoint the
government, call elections and sign bills into law. She is elected for
seven years and may be re-elected once. In practice, however, the
presidency is a weak and symbolic office. Even though some of the
holders of the office have been highly political figures, all chose not
to involve themselves in party politics and to concentrate on the
ceremonial role of the office. The first president was probably
chosen to ensure this. A Protestant professor of Gaelic literature,
Douglas Hyde, he could not have been further from partisan politics.
The prerogatives that the president does possess cannot be exercised
freely. Most must be carried out at the direction of the Taoiseach or
the government. The President can be, and has been, prevented from

travelling abroad, and major speeches need to be cleared by government.

The president does have some significant powers. Though she cannot refuse to sign bills, she can refer them to the Supreme Court to test their constitutionality before signing them. This does not give presidents a veto, but it does draw legal and public attention to a Bill. This prerogative has not been used very much, but one case caused severe criticism from a government minister who reportedly called President Ó Dálaigh 'a thundering disgrace' (what he actually said was much worse). It is indicative of the relationship that the president and not the minister resigned as a result of this disagreement. The other significant power is the right to refuse the request for the dissolution of the Dáil (lower house of parliament) by a Taoiseach who has lost his majority. Though it has never been used, its potential use may have been important in the formation of the 'Rainbow Coalition' in 1995. In this case the Labour party left the government of Fianna Fáil and a new government was formed without an intervening election. It was expected at the time that the Fianna Fáil Taoiseach, Albert Reynolds, would seek a dissolution of the Dáil, but the President sought legal advice as to whether she could refuse this, perhaps prompting him to resign without requesting a dissolution.

The Irish presidency was a rather inactive institution which tended to be occupied by Fianna Fáil politicians on the way out of political life. The office was purely symbolic but also quite anonymous. This changed in 1990 when in the first contested presidential election since 1973, Mary Robinson, a candidate supported by Labour and other left-wing parties, despite coming second to the Fianna Fáil candidate in the first count, went on to beat him when a third party's candidate's votes were distributed.

Robinson was an unlikely victor. A liberal academic lawyer who represented Trinity College, Dublin in the Irish Senate, she had tried and failed to get elected to the Dáil for the Labour party on a number of occasions. As a senator she consistently pushed a (for the time) radical liberal agenda proposing legislation on family planning, adoption and women's rights. She resigned from the Labour party in 1985 because she opposed the Anglo-Irish Agreement for ignoring the concerns of unionism.

Having won, she became much more activist than previous incumbents, or at least the media covered her activities much more than they had for previous presidents. Though remaining apolitical she became a champion of minority and emigrants' rights. She travelled

**Illustration 4.1    Mary Robinson**

Mary Robinson's election as President transformed the Presidency. It is still not an important office politically but has increased in visibility and symbolic importance. She has subsequently become best known for her advocacy of human rights throughout the world.

widely, highlighting poverty and debt in Africa and human rights abuses in many countries. She also used some of the few political prerogatives given to an Irish president. She allegedly angered the Labour party by referring a number of bills to the Supreme Court to test their constitutionality. What was most remarkable was the warmth and affection in which she was held by the Irish people. She appeared the archetype of what a successful Irish politician should *not* be, yet with over 90 per cent approval ratings, had she chosen to seek re-election, she would almost certainly have been returned unopposed.

Robinson transformed the presidency from an office in which Fianna Fáil elder statesmen were inactive to a much more visible and possibly important one for Irish people. She could do this in part because she was popularly elected. Her successor, also a female academic lawyer, although deeply conservative, has continued the trend of activism and it seems unlikely that future Irish presidents will revert to the semi-retirement that had previously characterized the presidency.

## The Houses of the Oireachtas

There are two chambers in the Irish parliament: Dáil Éireann (pronounced Dawl AIR-in) and Seanad Éireann (pronounced SHAN-ad AIR-in) are the lower and upper houses respectively. The Dáil, like lower houses in most of Europe, is the more powerful of the two chambers. It has 166 TDs (MPs) directly elected for up to five years from 43 constituencies of between three and five seats. The electoral system used (discussed in Chapter 5) is proportional representation by a single transferable vote. The Seanad or Senate has 60 members, most of whom are indirectly elected (by county councillors, TDs and other elected officials) through five vocational panels (Cultural and Educational, Industrial and Commercial, Agricultural, Administrative and Labour). These were meant to ensure representation of interests from all sections of society, but because the electors are party politi-

**Illustration 4.2    President Mary McAleese addresses the Dáil**

The Dáil is a U-shaped chamber in which the Taoiseach sits at the upper right-hand side, his cabinet ministers beside him and party TDs behind him. The leader of the opposition sits opposite the Taoiseach and the Ceann Comhairle (Speaker) sits in the centre. Deputies speak standing at their seat. Voting can now be done electronically from one's seat but for important votes TDs are counted walking through the Tá (yes) and Níl (no) lobbies.

cal, senators too are party political. Eleven senators are appointed by the Taoiseach and six are elected by graduates of two of Ireland's universities, the National University of Ireland and University of Dublin (Trinity College). The Taoiseach's right of appointment usually guarantees a government majority. The Senate's role is less to block government actions but to provide alternative views that the Dáil can then reflect on. How useful a function it provides is debatable, and many have called for the second chamber to be abolished outright – something most parties have agreed on.

For a bill to become law, the Dáil must pass it but the Senate can only delay its passage by sending it back to the Dáil. The Dáil is also superior insofar as some types of bills must be introduced in the Dáil. The Dáil's role is twofold, one is to legislate and the other to oversee the operation of government and hold it to account. In reality both houses are subject to government control. The two houses are dominated by the government through a number of mechanisms. First, timing is controlled by government, so opposition parties find it very difficult to have the time to push bills through. Second, the agenda of the Dáil is closely guarded by the government, so it is frequently the case that those trying to question the government are ruled out of order by the Ceann Comhairle (Speaker) who in practice is a government appointee. Legislation tends to emerge from the government, which has the resources to make policy. Only a tiny number of non-government bills have become law. Bills must go through five stages:

- The **first stage** is usually a formality where the bill is announced.
- At the **second stage** the broad principle of the bill is debated. This is an important stage, which often determines its ultimate acceptance or rejection.
- In the **committee stage** the bill is discussed in detail either in a specialist committee or in a committee of the whole house. Amendments at this stage must not conflict with the broad principle agreed at the second stage.
- The **report stage** allows the tidying up of amendments and new amendments may be proposed as long as they had not been rejected in the committee stage.
- The **fifth stage** gives formal and final approval to a bill before it goes to the Seanad for the **final stages**. The Seanad may accept the Bill or propose amendments, but these can then be rejected by the Dáil.

The government's dominance of the Dáil means that the Dáil has little influence. TDs have few resources to match those of government departments. Devices such as parliamentary questions, which are designed to allow the parliament to oversee the work of the government, are evaded. One former minister explained his attitude to answering parliamentary questions thus: 'if the other side don't ask the right questions, they don't get the right answers', and the chairman of a tribunal into a government policy on insurance of exports of Irish beef said that 'if the questions that were asked in the Dáil were answered in the way they are answered here, there would be no necessity for this inquiry' (cited in O'Toole,1995: 256, 241). Unlike in, for example, a media interview, ministers cannot be asked the same question again and again until it is obvious that they are refusing to answer. Ministers can answer whatever questions they wish to and the restrictive rules of the chamber allow few ways for a questioner to get an answer. Because government controls the Dáil agenda and time, it is difficult for opposition parties to propose any legislation that would have any chance of becoming law, and it is virtually unheard of for a government bill to be rejected, though at times it will be amended because of issues raised in debate. As well as Dáil time, the government also controls the information released to the public, so very often any debate will take place on the basis of information the government has chosen to release. The weak freedom of information regime makes it difficult for the Oireachtas to perform its function of government oversight. So a reasonable complaint can be made that recent legislation which has committed billions of euros of taxpayers' money received ill-informed debate because all the facts and figures informing the debate came from government rather than an independent body.

The opposition and even government backbenchers tend to be treated with a certain amount of disdain. The Dáil is not seen as an important institution where decisions are made, and the few people who watch Dáil debates on television will be struck by the emptiness of the chamber. There is rarely the sense of drama that one sees in the British House of Commons. Speeches are read out – though this is against the rules of the House – and most ministers' speeches are written by civil servants. Few speeches inspire debate outside the House. Much of the blame for this is laid at the feet of the electoral system (see Chapter 5). Gallagher (1987) has argued that the fact that backbench TDs and the opposition have so little control of public policy causes apathy around the work of the Dáil and Seanad among politicians and the public alike.

*Table 4.1*    Irish governments since 1954

| Year | Party/parties in government | Taoiseach | Government type |
|------|-----------------------------|-----------|-----------------|
| 1954 | Fine Gael, Labour | John A. Costello | Majority |
| 1957 | Fianna Fáil | Éamon de Valera Seán Lemass (1959) | Majority |
| 1961 | Fianna Fáil | Seán Lemass | Minority |
| 1965 | Fianna Fáil | Seán Lemass Jack Lynch (1966) | Majority |
| 1969 | Fianna Fáil | Jack Lynch | Majority |
| 1973 | Fine Gael, Labour | Liam Cosgrave | Majority |
| 1977 | Fianna Fáil | Jack Lynch Charles Haughey (1979) | Majority |
| 1981 | Fine Gael, Labour | Garret FitzGerald | Minority |
| 1982 (Feb) | Fianna Fáil | Charles Haughey | Minority |
| 1982 (Nov) | Fine Gael, Labour | Garret FitzGerald | Majority |
| 1987 | Fianna Fáil | Charles Haughey | Minority |
| 1989 | Fianna Fáil, Progressive Democrats (PDs) | Charles Haughey Albert Reynolds (1992) | Majority |
| 1992 | Fianna Fáil, Labour | Albert Reynolds | Majority |
| 1994* | Fine Gael, Labour, Democratic Left | John Bruton | Majority |
| 1997 | Fianna Fáil, PDs | Bertie Ahern | Minority |
| 2002 | Fianna Fáil, PDs | Bertie Ahern | Majority |
| 2007 | Fianna Fáil, Greens, PDs | Bertie Ahern Brian Cowen (2008) | Majority |
| 2011 | Fine Gael, Labour | Enda Kenny | Majority |

*The Bruton government replaced the Reynolds government without recourse to an election.

The Dáil also has the role of overseeing policy proposals that have been agreed at EU level, but as we shall see in more detail in Chapter 8, EU policy cannot be amended by the Dáil and the multi-national nature of EU decision making makes any practical oversight difficult. The best that the Dáil can do is to look at the way the Irish government chooses to transpose EU law into Irish law, but in truth few Irish legislators have sufficient interest or resources to carry out the function properly.

## The Taoiseach and cabinet

If the Oireachtas (the Dáil, Seanad and presidency) has little policy-making power, where is this power situated? The answer is straight-forward – in the government. However the way in which government policy is made and the distribution of power within the government is complex and not always clear. This is partly because much government activity takes place behind closed doors. The government is made up of the Taoiseach (prime minister, literally chief) who is appointed by the president on the nomination of the Dáil; the cabinet, which is appointed by the President on the nomination of the Taoiseach; and the ministers of state or junior ministers, appointed by the Taoiseach. These must be members of either the Dáil or Seanad, and in practice they are nearly always TDs. This group provide the political leadership for a number of departments of state, which specialize in certain areas such as finance, foreign affairs, enterprise and employment, justice and health. The ministers are supported by an extensive bureaucracy that both provides policy formulation advice and implements those policies.

Government decisions are made by the cabinet, whose meetings are chaired by the Taoiseach. Policies emerge from a relevant department and a briefing document is circulated to all other departments for discussion. Only interested departments will comment, and it is hoped that difficulties and conflicts are ironed out at this stage bilaterally, often in meetings between civil servants. The policy is then put on the agenda of the cabinet for discussion. If the issue is uncontroversial it may be approved quickly; however, many issues which are politically sensitive may cause a meeting to last for hours and decisions may be postponed pending further discussions. Decisions once made are subject to collective cabinet responsibility. This means that all ministers, even those who disagreed with the policy in the cabinet

**Illustration 4.3   Taoisigh Charles Haughey (*left*) and Garret FitzGerald (*right*)**

These two men dominated the political scene in the 1980s and their contrasting styles, which continue to fascinate the Irish people today, are reflected in their official portraits (see Box 4.1).

meeting, must publicly support the policy. It is now common for ministers to make their position so clear in advance of the meeting that most people know their true feelings even if they go through a charade of defending a policy they opposed.

It is not clear who has most power in the cabinet. It is alleged that the Taoiseach is a very powerful figure within the government, and there is no doubt that he is an important figure. However Taoisigh (prime ministers) have no direct policy-making powers: they cannot change policy without the agreement of other figures, such as ministers and the cabinet. Ministers are powerful within their own areas and it is difficult to see how a policy could be passed against the wishes of the relevant departmental minister, but ministers sometimes see their pet projects rejected and amended by cabinet. Taoisigh too might be thought to have a veto, and can certainly postpone decisions through their role as chairman of cabinet meetings. As the only cabinet figure without a portfolio, the Taoiseach can co-ordinate government business, and has time to get involved in the areas he (they have all been men) is interested in. His position allows him to demand information from departments. He can also call elections when he wishes, which allows him, as party leader, to maximize his electoral advantage. However, Taoisigh are usually categorized as being either 'chairman or chief' – someone who manages conflict or someone who can impose his will. The rationale behind this categorization is that the Taoiseach can sometimes control many of the important political actors through his ability to hire and fire ministers, but at times owes his position to these actors. The Taoiseach is also usually the leader of the majority party in government and can control the careers of his party's TDs. In reality most Taoisigh are closer to the chairman role. For instance Éamon de Valera who earned himself the epithet 'Chief' always only called decisions if there was a consensus. Another Taoiseach, Charles J. Haughey, liked to be called 'Boss', and his press secretary once used a reference to Mussolini, the Italian fascist leader, '*un Duce, una voce*', when describing the nature of leadership control in his government. Yet despite Haughey's reputation as a dictatorial leader he faced many constraints, not least because of divisions in his party. Power relations are further constrained as coalition politics has become the norm, so Taoisigh are forced to cede to the demands of their coalition colleagues. This makes government more obviously a system of compromises. For instance in the aftermath of the property collapse, the Fianna Fáil-led government wanted to reintroduce tuition fees for university students in order to reduce the fiscal deficit. Their coalition partners, the Greens, objected to this proposal and as a result it was not pursued.

## The bureaucracy

As the British civil service system was transferred without significant change into the new state, the ethos and culture of the Irish civil service is very much like that of the UK civil service. It is much smaller of course: of the almost 380,000 public servants, just over 34,000 are civil servants. The main structure of the relationship between politicians and bureaucrats is one in which the minister is the 'corporation sole' providing the legal character for the department. For this reason letters from departments begin with 'The minister has instructed me to . . . ', even though the minister probably had no knowledge of the correspondence. C.H. Murray (1990), a former Secretary General of a department, pointed to 'the anomaly that the Minister is the legal head of the Department but not a full-time exec-

**Box 4.1   Charles Haughey and Garret FitzGerald**

In the 1980s two politicians dominated Irish politics. One of FitzGerald and Haughey held the position of Taoiseach throughout the decade. Both were born in 1926 and educated at University College Dublin, but where FitzGerald was the intellectual, Haughey was the pragmatist. FitzGerald came from an upper middle-class family, the son of a cabinet minister in the first post-independence government. He often gave the impression of being a woolly academic (he is alleged to have said in a cabinet meeting, 'That's all very well in practice, but what about in theory?') but was undoubtedly more driven that he sometimes showed. Haughey by contrast came from a working-class family, and with undoubted intelligence achieved a university scholarship and married the daughter of a leading Fianna Fáil minister.

As Taoiseach, FitzGerald pushed social democratic policies within his sometimes reluctant party. He tried to bring about a 'constitutional' crusade to liberalize Irish society making it more attractive for Unionists. Haughey opposed this, maintaining the traditional nationalist and Catholic approach favoured by his party. As a young minister he was seen as progressive but was sacked when it was alleged he was involved in a plot to import arms for the nascent Provisional IRA. This reversion to traditional nationalism surprised many. If he did little to modernize Irish society, Haughey more than most helped modernize the Irish economy. He brought public finances under control in the late 1980s and redeveloped many rundown areas of Dublin. In government they displayed contrasting styles. Fitzgerald ran cabinet like a university seminar, with meetings lasting whole days, whereas Haughey kept meetings short and business-like.

Their private lives also differed. FitzGerald had a reasonably modest lifestyle and remained devoted to his wife, whereas Haughey used his position to build up great wealth, living in a large mansion outside Dublin. He had a long-running affair with a gossip columnist, but managed to keep this out of the public eye until after his resignation. Haughey died in 2006 with his reputation in ruins after many years of investigations into his financial affairs. He continues to provoke a passionate defence among his many loyal supporters.

utive, whereas the full-time executive is not legally responsible for the actions or omissions of the Department'. Though this has changed somewhat, the Secretary General now being charged with the accounting function, it is still broadly true.

One area where the influence of the UK has continued is the way the Irish civil service looks to and copies the UK for solutions to similar problems. This inclination has probably subsided since

Ireland joined the EEC, as the EU now exposes Irish policy makers to influences beyond London. Two other salient points of comparison with Britain are the civil service's tradition of non-involvement in party politics and its culture of secrecy. Irish civil servants above certain grades, like their British counterparts, may not be members of a political party. They are expected to serve the government of the day (whatever political hue it may have) with professional and unbiased advice, allowing the government to make its decision in full knowledge of the facts. That said, and despite the public platitude of politicians about the quality of the service, privately many ministers complain about being blocked by civil servants averse to change. There have also been allegations that some senior civil servants lean more towards one party than another. Yet there is little demand to change the current practice, and it would be an exaggeration to suggest that there is a serious problem of impartiality.

The Irish civil service also operates under a culture of secrecy, which it would rather term confidentiality. The Official Secrets Act 1963 prohibits civil servants from communicating official information without express authority. The position of the government is also protected by a tradition of limiting the amount of information the civil service is inclined to give, even when authorized to do so. A civil servant was allegedly sent a congratulatory memo from his superior for having confused a deputy asking questions (*Dáil Éireann*, Vol. 445, Col. 539, 2 September 1994). This culture of secrecy and protection of the minister means that not only is it difficult for the Dáil to oversee what a cabinet minister is doing, it is also difficult for his government colleagues.

One way in which the Irish civil service differs markedly from its British counterpart is in the background of the top civil servants. Recruitment is by means of open competition. Unlike Britain where it is common for top civil servants to have an Oxbridge (an amalgam of Oxford and Cambridge, the UK's two most prestigious universities) education, Irish civil servants are more likely to have been educated at a Christian Brothers' School, and only more recently has it become common for higher civil servants to have university degrees.

The products of this education were 'intellectually able and hardworking but rather narrowly practical in their approach' (Chubb, 1992) and the ethos of the Irish civil service was conservative. This apparently had the effect for some time that the ethos of the service was against initiative. However some civil servants have had remarkable influence on the Irish state, not least T.K. Whitaker, who arguably wrote the blueprint for the modernization of the country (see Chapter 6). Even so, the civil service is continually criticized for being too concerned with the urgent to the detriment of the important: that is, the Irish civil service have been efficient administrators, but have not had the time or inclination to plan for the future. The banking collapse and the economic crisis also revealed a lack of expertise and capacity on the part of the civil service. For many years the Department of Finance had assured all that the housing bubble was nothing to worry about. It continually predicted a soft landing, but at the same time used the money from the expanding tax revenue to increase spending. It was revealed later that there were only four fully qualified economists in the department, and the rules of appointment to the civil service prevent the department from hiring more.

There are also concerns that the Irish public sector is not very efficient, and that this has an impact on the behaviour of politicians. While the public sector is not overly corrupt (though in property development planning there are frequent assertions that both officials and politicians have taken bribes), it is difficult for Irish citizens to question bureaucratic decisions without engaging in a time- consuming process. Many find it much easier to contact local TDs who can then cut through the red tape. The bureaucracy acknowledges this by giving TDs special privileges to skip queues which their constituents willingly exploit.

There has been a move in recent years to decentralize the Irish civil service, which is notable mainly for the fact that it was announced without any serious debate and ignored the government's own National Spatial Strategy. Nor is decentralization an attempt to decentralize power. The Irish state, like Ireland in other areas, is dominated by Dublin. All major decisions are made in Dublin and although there are regular local elections and a range of county, city and urban district councils with elected local representatives, Ireland has no local government to speak of. The Irish local government system, which has few independent funding resources, is an administrative system which provides some basic services such as water supply and treatment, and waste collection. The other area it has some power over is planning (see Chapter 2). Local government under British rule had seen endemic corruption and the (undemocratic) system of county and city managers was used to put an end to this and remove political influence and political patronage. However, this has happened at the expense of any local democracy and may in part explain the failure of other Irish cities to compete with Dublin in size, economic growth or importance. The absence of responsibilities at the local elected level is partly a logical response to a relatively small country's needs. Ireland is smaller than most Italian regions, so it would make little sense to devolve power over social services to local councils. However, many state services are devolved to local level,

---

**Box 4.2   Northern Ireland's political institutions**

In April 1998 the Belfast or Good Friday Agreement (GFA) was signed between most of the parties in Northern Ireland and the British and Irish governments. Between 1921 and the outbreak of the Troubles, Northern Ireland was ruled locally but with a system that ensured the Official Unionist party had a monopoly on power. Northern Ireland had been governed by direct rule from Westminster since 1972. This gave all power to a minister in the British government to govern Northern Ireland with the support of the Northern Irish civil service, and since the 1985 Anglo-Irish Agreement, some consultative power to the Irish government. The GFA restored power to local politicians within a series of power-sharing institutions. There is an elected 108-seat assembly which sits at Stormont (outside Belfast); an executive which comprises ministers from all the major elected parties chaired by a First Minister and Deputy First Minister, each of whom must resign should the other resign; a new North South Ministerial Council which allows for some all-island policy agreements; a new British-Irish Council to bring together representatives from devolved administrations in the UK and the two governments; and a new British-Irish Agreement to replace the 1985 Anglo-Irish Agreement.

The first government was set up on 1 July 1998 with David Trimble (Ulster Unionist Party – UUP) and Séamus Mallon (SDLP) as the First and Deputy First Ministers of a government with Sinn Féin and DUP (Democratic Unionist Party) ministers. Devolution was suspended on a number of occasions because of issues of IRA decommissioning and its ceasefire. These problems continued and even though there were assembly elections, the power-sharing institutions were only restored in May 2007 when Protestant arch-unionist the Reverend Ian Paisley and the former Chief of Staff of the IRA, Sinn Féin's Martin McGuinness, were elected as First and Deputy First Ministers. This government of the extremes, although particularly unlikely, worked well, as both indicated a willingness to act pragmatically in Northern Ireland's interests. Nor do the two parties differ greatly on ordinary political issues. However other issues such as granting the Northern Irish government power over security caused problems within the government and the extent to which the system institutionalizes and stabilizes the division in Northern Ireland rather than resolving it is questionable.

but policy control is maintained by central government. So, for example, there were until recently regional Health Boards which were charged with administering health services in different parts of the country but which were responsible to the Minister for Health.

## 'Agencification' in Ireland

As we have seen, the Irish government relies on a number of executive agencies. One major change the Irish state has undergone in the last thirty years is the increase in the number of these agencies. Under the traditional governmental model of ministerial responsibility, ministers as heads of departments of state directed bureaucrats under their immediate control. The political head was then accountable to the people for the state's actions. There were always some executive agencies outside this system, usually for the good reason that their independence was protected from party political interference; to enable the recruitment of non-civil service experts, agencies such as the Central Statistics Office or the Met Office were outside direct departmental control. There has been a move, internationally, to New Public Management which is an attempt to modernize the delivery of public services by freeing them from political control. Governments have therefore moved towards the privatization of some services that the state once performed; for instance the Irish state airline, Aer Lingus, was sold in 2006. Some services have been contracted out, so road building, which the state used to undertake directly, is now done by private companies who are paid by the state, and executive agencies are entrusted with certain tasks.

It is estimated that there are now 600 such agencies implementing government policy, 60 per cent of which have been set up since 1990. While many of these are in fact institutions such as universities, museums, theatres and hospitals which are funded by government but act independently, many others seem to be charged with making policy decisions. One of the largest, the Health Service Executive, can make decisions to close hospitals or place a moratorium on staff recruitment. While such agencies may indeed increase efficiencies, and this is increasingly questioned, there are some issues about the extent of democratic control. If ministers can merely claim that decisions are made elsewhere, the agencies cannot be held responsible or responsive to public demands. Equally there is the problem that appointments to these bodies are made on an ad hoc basis which

**Illustration 4.4  The Four Courts**

The Four Courts in Dublin city centre is the seat of judicial power in Ireland. It was destroyed in the civil war and later rebuilt, but most of the legal records dating from the 12th century were destroyed.

means that there is little openness as to how appointments are made and many complain that nepotism and party political interest trump the national interest.

The economic crisis has put pressure on the public sector generally, which had enjoyed large and unsustainable pay rises. Their high state-secured pensions were also a problem. Most public servants took pay cuts of up to 15 per cent and an embargo on recruitment in the public sector was introduced. Reports were issued which called for the closure or amalgamation of a number of agencies, but there was little appetite for major reform of the way public sector workers are recruited or can be dismissed.

## The judiciary and justice system

Ireland is a common law jurisdiction. Common law consists of thousands of judicial decisions made over time with a practice of precedent, meaning that a court is required to follow an earlier, similar decision. Judicial decisions are, therefore, attributed the force of law. The common law system is also adversarial, in that each side seeks to influence an independent scrutineer, either a judge or a jury. The jury system allows someone to be tried by a group of their peers, although its independence is often questioned and it has been abolished in Ireland for certain types of cases. This contrasts with the civil law system, a predominantly continental European legal system based on comprehensive codes, where judges have a greater (more inquisitorial) role in the conduct of trials, but where precedent does not play such a crucial role in the system. In many civil law systems juries are either not used or used sparingly and not regarded as safe (on the reliability of jury trials, see Dawkins, 1997). Another important aspect of the common law tradition is the importance of individual rights over communitarian ones – the needs or desires of society as a whole.

The Irish legal system is not native to the country. Ireland had a system of Brehon laws which were ancient Gaelic laws overseen by druids and handed down through word of mouth. These laws were quite progressive, granting the right of divorce and treating men and women equally. After the Anglo-Norman invasion the Brehon Laws were challenged, especially on the east coast, and finally fell into disuse by the early 1600s.

There are a number of types of court, which do not differ so much in character, but rather in the subjects on which they can adjudicate. There are District Courts which are used for minor offences, and can only impose limited awards, fines or custodial sentences. The Circuit Courts, which are also regional in nature, can impose greater sentences and sanctions but are still limited. The High Court is used for serious criminal offences and for more important civil litigation. Apart from two unusual exceptions the Supreme Court is a court of appeal, though not the court of final appeal as the European courts are superior. A Special Criminal Court, which provides for non-jury trials in the cases where juries are likely to be biased or interfered with, also exists. These were introduced in the early 1970s as a temporary measure because of the difficulty of securing convictions against IRA and other nationalist paramilitaries, but they continue to exist today.

The legal profession in Ireland is divided into two branches, barristers and solicitors, a distinction continued in very few common law jurisdictions. In Ireland, significant differences exist between the branches of the profession as they operate at present. Prior to 1995, solicitors were allowed to become District Court judges only; barristers alone were entitled to be appointed as superior court judges. The

Courts and Court Officers Act 1995 made solicitors eligible to become Circuit Court judges, with the further possibility of 'promotion' to the High/Supreme Court.

Judges are appointed by the government, and are often members or supporters of the party in government, particularly in the lower courts. Judges tend to be middle-class, middle-aged men, with the interests and values of this group. Though there has been little research on whether judges act in a partisan manner, and there is little evidence that they behave in a party political way, they do impose their values on their decisions. Within their own system senior Irish judges are said to be among the most politically active in the world. Since the 1960s senior Irish judges have taken a decidedly activist approach to the opportunities of judicial review, essentially reinterpreting the constitution to enunciate rights that are not specified in the constitution. So, for instance, the right to 'bodily integrity' which is not mentioned in any legal document is now a constitutional right that the state is obliged to respect for its citizens. This was encouraged by the leader of the government that appointed these early activist judges (Morgan, 2001: 12), but it is now the case that the courts provide a real constraint on government policy making by tending to guarantee the rights of individuals over the rights of parliament to make policy for the common good. Judges would contend that they are merely offering literal readings of the law and that their ideology or interests have little to do with their judgements. Despite the judicial appointments system being both highly politicized and partisan, there seems to be little evidence that the judiciary itself makes partisan decisions. But it is obvious that certain liberal judges make liberal decisions and certain conservative judges make conservative decisions. The judiciary's freedom to make decisions is sometimes driven by political inactivity, for instance in dealing with abortion (see Box 4.3). Perhaps because these do not seem to be related to the political party, unlike in the USA there is little debate about the power of the judiciary or their potential influence on public policy.

The legal and justice system's independence means that there is little (effective) political interference in the judicial process. The importance of individual rights has led to an open, free and fair legal system which gives a degree of confidence to those investing in the country that politically driven or wilfully biased decisions will not be made. Rights such as *habeas corpus* – demanding that the state must grant a person the right to petition a court – guarantee the individual protection from arbitrary state action. However, it may also make the

**Box 4.3    Abortion, the courts and politics**

Abortion has always been an emotive subject in Ireland and though many groups try to politicize it, politicians on the whole prefer to resist these demands. Abortion was banned from 1861, though continued to be provided illegally. Since it was legalized in Britain, thousands of Irish women have travelled there to terminate their pregnancies each year. By the 1980s the religious right in Ireland, worried that the courts might interpret the right to an abortion under the constitution along the lines of the *Roe v. Wade* case in the USA, succeeded in getting a commitment from the two main party leaders that they would introduce an explicit constitutional ban on abortion, in order to safeguard the legal ban already in place. Producing a form of words proved difficult, and no cross-party consensus emerged. A proposal was put to the people that was opposed by the government but supported by Fianna Fáil in opposition. It acknowledged 'the right to life of the unborn...with due regard to the equal right to life of the mother'. It was easily passed by a majority of two to one. The issue came to a head again when in 1991 the Attorney General applied for an injunction to prevent a 14-year-old girl travelling to Britain for an abortion having been raped by a family friend. Her parents alerted the Gardaí (police) because they wanted to use the foetus as evidence against the rapist.

The High Court granted the injunction in the 'X' case, citing that the certainty of harm to the unborn was of a different magnitude to the risk to the life of the girl. The Supreme Court reversed this decision on the grounds that the mother's threatened suicide gave her the right to travel. This implied that the thousands of Irish women who travelled to the UK for abortions every year could be restrained unless they could demonstrate they were suicidal. This crisis led to referendums granting the right to travel and the right to information about abortion.

The problem re-emerged in 1997 when a 13-year-old rape victim in state care applied to leave the state in order to have an abortion. The judgement granted her the right to travel on the grounds that an abortion would be legal in Ireland. This opened the possibility for legalized abortions in Ireland, but politicians are reluctant to legislate to clarify the issue.

control of crime more difficult; for instance, securing convictions is complicated by the fact that the Garda Siochána is constrained by a constitution that is so strong in guaranteeing the rights of individuals. This makes certain law enforcement techniques that are common in other jurisdictions legally questionable in Ireland. The Irish have been willing and able to restrict common individual rights, so censorship was common, and until the mid-1990s a section of a

Broadcasting Act meant that members of Sinn Féin were not allowed to speak live on TV or radio and, more ridiculously, had to have their voices dubbed.

Some have questioned whether the Irish governmental system works or not. It is possible to observe that the government has too much power over policy making and that there is too little input from policy experts. A number of spectacularly poor policy decisions were made in the 2000s, ultimately leading to the financial crisis in Ireland being deeper and lasting longer than in other countries. The voices of other groups – parliamentarians, opposition parties, (certain) interest groups, think tanks or academics were never listened to. The calls for reform of the political system indicate that many blame the institutional architecture discussed in this chapter. It is arguable that civil society in Ireland is quite weak in terms of influence, but as we shall see in the next chapter, some groups have significant power.

# 5

# Politics and Civil Society

Though Ireland's political institutions have been stable over the lifetime of the state, even remaining broadly similar on achieving independence, the people and groups that inhabit the Irish political institutions and many of the norms regarding politics have undergone some significant changes in the last three decades. And how the state relates to society and groups within society has also changed. For instance some groups, such as trade unions, are now given a special place in the policy-making process. How people relate to each other is what might be meant by society, and how they relate in terms of the public sphere or public decisions can then be thought of as civil society. In civil society, groups will be prominent which are not prominent in our 'normal' social lives. So people come together in organized groups, such as community groups, interest groups and political parties, to achieve certain aims, such as to clean up a neighbourhood, change a state policy or run the state. Civil society encompasses all those non-state actors who interact to achieve certain ends, including those who influence or seek to influence the state itself.

Irish civil society groups, cultural and political nationalists, were important in Ireland's achieving independence. Civil society is considered important because where an active civil society exists, it indicates that people have multiple opportunities to engage in the political process (not just deciding whether and how to vote in periodic elections). A vibrant civil society is thought to be important for the survival of a democracy, as it indicates that people are engaged and generally supportive of the state, but it can also act to counterbalance state power. Given that some have remarked at the stability of Ireland's democracy, we would expect to see that there is an active civil society in Ireland. Apart from the high level of church membership, which will be discussed in Chapter 7, civil society is quite passive in Ireland, and membership of voluntary groups and political parties is low and falling.

It has been suggested by a left-wing think tank, Tasc, that the absence of strong civil society groups who are active and engaged in an open public policy process was one of the causes of the economic crisis in Ireland. As we shall see, a form of policy making known as social partnership brought together trade unions and employers to give both a great deal of power in policy making but at the expense of open debate about the direction of economic and social policy.

Civil society is closely related to the idea of social capital, which is the reserve of trust, norms and social networks that exist in a country and enable the efficient and peaceful operation of democracy. Social capital might be useful for economic and political development, and the greater the levels of interaction people have, the more trust increases, and the more efficiently the economy and other social interaction can run, without the need for significant state intervention. It is noticeable that the homogeneity of Irish society – where there are few divisions, and many people share the same basic expectations of each other – makes Ireland a pleasant place to live and contributes to the generally low crime rate and societal stability.

How these civil society groups interact with the state is often categorized into two distinct types, corporatism and pluralism. In a corporatist state there will be established means by which certain groups have the right to speak with and be listened to by government. These groups will tend then to be respectful of other (competing) groups' views and opinions. Government in turn will seek a policy that is an acceptable compromise between these groups. In a pluralist framework no groups are given the *right* to speak with government and all will compete for the government's ear. Government can choose to listen to or ignore whomever it wishes.

This chapter will outline the main groups in civil society and how these interact with the state in Ireland. The most prominent groups are of course political parties, and the chapter examines how these compete for elections. Central to the way in which politics acts at both a formal and informal level are rules. The last chapter outlined some of the formal institutions and rules, but informal norms and rules are also important, and these are discussed in the next section.

## Political culture

A country's political culture refers to the way in which the politics operates and rules are enforced, and the attitudes and beliefs of the people regarding the political system and its actors. Political culture imposes constraints or freedoms on what is politically acceptable behaviour (for instance, in some countries it is acceptable for the army to put pressure on government even if this is technically illegal). When the political culture and the political institutions are incompatible, then the viability of the state might be threatened.

When we think of the practice of politics in Ireland, a number of ideas are often suggested, most notably nationalism, conservatism, authoritarianism and peasant culture. Nationalism is probably central to the culture in any nation-state. As we saw in Chapter 1, different groups have for a long time propagated the idea of the distinct Irish nation. What this means now that Ireland has independence is less clear. Certainly it is rare that political parties or politicians challenge the perceived need to re-unify the country, though there is disagreement about how that might be brought about. Another feature might be that the Irish are typically patriotic. Survey evidence shows that the Irish are indeed more proud than most other peoples in the world. According to 2002 World Values Survey (WVS) data, nearly 73 per cent of Irish people are very proud of being Irish; this compares with Czech Republic 26 per cent, Britain 51 per cent, and the USA 72 per cent. Nationalism can manifest itself in a chauvinistic sense and can lead to racism or distrust of foreigners. Irish nationalism might reasonably have been defined as anti-Britishness rather than Irishness in the past, though the extent to which the Irish remain anti-British is debatable. A 2003 survey of young people's attitudes found that Irish adults under 40 years of age felt closer to people from Britain than from Northern Ireland.

Conservatism as a political culture rather than an ideology might refer to the role of the state in society and the extent to which the state should involve itself in people's lives. WVS data shows that Irish people are on the whole slightly less in favour of state intervention than in other western European countries and that they are more likely to emphasize personal responsibility for their own economic position than in the past. Another tendency that people speak of in Ireland is distrust of the state, and we can see that Irish people are generally less satisfied with democracy than people in other western countries (Newton and van Deth, 2005: 146), though when asked to rate the political system the Irish are not exceptionally negative. One of the reasons for this alleged distrust of the state may be that the state was associated with Britain for so long that 'cheating' the state is an acceptable form of nationalism. However survey data shows Irish people to be likely to find under-declaring income tax unacceptable.

Conservatism might also be linked to support for traditional values, and the WVS survey finds that Irish people have attitudes that emphasize the role of the church in their lives and generally support Catholic social teaching. So 27 per cent of Irish people, for instance, mention that they would not like to have homosexuals as neighbours, a figure more in line with southern or eastern Europe than north-west Europe. Though this type of authoritarian attitude is declining, it does demonstrate the tendency of Irish people to feel that people should be able to impose their views on others. An early study of political culture found that 61 per cent of Irish people thought imposing their values on minorities was acceptable (Raven and Whelan, 1976).

Though peasant culture may no longer operate, certain aspects of the relationship between landlord and tenant that were important in Irish society may have continued until more recent times. Certainly it may be thought that kinship and loyalty to one's own group is still important, and it has been argued that a major political party, Fianna Fáil, has a culture of loyalty in which dissent would not be shown to outsiders. However, that culture of loyalty, if it exists, is probably determined by internal party rules and the resources at the disposal of the party leader to enforce this loyalty. Also linked to the peasant culture is the idea of clientelism, which is frequently mentioned by political commentators (this can be found by searching the *Irish Times* archive). Clientelism refers to a practice where those in state positions use them to distribute benefits to 'clients' who may be party supporters. Clientelism can then be used to bolster electoral support or organization. In fact there is little evidence of clientelism in Irish politics; rather, what people mean when they refer to clientelism is brokerage. This is the practice, common in Ireland, in which politicians assist citizens in their dealing with the state. So a person who wishes to apply for state support, such as public housing, may find it easier and quicker to approach their local TD who will have better access to the bureaucracy.

When it comes to trust – central in the idea of social capital – the Irish are more trusting of fellow citizens than people in other western countries, but trust in some state institutions such as the government and the Dáil is low (just a quarter of the population has high trust in them) (Garry, 2006: 65). The police force, the Garda Siochána, has high levels of trust from nearly 60 per cent of the population.

There is some inconsistency in the results of this survey, and this inconsistency is reflected in what different writers say about Irish political culture. A general problem with the idea of political culture is that it tends to be measured through surveys which in fact measure declared attitudes rather than the underlying nature of the people and the state. Nor can we be sure that culture is not caused by some factor which changes easily over time.

One of the most notable features of the Irish political culture is its apparent passivity. When in many countries undergoing similar economic strains, riots and wide-scale strikes were commonplace, the Irish seemed not to display anger. In the 2011 election, however, the Irish revealed a quiet anger through the ballot box by punishing the party that had dominated Irish politics for the previous 80 years. It might be argued that because of the electoral system it meant that Irish politicians are remarkably close to their electorate. Certainly we can see that the Irish political culture if nothing else is a democratic one.

### Elections

We saw in Chapter 3 that there are no deep, structural divisions in Irish society. As a result there are no obvious bases on which the party system is formed. Some have argued, however, that the electoral system ensures that the focus of electoral competition is personal and localist. Electoral systems are generally categorized into one of two groups, proportional systems and majoritarian systems. Proportional systems tend to convert votes into seats in a proportional manner, so a party that gets 15 per cent of the vote might expect to get about 15 per cent of the seats in parliament. Majoritarian systems give the seat to the largest party in a constituency, regardless of relative size, and so will give a seat bonus to larger parties. The Irish electoral system uses proportional representation by single transferable vote (PR-STV) to elect TDs to the 166-seat Dáil. It was first used in Ireland in 1919 for a local election, but then extended to the whole country in the new Free State elections. The logic behind using this unusual voting system was the fear that if the first-past-the-post system used

**Illustration 5.1   A ballot paper for the 2011 Dáil election**

Voters in Ireland must rank order the candidates who are elected using a complex system of counts and vote transfers. The counts can go on for many days and are filled with political drama. 'Tallymen' watch the count closely in order to get an idea of the result before it is officially announced. Efforts were made to use electronic voting but these were shown not to be secure and many would have regretted losing the excitement of the election count.

previously to elect the Irish seats to Westminster were used, there would be no chance for representation of the Protestant minority in the Irish Free State. There have been a number of attempts by Fianna Fáil to change the system back to the UK system but these were rejected by the voters in referendums.

The system requires voters to rank order candidates, indicating a 1 for the most preferred candidate, 2 for the next most preferred and so on (see Illustration 5.1). A voter need only indicate one vote, but given that in Ireland there are between three and five seats allocated in any one of the 43 constituencies, and one's first choice may not get elected, it makes sense to continue allocating preferences down the field. It is possible that one's vote can be used a number of times, to help elect a number of people. The counting can be a long process. The first count sets out how many number 1 votes go to each candidate. A quota is worked out which is the total number of valid votes divided by one plus the number of seats, with one then added on. So in a three-seat constituency with 40,000 valid votes, the quota will be 10,001. Any candidate reaching this number will be elected and his/her surplus votes (anything above the quota) will be distributed to the next placed candidates on the ballot paper. When there are no surpluses to distribute the lowest placed candidates are eliminated. This process continues until all the places are filled.

The impact of the electoral system is unclear. Many argue that it forces Irish legislators to do excessive brokerage or constituency work. Certainly many TDs spend much more time on their constituencies than in many other countries and Irish parliamentary debates are not known for their incisive points on national policy. The argument is that because TDs from a party have to compete against candidates from the same party for the electorate's support they are forced to compete in terms of constituency service. This argument does not take into account the fact that parties usually divide up the constituency between candidates or that there is nothing to stop candidates from competing in terms of national policy debate. Gallagher (1987) has convincingly argued that PR-STV is not the cause of brokerage. The causes of this may be that the Dáil is weak as a legislature, or that because there are few ideological divisions between the parties, they must compete on 'valence' issues – features of an object we evaluate positively or negatively – such as personality and organizational competence. That said, the Irish National Election Survey shows that the Irish are quite happy to have their TDs act as brokers between them and the state bureaucracy.

## Parties and the party system

Although much has changed in Irish society, the political party system after the 2007 election looked remarkably like the one in the 1920s. Though some new parties had entered the fray, there were still two large parties, Fianna Fáil and Fine Gael, and a comparatively small Labour party. The smaller parties, which tend to have a short lifespan, have cycles of support, becoming strong when the established parties are seen as ineffective at dealing with the country's problems and weakening when the main parties are seen as effective. Ireland is also unusual in having a powerful group of non-party deputies. In 2002 a particularly weak Fine Gael opposition lost a large number of seats to smaller parties and independents. The 2007 election saw a consolidation of support for the two main parties, mainly at the expense of smaller parties and independents. But by 2011 the party system had changed significantly, it being one of the most volatile elections in Europe's post-war history. But an unusual feature is that all the political parties were still the same ones that existed 80 years earlier.

Nearly all of the parties in Ireland are descended from Sinn Féin (see Figure 5.1), with only the Green Party having no link to Sinn Féin or one of its offshoots. This might indicate that nationalist politics is of central importance in Irish political competition, but the issue of the link with the UK and Northern Ireland is not now subject to much political debate. Since the early 1990s all parties are agreed on a common strategy of non-aggression and efforts to facilitate peace in Northern Ireland. However the roots of party competition do lie in the policy dimension of nationalism and attitudes to Britain. Fianna Fáil would have been seen as more 'green' or more nationalist on the Northern Ireland question than Fine Gael. The two parties competed in other areas, with Fianna Fáil representing the 'small holder' or small landowner, and Fine Gael representing the professions and larger farmers. However, many have questioned whether there is any real programmatic or policy difference between the two parties, which both appear remarkably conservative on economic and social issues.

The Irish party system for most of the history of the state was dominated by one party, Fianna Fáil, which ruled alone for long periods interrupted by a coalition of the other parties. These coalitions often lacked cohesion, considering they are based on a large Fine Gael base with Labour and sometimes other parties added. One

*Figure 5.1*    Genealogy of Irish political parties

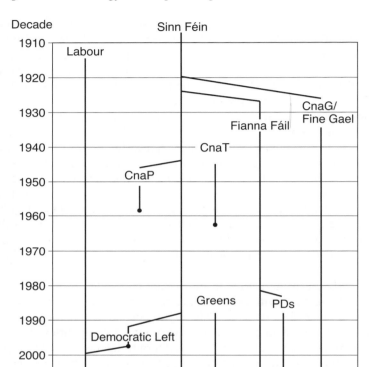

of the most unstable governments was the 1948 government of Fine Gael, two Labour parties, Clann na Poblachta (a small socially leftist republican party), Clann na Talhman (a farmers' party) and a group of independents.

A major change to the Irish party system took place in 1989 when Fianna Fáil entered a coalition government for the first time. Up to that point it had been a 'core value' of the party that single-party government was superior to coalition and that it would not form part of a coalition government. From 1987 to 1989 a Fianna Fáil minority government ruled with the support of Fine Gael on the basis that it would address the parlous economic situation Ireland faced. This arrangement had been reasonably successful, but Charles Haughey,

**Box 5.1   Northern Ireland's political groupings and the peace process**

Political parties in Northern Ireland are divided on religious/cultural lines. The Protestant/ unionist majority is represented by the Ulster Unionist Party (UUP) and the Democratic Unionist Party (DUP). Catholics/nationalists vote for the Social Democratic and Labour Party (SDLP) and Sinn Féin. The UUP and the SDLP were seen as the more moderate parties representing the two sides and both dominated politics during the Troubles from the 1970s to the late 1990s. The Ulster Unionists had traditionally dominated politics in Northern Ireland and were linked to the Protestant Orange Order, a group set up to celebrate William of Orange's victory over James II's forces. Both were dominated by upper-class gentry who ran Northern Ireland with weak nationalist party opposition. The SDLP was formed in 1970 out of the civil rights movement. When in 1988 the SDLP leader, John Hume, agreed to hold private talks with Sinn Féin, which is linked to the Provisional IRA, the group many blame for the length and bloodiness of the Troubles, it started a peace process that would lead to Sinn Féin and the radical British nationalist DUP sharing power. The Belfast Agreement signed on Good Friday in 1998 was passed by a referendum in the North and the Republic, but the DUP campaigned against the deal. Gradually the two more radical parties have overshadowed their more moderate stable-mates. Indeed it is uncertain that the SDLP or UUP will survive as viable political groupings.

The DUP was founded by the Protestant clergyman Ian Paisley, who was virulently anti-Catholic. His radicalism and a strong base in the church he founded meant that he was able to capitalize on unionist uncertainty about the power-sharing deal. The party's electoral strength meant that it and Sinn Féin were both essential to any eventual settlement. Both sides appeared to bargain hard, but also made significant compromises to eventually allow Martin McGuiness and Ian Paisley to share power in government.

the Taoiseach, used his constitutional right to dissolve the Dáil and cause an election. The election failed to give Fianna Fáil the overall majority Haughey expected and wanted, but after the election Fine Gael refused to revert to the strategy of supporting a minority Fianna Fáil government. Haughey negotiated with the Progressive Democrats (PDs), a small liberal party which had split from Fianna Fail a few years earlier, and the two parties entered coalition.

From 1987 to 2011 Fianna Fáil had been part of every government but one. The reason for this lay in Fianna Fáil's position in the Irish party system. Fianna Fáil regularly received 40 per cent of the vote and from 1932 until 2011 was always the largest party. Forming a government without Fianna Fáil required all or nearly all other parties and independent TDs to support an alternative government. Figure 5.2 shows how central Fianna Fáil is to politics on the main economic (horizontal) dimension. Forming a government of all parties from Sinn Féin to the PDs would have been close to impossible, whereas Fianna Fáil could have coalesced with one or two of the smaller parties – the government elected in 2007 was between Fianna Fáil, the PDs, and the Greens.

The economic crisis put severe pressure on Fianna Fáil's coalition of support that had spanned left and right. By 2009 the party was behind Fine Gael in local and European elections, and an election in early 2011 saw the party come third at an election behind Fine Gael and Labour. The decline of Fianna Fáil from its dominant position will be one of the legacies of the crisis.

Figure 5.2 shows that the majority of Irish voters are economically centre-right, whereas there is more variation on the less salient dimension of social liberalism. It will also be evident, and perhaps, surprising that the two largest parties are so close together. A look at the history and development of these parties might help explain this.

*Fianna Fáil*

Fianna Fáil was established in 1926 by Éamon de Valera and others in anti-treaty Sinn Féin who split with Sinn Féin on the issue of abstaining from the Dáil. Though he initially contemplated leaving public life, de Valera, or Dev as he was popularly known, was persuaded to set up a new political organization which would challenge the treaty and the new Free State government from within the political process. Fianna Fáil quickly became organized nationally and ran for election within a year of being formed, almost becoming the largest party. Its stated aims at its foundation were:

- Securing the political independence of a united Ireland as a republic.
- The restoration of the Irish language and the development of a native Irish culture.
- The development of a social system in which, as far as possible, equal opportunity is afforded to every citizen to live a noble and useful Christian life.

*Figure 5.2*   Irish party and voter positions as estimated by voters, 2002

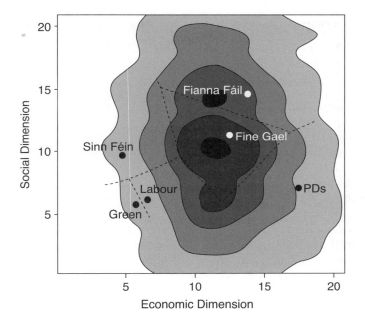

*Note*: The economic dimension measures willingness to increase taxes to fund
spending (0) to willingness to cut spending in order to allow tax cuts (20). The
social dimension measures attitudes to homosexuality and abortion, with lower
scores representing a more liberal position. The figure can also be read like an
Ordnance Survey map where darker areas represent more densely populated
positions, so the most popular position among Irish voters is the dark circle just
south-west of Fine Gael.

*Source*: Benoit and Laver (2005).

- The distribution of the land of Ireland so as to have the greatest
  possible number of Irish families rooted in the soil of Ireland.
- The making of Ireland an economic unit, as self-contained and self-
  sufficient as possible – with a proper balance between agriculture
  and the other essential industries.

It initially tried to exploit Cumann na nGaedheal's (later Fine Gael)
dependence on Protestant bankers and businessmen in its attempt to
get the new state up and running. As such it appealed to Gaelic

Ireland, and attracted support from many radical social reformers – in turn Fine Gael tried to allege that Fianna Fail was a threat to the state, capitalism and Catholicism. In truth de Valera was a conservative Catholic and no socialist. Though the initial policies of Fianna Fáil were reforming, many policies were (at least with hindsight) counter-productive nationalist measures, such as the starting of the economic war with Britain.

Despite causing a recession, the party quickly consolidated its position as the largest Irish party and enjoyed uninterrupted rule for 16 years. Meanwhile many of the more reforming members became disillusioned with the party, though it still maintained an image as the party of the true nationalist. After 16 years' rule there was a feeling that it had become stale and that it lacked policies for the nation's problems, and it lost power twice in the late 1940s and 1950s. Part of the problem was that there were people with different ideas about running the country in the party and de Valera's innate conservatism (and possibly his fear of a split in the party) meant that neither side won out. When Seán Lemass took over he promoted younger men to cabinet and introduced some more radical measures, such as the free education scheme. After his retirement the party settled on a compromise candidate, but problems emerged on the outbreak of the Troubles, when it became evident that there were two different views in the party on how to tackle the problem. The Arms Crisis (when a number of ministers were dismissed and others resigned in a dispute about the extent of authorization for the import of arms for the nascent Provisional IRA) exposed these divisions further, and the split came to a head in the 1980s when, under Charles Haughey's leadership, a number of members were expelled who went on to form the PDs. The party has since become more accommodating to the views of Northern Ireland's unionists and under Bertie Ahern it re-emerged as a competent electoral machine.

As a centrist party it is sometimes difficult to identify the ideology of Fianna Fáil. The name of the party was in part chosen because it was difficult to translate and not identifiable with a particular ideology. Members of the party often boasted that it was a 'national movement' rather than a political party. Many on the left would argue that it is a right-wing party, whereas some in Fianna Fáil put an emphasis on policies of social justice; indeed Bertie Ahern, the leader of Fianna Fáil and Taoiseach, once claimed (to much mockery) that he was one of the few socialists in the Dáil. Its support base is remarkably heterogeneous. It draws votes almost equally from the urban

**Illustration 5.2   Irish election posters in 2011**

Irish elections are characterized by large numbers of posters. These show how candidates are central to Irish parties' campaigning.

working class and middle class as from farmers. What is certain is that it has failed to achieve any of its initial goals. Ireland is still partitioned; the language is all but dead; income inequality has grown; Ireland is increasingly urbanized; and far from being self-sufficient, it is one of the most globalized countries in the world. Fianna Fáil would argue that it is a pragmatic party which recognized that certain goals were outdated, and Fianna Fáil continued to be one of the world's most successful political organizations. In 2007 it announced that it would investigate the possibility of running for election in Northern Ireland, thus becoming the second (serious) all-island party after Sinn Féin. At the same time its popularity was reaching all-time lows. The economic crisis was widely blamed on Fianna Fáil and in government it struggled to offer solutions. In the 2011 election voters roundly blamed Fianna Fáil for the economic collapse and reduced it to the third largest party, and its worst result since its foundation. It is clear that Fianna Fáil would never return to the dominance it had once had, and that it would now be just another party. Where that party would position itself is more difficult to tell. Many spoke about returning to the party's roots, but exactly what that meant was less clear. It had survived as a catch-all party because it was so large. As a much smaller party it will need to distinguish itself somehow.

*Fine Gael*

Fine Gael is descended from an amalgamation of the original pro-treaty party of Cumann na nGaedheal and a small party, the National Centre Party, earlier the Farmers' Party, and the National Guard or Blueshirts, an organization designed to protect pro-treaty forces when Fianna Fáil came to power. It took over the job of governing at the start of the state and though it managed the task of stabilizing the state it arguably did so at the expense of radical reforms, becoming easily labelled a conservative party. The necessity of working with established Protestant families to stabilize the state also gave it a tinge of 'West Britonism' (the idea that someone or something apes the behaviour or attitudes of the British) that lasts to this day. It was also unfortunate in that its two likely natural leaders, Michael Collins and Arthur Griffith, died before the party was established. It became for some the party of business and large farmers, tending to perform better in the east of the country than the west, but in perpetual opposition it lost support, by 1948 receiving less than 20 per cent of the vote. A number of spells in government with parties on the left also added to confusion about its identity and purpose. From the 1960s a number of young intellectuals in the party tried to shift the party to the left and its most successful leader, Dr. Garret FitzGerald, regarded himself as a social democrat. He attempted to reposition it as a socially liberal party, but some of these efforts failed. Fine Gael has always suffered from being dependent on the fortunes of Fianna Fáil. It has only been able to form a government with parties on the left and the question of why someone would support this conservative party, when Fianna Fáil too is a centrist non-ideological catch-all party has been raised. Since 2002 there has been something of an upturn in the party's fortunes, linked to Fianna Fáil's decline. In 2011 general election, capitalising on the unpopularity of Fianna Fáil it became the largest party, forming a coalition government with Labour. Still it only received 36 per cent of the vote, and entering government at a very difficult time, it will no doubt lose support.

*Labour*

The Labour party is one of oldest parties in the Republic, founded in 1912. Its decision to abstain from the 1918 general election after a major enfranchisement is sometimes cited as one of the reasons for its failure to challenge the two largest parties. The absence of anti-treaty Sinn Féin from the Dáil in the early years of the state cast it in the role of main opposition party but it failed to build on this opportunity and was damaged by the electoral success of Fianna Fáil. The party has also suffered a number of splits between radical and conservative members. These splits have sometimes occurred over whether it should enter coalition arrangements. Before the 2007 election, Labour had the possibility of overtaking a weakened Fine Gael as the second largest party, but its decision to enter a pre-election pact with Fine Gael arguably gave Fine Gael a boost at Labour's expense. By 2010 it looked more likely that Labour could make the breakthrough it continually predicts for itself, but its result in 2011 must have been a disappointment to the party. There was no shift to the left by the Irish. Its decision to enter a coalition with a centre-right party also meant that it would not forge a left-right split in Irish politics.

The position of the Labour party and the left in Ireland is intriguing. Though the party systems of European countries vary greatly, most countries have a large social democratic or socialist party. The extension of the franchise in the first half of the twentieth century, and the coming of socialist ideas with their interpretation of class structure, led to the growth of mainstream left-wing parties. At this time an Irish Labour party was formed, but it never saw the growth that its sister parties in Europe saw. It has averaged about ten per cent support. Ireland's nationalist parties Fianna Fáil and Fine Gael, on the other hand, have been remarkably strong with support from across the class divide. Why the left has been so weak has been a mystery to political scientists. A number of reasons, have been offered however.

- *The Labour party became irrelevant by not involving itself in the 'national question' (of the relationship between Britain and Ireland) or the 1918 election.* By opting out of this defining election, Labour may have effectively sidelined itself from the new political agenda and allowed nationalism to take precedence over socialism. One problem with this interpretation is that by 1922 Labour received over 20 per cent of the vote nationally, more than anti-treaty Sinn Féin (later Fianna Fáil).
- *There were not enough working-class people to support a socialist party.* Ireland was essentially a rural country with a great number of people living and working off the land. Land ownership was comparatively high and these small landowners would have been naturally wary of socialist ideas of collectivization (even if these were not current in Ireland). Mair (1992) has shown that enough people identified themselves as working-class, but this failed to materialize into class voting.
- *The Irish as Catholics were naturally wary of socialism.* In many countries the Catholic Church is associated with conservative parties and antipathetic to socialist teachings which it saw as alien to Catholicism. In Ireland, the church successfully aligned itself with a nationalist cause and so the revolution was a Catholic revolution as well as a nationalist one. The division, common in other countries, between Catholics and revolutionaries did not occur (on a large scale) in Ireland. As a result there was little anti-Catholic feeling and the church remained influential, depriving a left-wing party of a constituency to mobilize.
- *The fractious nature of the left in Ireland.* In the past the left has been represented by a number of small parties. Even the main left-wing party, the Labour party, was split between urban liberal socialists, conservative rural representatives and militant Marxists. One of the problems the Irish Labour party continues to have is that

it could be thought of as two parties in one. It has always had strong support in some of the larger country towns and among farm labourers, but the TDs elected in these rural areas tended to be arch-conservatives who rarely supported socialist policies. Contrast these with some of the TDs elected in urban areas, who were middle-class liberal intellectuals who were influenced by European left-wing thinkers. There have also been tensions with more militant members of the Labour party who opposed the Labour party's policy of coalescing with Fine Gael.

- *Fianna Fáil was a left-wing party.* In 1932 when Fianna Fáil entered government it did so on the promise of radical social reforms, some of which received initial support from Labour. Many of the early members of Fianna Fáil regarded themselves as left-wing and Fianna Fáil as a left-wing party. Fianna Fáil, it could be claimed, helped build a reasonably strong social welfare system and enabled the involvement of social partners such as unions in key policy making. However it is clear that Ireland is not an egalitarian society.
- *Irish brokerage politics.* Some have argued that the nature of brokerage politics in Ireland, where individuals go to their elected representatives to have certain problems solved individually, means that there is less incentive for or possibility of collective class action.

## Smaller parties and independents

Apart from the three established parties, Ireland has had a number of small parties, some of which have been highly influential. The parties tend to come and go in waves. The first wave was arguably in the 1920s before the political and party system settled down. In the 1940s another wave came, which lasted until the early 1960s. During this period Clann na Poblachta was formed by republicans disillusioned with Fianna Fail's conservatism. Though it received over 13 per cent of the vote and entered government in 1948, it soon split and rapidly diminished. A longer-lasting party was Clann na Talmhan, a farmer's party, which had its support base in the west of Ireland and took most of its support from Fine Gael. Like Clann na Poblachta, the experience of government made Clann na Talmhan defunct.

The next wave of parties emerged in the 1980s. The Troubles had caused the Belfast-based IRA members to split from its Dublin-based leadership and form Provisional Sinn Féin and the Provisional IRA.

These did not take part in the political process, but the remaining Official Sinn Féin took a decidedly leftist turn, becoming Sinn Féin – The Workers' Party, later just The Workers' Party. It had some parliamentary representation in the 1980s, but split again after the fall of the communist regimes of Eastern Europe, as most of the party's TDs left to form Democratic Left. It entered government with Labour and Fine Gael between 1994 and 1997 but later merged with the Labour Party. Provisional Sinn Féin, known now as Sinn Féin, had been the political wing of the more important IRA. Its first forays into electoral politics were during the hunger strikes of the 1980s, and while it made consistent electoral progress in Northern Ireland, it was only after the IRA ceasefires and the Good Friday Agreement that Sinn Féin started to gain support in the Republic. Its progress was slow but by 2011 it was the fourth largest party and close to Fianna Fáil.

Another prominent party that emerged in the 1980s is the Progressive Democrats (PDs), founded by some expelled members of Fianna Fáil. The party differed with Fianna Fáil in being decidedly neo-liberal in its economic approach, liberal in its social views and conciliatory towards northern unionists. It took 14 seats in its first election in 1987, but since then the party's support has fluctuated downward. However it, more than many parties, has been successful in achieving its policy goals. It first entered government from 1989 to 1992 and then was in government from 1997, always with Fianna Fáil. Its tax reform agenda was implemented and is now accepted by most mainstream parties. In 2007 the party lost six seats, and though it entered government, it disbanded in 2009.

The Green Party was founded in the early 1980s, but only made a real electoral breakthrough in 2002, winning six seats. Like Green parties throughout Europe it is an environmental party which campaigns on issues such as climate change. Though disappointed with its performance, it took the bold step of entering government with Fianna Fáil, a party it had often criticized. This decision proved costly as it lost all its seats at the 2011 election.

Another unusual feature of Irish politics is the large number of independents who run and are elected to the Dáil. The candidate-based electoral system enables this, and the Irish at times elect non party candidates in large numbers. Most of these tend to be 'local promoters' who attempt to secure the delivery of goods to their constituency. In 2011 a large number of 'nationally-focussed' independents emerged, but because they wielded no influence on government, we might expect this wave of independents to ebb.

**Box 5.2 Corruption and Irish politics**

In July 1999, at the Flood tribunal into planning corruption in County Dublin, one-time Minister for Foreign Affairs Ray Burke described TDs' salaries as so inadequate that fundraising was an unfortunate fact of political life. He said that it left politicians open to allegations like those levelled against him and he urged the tribunal chairman to consider this in his final report (Proceedings of the Flood Tribunal, 9 July 1999). Three years later and after a number of spells in prison for contempt of court he was found to have received corrupt payments. His case was seen as minor compared to that of former Taoiseach Charles Haughey who was found to have received at least €11 million in questionable payments. A number of tribunals into various matters of corruption or improper political process continue to trawl through politicians' finances, including those of Bertie Ahern.

Whether Ireland is a corrupt country is debatable. On a score of perceived corruption, Ireland is regarded as one of the least corrupt countries in the world (Transparency International Report, 2010). Certainly it is not culturally acceptable to bribe public officials for services one is entitled to as can be observed in other countries. Why might it be that corruption has become so associated with Irish politics?

Most of the corruption alleged to occur in Ireland has to do with the planning process. It has been suggested that where the state can make decisions which have great economic consequences for the subject of the decision, corruption is more likely. In a relatively liberal economy such as Ireland's is today, this affords little opportunity, except in the area of construction. Land is typically zoned for certain types of uses, such as agriculture, residential or commercial. A change in the zoning of the land, a political decision, can have enormous consequences for the value of the land. In addition the density at which land can be built on also affects its value. This allows land speculators with political connections to buy agricultural land and get it rezoned, thereby making a huge profit. Haughey, however, received payments from wealthy business people, which they argued were merely supporting the financial needs of a friend, but were possibly because he made decisions in the 1980s which directly assisted them in building up their fortunes.

## Interest groups

The centrality of government and weakness of parliament in Irish policy making leaves some room open for policy influence through interest groups. The Catholic Church was by far the most powerful interest group, but its power waned from the 1990s. Irish policy making in the 1930s was designed to be corporatist, seeking to bring social partners such as employers' organizations and trade unions into the policy-making process. The medium for this was then the Senate, though this quickly and predictably became a party political chamber. Corporatism in Ireland actually means wage agreements. These started in the 1970s but were largely unsuccessful, and it was only in the late 1980s that Irish governments under Charles Haughey successfully combined changes in the tax regime to temper the wage demands of unions.

Social partnership has been credited with bringing about the economic miracle that led to what became known as the Celtic Tiger by introducing wage restraint and improving industrial relations in the state. But critics complain that it had too much power and that it kept private much of the policy debate that should occur in public. When put under pressure by the economic crisis, the whole social partnership system came close to collapse, leading to questions as to whether it was just a means of buying industrial and political peace at too high a price for the state.

Outside the area of wage control, social partnership is limited, and a more pluralist system of interest group relations prevails. Interest groups in Ireland tend to be economic in their focus. As such their main focus is attempting to influence the Minister for Finance to make certain provisions in the budget. Other interest groups such as pro-Life groups, usually supported by the Catholic Church, have also been highly active and generally successful in lobbying the state, whereas liberal groups seeking protection or extension of certain rights have relied on the courts to achieve their goals. Some other groups representing professions, such as the Irish Medical Organisation, the Law Society and the Institute of Chartered Accountants, are powerful because they regulate important professions in Ireland.

An example of the influence of interest groups can be seen in the success of groups representing motor companies in introducing a car scrappage scheme. While in other European countries where cars are manufactured, car scrappage schemes where vehicles over ten years old are replaced by new vehicles makes some sense, in Ireland it makes little sense as it is a subsidy to the wealthy to send large amounts of money abroad. There was little debate about it in parliament and no analysis of the scheme was released to the public. Yet in 2009 the Irish government introduced the scheme after lobbying by these groups.

*Construction industry unions*

Traditionally one of the largest industries in Ireland is construction, which at its height represented as much as 20 per cent of GDP (compared to a European average of about 12 per cent). It is, unsurprisingly, a powerful government lobby group and thought to be a major source of funding for the political parties, especially Fianna Fáil. The main organization representing the industry is the Construction Industry Federation, which lobbies government mainly on ensuring a large spend on infrastructure projects and on stamp duty – a tax paid by purchasers which can be up to nine per cent of the value of a property. The fact that new homes were exempt from this tax meant they could increase the price of new homes to match those of the existing housing stock. It has been largely successful in achieving its goals, and this is thought to be related to the significant funding builders and developers have given to parties, in particular Fianna Fáil. There is widespread suspicion that it was this close relationship that led to the policies which seemed to fuel the building boom at a time of already strong growth.

*Employers' organizations*

There are a number of employers' organizations, the most important of which, the Irish Business and Employers Confederation (IBEC), has over 70 sectoral groups associated to it. It has assumed a great deal of influence since the late 1980s because of its central role in national wage agreements. Its main goal has been to temper wage demands of workers, and to create a more flexible labour market. Its importance, therefore, is not dependent on certain types of government being in power, but rather derives from its influential position as an agent of social partnership.

*Labour organizations*

There are about 60 trade unions in Ireland, most of whom are affiliated to the Irish Congress of Trades Unions (ICTU). In total about half a million or less than a third of workers are members of trade unions, a proportion that continues to decrease. Within Europe Ireland is about average in terms of union density. The largest union in Ireland is SIPTU, with 200,000 members in virtually all sectors of the economy. It has links with the Labour Party and is one of the main supporters of the social partnership process. ICTU represents labour in social partnership talks, and is sometimes seen as close to Fianna Fáil. Unlike in the UK, ICTU has a high degree of authority over affiliated unions. The logic of union membership is sometimes questionable, given social partnership, as the benefits negotiated are distributed regardless of union membership. Industrial disputes were at a historically low level; this is partly explained by the labour movement's participation in the social partnership process. Therefore while recent legislative changes have been unfavourable to unions, their political influence remains comparatively strong. With the economic crisis, the social partnership process collapsed and unions reverted to causing a series of strikes in the public sector. These tended not to have support among the general public, and it is common for people to complain about the favourable treatment public sector workers receive and the high level of influence of unions representing them.

### Irish Farmers' Association

Though agriculture is no longer an economically significant industry in Ireland, the Irish Farmers' Association (IFA) remains a strong interest group. With about 85,000 members, it has been influential in ensuring that Irish governments have been at the forefront of the defence of the EU's Common Agricultural Policy (CAP). It has also been able to dilute some of the more demanding new policies from the EU, but this influence cannot be taken for granted as agriculture continues to decline in importance and environmental concerns become more pressing.

### Others

There are many other civil society organizations which sometimes attempt to lobby government on various issues. Often these are local groups which are aimed at preserving services in their area. Hospital groups have had a high profile and at times have successfully fielded candidates in general elections. Of national interest groups, the Vintners Federation of Ireland, which represents bar owners, has been seen as successful in preserving a highly regulated industry, but it failed in its attempt to block the ban on smoking in public places. Another vocal lobby have been environmental groups, which have often combined with local groups to object to road building programmes. These have been largely unsuccessful, and have had to resort to the courts to seek any concessions; the participation of the Green Party in government does not seem to have changed this.

## The media

Media systems have been categorized by Hallin and Mancini (2004) into three types – a democratic corporatist model in which the media is tied to organized social and political groups; a polarized pluralist model in which the media is integrated into party politics; and a liberal model in which market mechanisms dominate. The first two models are thought to prevail in northern Europe and southern Europe respectively, while the third is meant to be typical of Anglo-American democracies of which Ireland is considered to be one.

In analyzing media ownership, the existence or otherwise of a market depends on the type of media. Television and radio were dominated by the broadcaster RTÉ, which is state-owned but independent of government, being financed through advertising and by a licence fee. It controls three radio stations and three television stations – one of each broadcasts in the Irish language. More recently new entrants have been allowed into these markets, which are regulated by the Broadcasting Commission of Ireland. This means that there are now many national and local radio stations catering for different market demands. In television new commercial TV stations have emerged catering for a younger 20–35 age group. The radio market has seen some concentration with one businessman, Denis O'Brien, building up a portfolio of stations.

Given the proximity of Britain, many Irish homes on the east coast and near the border with Northern Ireland could receive transmissions from domestic British channels. In the last twenty years new technology means that the rest of the country can receive these also. Therefore it is unsurprising that the output of the Irish broadcast media does not differ significantly from its British equivalents. Many programmes are bought in from the UK or the USA, and many domestic programmes are remakes or copies of foreign programmes. The exposure of Ireland to British TV channels mean that the Irish government's control over broadcasting policy has by and large become redundant. It can insist on certain broadcasting rules, but given the ability of Irish viewers to switch to the UK stations, rules that significantly restrict Irish broadcasters' freedom might risk losing a domestic Irish market. However there are rules which ensure

**Illustration 5.3    The front pages of Irish newspapers**

The papers show the reaction to the IMF bailout. Some British newspapers, such as the Sunday Times and the Daily Mail, have Irish editions which sell well in Ireland.

that broadcasters cover a certain amount of current affairs. This free media is one of the few ways political parties can use the broadcast media as political advertising is banned. The rapid expansion in the number of channels from the start of this century may have the effect of weakening Ireland's social glue, as there are fewer media events that the whole nation sees and can feel part of.

In terms of press ownership, apart from the *Irish Times*, which is controlled by a non-profit trust, all major national papers are privately owned and operating for profit. The papers are independent of political parties, although a paper which closed down in the 1990s, the *Irish Press*, was controlled by the de Valera family and was seen as a mouthpiece for Fianna Fáil. The biggest selling broadsheet is the *Irish Independent* which has daily sales of about 150,000, compared to 110,000 for the *Irish Times*. The *Independent* is controlled in part by Sir Anthony O'Reilly and Independent Newspapers plc which until recently owned papers in the UK, Australia and South Africa. This company also controls many local papers. The *Irish Times*, a paper which was linked with Protestant interests, is now the most serious newspaper and the one which might represent the liberal intelligentsia if Ireland possesses such a group. However in recent years it has expanded its market share in part by catering for a growing consumerism, especially in property (features on shopping trips to New York can be found, for example). Generally the media is obsessed with consumerism, and all papers and broadcasters covered the opening of Ireland's first IKEA shop in Belfast as a major news story. Ireland is also unusual in having a high penetration of foreign newspapers in its market. British papers sell significant numbers in Ireland, and their coverage of British celebrities and English soccer is only partially tailored to suit the Irish market. *The Sun*, the *Mirror* and the *Daily Mail* become the *Irish Sun* and *Irish Mirror* and *Irish Daily Mail*, but little else changes except for a focus on Irish sport, celebrities and the removal of anti-Irish commentary.

One feature of the British press that has not travelled to Ireland is the partisanship of the press coverage of politics. Whereas in the UK certain papers are close to particular parties, apart from the *Irish Press*, only one paper has just once explicitly called for people to vote a certain way at elections. Irish journalists are also thought to be left-leaning (Corcoran, 2004) and the proprietors right-leaning. There are some highly opinionated periodicals, such as the now defunct right-wing *Magill* and left-wing *Village*, but these tend not to involve themselves in party politics.

There is little tradition in Ireland of investigative journalism. Notwithstanding the murder of a prominent journalist covering the criminal underworld, Veronica Guerin, which was later made into an eponymous film, Irish papers might be criticized for being tame. Certainly though many people openly questioned the financing of former Taoiseach Charles J. Haughey's lifestyle, none of the papers attempted to uncover or publish allegations about what were subsequently discovered to be his corrupt actions. This timidity is in part due to the libel laws which make publishing allegations financially risky.

# 6

# The Economy

From the 1990s the Irish economy underwent changes so rapid and widespread that they were unlike those in almost any another country in the world. In the 1950s some questioned whether Ireland was capable of governing itself. In the 1980s, though it was not a third world country, arguments could be made that it was firmly in the second world, and that only its geographic position in western Europe and the high expectations of its population made it usually described as first world. With Portugal it was among the poorest countries in western Europe. However by the turn of the twenty-first century Ireland had overtaken most other countries in terms of wealth, having achieved remarkably strong and consistent productivity growth. Ireland became the stuff of legend and economists and policy makers flocked to Ireland to praise it and study what it had achieved. Given that achieving growth is the Holy Grail for nearly every poor country, Ireland was held up as a paragon of good economic management.

Between 1993 and 2005 Ireland had an average annual nominal GDP growth rate of eight per cent, compared to growth rates closer to two per cent in other European countries. Even if we account for the relatively high inflation which should be taken away from the nominal growth rate to estimate the real growth rate, Irish growth was remarkably strong. In that time Ireland rose from about 80 per cent of the average per capita GNI of the EU-15 (the members of the EU in 1995) – to over 120 per cent the EU-15 average. Ireland's earnings per person (see Table 6.1) made it among the wealthiest countries in the world (of the EU countries only Luxembourg, Austria and the Netherlands were wealthier in 2008). The number of people employed increased by over 600,000 and the unemployment rate fell from 16 per cent to four per cent – a rate many economists regard as full employment.

*Table 6.1*  Ireland's earnings, 2004–9

| Description | 2004 | 2005 | 2006 | 2007 | 2008 | 2009† |
|---|---|---|---|---|---|---|
| | | | | | | € million |
| Gross Domestic Product (GDP) at current market prices | 149,344 | 162,314 | 177,343 | 189,374 | 179,989 | 159,646 |
| Gross National Product (GNP) at current market prices | 126,465 | 138,053 | 154,078 | 162,853 | 154,672 | 131,241 |
| Gross National Income (GNI) at current market prices | 127,929 | 139,859 | 155,387 | 164,062 | 155,985 | 132,601 |
| Gross National Disposable Income at current market prices | 126,858 | 138,318 | 153,574 | 161,863 | 153,518 | 130,340 |
| Chain linked volume measures | | | | | | |
| Gross Domestic Product at constant market prices (referenced to 2008) | 158,223 | 167,742 | 176,669 | 186,609 | 179,989 | 166,345 |
| Gross National Product at constant market prices (referenced to 2008) | 135,918 | 144,030 | 153,398 | 160,299 | 154,672 | 138,161 |
| Gross National Income at constant market prices (referenced to 2008) | 137,258 | 145,532 | 184,861 | 161,497 | 155,985 | 139,476 |
| Per head of population (€) | | | | | | |
| GDP at current market prices | 36,919 | 39,265 | 41,828 | 43,645 | 40,702 | 35,801 |
| GNP at current market prices | 31,263 | 33,396 | 36,341 | 37,532- | 34,977 | 29,431 |
| GNI at current market prices | 31,625 | 33,833 | 36,649 | 37,811 | 35,274 | 29,736 |

† Preliminary

*Source:* Data from Central Statistics Office, *National Income and Expenditure* (2010).

Economic growth can come about in a number of different ways, which Szirmai (2005: 69) lists as:

- Discovery of riches and natural resources
- Increased effort
- Saving and capital investment
- Education leading to increased added value
- Theft
- Efficiency
- Technological change.

Ireland probably used most of these strategies (except perhaps theft) to achieve its remarkable economic growth rates, but the overarching approach was to increase trade. As we saw in Chapter 1, soon after independence the Fianna Fáil governments attempted to introduce a homely rural-based economy based on some utopian idealization of seventeenth-century rural life. Key to this was self-sufficiency and the protection of Ireland from outside mass industrial influence. Restrictions were placed on the foreign ownership of industry, though even economic nationalists recognized the need to import British coal and to export agricultural products. There was no attempt at mass industrialization. These policies failed completely and in light of the mass emigration and poverty of the 1950s, a new political direction was pushed by Seán Lemass, who took over as Taoiseach from de Valera in 1959, opening the country up to competition and freer trade partly in preparation for Ireland's prospective EEC membership. This caused mild industrialization and economic growth between 1959 and 1972. The international oil crises and poor policy decisions, such as the decision to fund tax reductions by increased borrowing, caused a crisis of confidence in the Irish economy and meant Ireland reverted to high levels of emigration and unemployment in the 1980s. The government's increased spending failed to lift Ireland out of recession, and instead reduced confidence in the economy and the state's ability to deal with its problems.

The attempts of the Fine Gael–Labour government to get public spending under control failed to have much impact on the economy. Ireland was in a vicious circle of emigration, which though limiting the rise in unemployment also removed pressures that might stimulate growth. That Ireland was a regional economy tied to and following its larger neighbour, the UK, was problematic given the fact that the UK was in economic decline for much of this time. Although

Ireland's growth rates matched those of Britain, Ireland was starting from a much lower base. When in 1987 the new Fianna Fáil government started large cutbacks to public services despite protests from the public, this increased confidence internationally and within the country showed that Ireland was at least taking its problems seriously. Simultaneously tax rates were reduced as part of an agreement between business lobbies, trade unions and government, whereby wage increases would be capped. As well as delivering real wage increases from falling taxes, there was comparative industrial peace with very few days lost due to strikes. Over time increased investment in the economy and the location of foreign businesses in Ireland increased employment. With this, tax revenues increased, though tax rates continued to fall, stabilizing the economy and eventually reducing the previously high levels of government borrowing.

Ireland's membership of the European Union, which had formed a single market where goods, services, capital and people could travel freely, allowed Ireland to market itself as a region within a much larger European economy. The trade liberalization, infrastructural investment and membership of the Euro all contributed to the export-led growth Ireland experienced. Instead of the 'Irish disease', people were now referring to the Celtic Tiger and the 'Irish miracle'. By the early 2000s it became clear that domestic demand – funded by borrowing – rather than exports was driving economic growth. In addition soaring house prices put pressure on employers to cede to wage demands. In this the state led the way, as the expansion in government spending was largely accounted for by pay increases. By 2007 the collapse in the world economy, the collapse in domestic property prices and government overspending created a situation where the economy was going to either have to jam on the brakes or hit a brick wall. Which it did is a matter of opinion, but either way it was unpleasant.

This chapter will focus on the Irish economy, beginning by studying its nature at independence, tracing the policies of successive Irish governments. The picture will emerge of an economy shaped by politics, where political decisions, both good and bad, drove the Irish economy. This will set the scene for the second part of the chapter, which will outline and offer explanations for what is commonly referred to as the Celtic Tiger. This will include a discussion of membership of the EU single market, EU financial support, US investment and the liberalization of the Irish economy. We then look at what went wrong and if there is any prospect of recovery.

## The structure of the Irish economy

Ireland is a liberal capitalist economy in which most income is earned
through and where most people work in the private sector. About
370,000 of the nearly 2 million people employed in Ireland work in
the public sector. Traditionally economies are categorized in three
areas, agriculture, manufacturing and services. Agriculture, for a long
time the main source of Ireland's economy, now accounts for just two
per cent of income, and about five per cent of employment (see Table
6.2). That said, meat exports, in particular beef, are an important part
of the Irish economy. Food processing is one of the few genuinely
indigenous industries.

Most people employed in Ireland are engaged in the service sector.
The service sector – including banking, insurance, retail and tourism
– also accounts for the bulk income that Ireland earns each year.
Ireland came late to manufacturing; it was only in the 1960s that
manufactured goods exceeded agricultural goods as the largest category of Irish exports. From the late 1980s Ireland targeted specific
manufacturing industries for development, especially pharmaceuticals and computers. Less and less economic activity is made up by
manufacturing, which has transferred to countries in Asia (particularly China) and central and eastern Europe with lower wage costs.
Industry accounts for a quarter of Ireland's income annually, and of
this a third is in chemicals and pharmaceuticals. Computer manufacturing had been important but with the closure of the Dell plant in

*Table 6.2*    Employment per sector, 2009

|  | *2009* |
| --- | --- |
| Agriculture | 97,200 |
| Industry | 413,800 |
| Services (incl. public service) | 1,427,500 |
| Total employed | 1,938,500 |
| Participation rate    62.5%    Unemployment rate    11.5% | |

The participation rate is the ratio between the labour force (the number
of people employed and unemployed) and the overall size of their cohort
(national population of the same age range).

*Source*: Data from Central Statistics Office, *Quarterly National Household Survey
Q2* (2009).

2009, nearly all manufacturing ended. There was a shift away from so-called screwdriver industries to higher-end jobs in the services sector, particularly IT and financial services, where research and innovation are important. The construction industry became highly important, and on some measures constituted a quarter of Irish GNP in 2006, many times what it is in most other countries. Many of the migrants from eastern Europe worked in construction.

Like most modern western economies, Ireland is a mixture of free market capitalism and state intervention. The Irish state accounts for about 33 per cent of GDP, lower than most other OECD countries (average 42 per cent), though if taken as a percentage of GNP then it is 39 per cent (see Box 6.1). The Irish state has expanded in size and scope, but like most other countries in Europe it represents a smaller proportion of the overall economy, which was expanding. State spending grew by an average of 4.5 per cent a year in real terms between 2000 and 2006. The state spent nearly €56 billion in 2008, and of this the social services discussed in Chapter 3 – social welfare, health and education – accounted for over half of public sector spending (see Figure 6.1). The increased spending in real terms has, however, had little impact on the quality or range of services. That almost €20 billion went to pay the salaries and pensions of public sector workers might indicate that the problem is that staff are overpaid rather than the services underfunded. The debate is ongoing about the nature of the state – whether it should be the primary provider of services or whether it should merely facilitate the provision of services.

The Irish state raises this money by imposing taxes on people's activities. Income tax and value added tax (VAT – a sales tax, with rates of up to 21.5 per cent) together collected over 60 per cent of revenue. Excise duty, an extra tax on tobacco and alcohol, and corporation tax, a tax on the profits of businesses, make up a further 25 per cent. Stamp duty, a tax on, among other things, housing transactions which could be up to nine per cent of the cost of the house, was also an important component of the Irish revenue stream, but the collapsed housing market and reduced rates and increased exemptions make this a less important source of funds. In 2008 the government did not receive enough to cover its spending commitments, and its large deficit was funded by borrowing on international financial markets. The cost of that borrowing increased as Ireland's credit rating was downgraded – meaning that the markets thought there was a greater risk Ireland might default on its debt, something it has never done.

---

**Box 6.1   Problems of using GDP as a measure of wealth**

When we measure a country's wealth we usually look at the GDP, which stands for gross domestic product. GDP represents the monetary value of all goods and services produced within a nation's geographic borders over a specified period of time. Less frequently used alternative measures are GNP (gross national product) and GNI (gross national income).

GNP and GNI measure the income of the country's citizens regardless of where it was earned, so a US company that makes computers in Ireland will contribute to Ireland's GDP but to the USA's GNI. For most countries GNI/GNP and GDP are quite similar, and GDP is often used to measure wealth without creating problems. Because of Ireland's high reliance on foreign direct investment (FDI), much of Ireland's created wealth ultimately ends up in other countries, principally the USA. For this reason there is a large discrepancy between Ireland's GDP and Ireland's GNI (see Table 6.2 for an illustration of how each of these are formed). Where Ireland's GDP was €182bn in 2008, GNP was €155bn (about 86 per cent of GDP). Therefore when looking at figures as a percentage of GDP for Ireland one needs to be cautious. Frequently, on that measure, Ireland may underspend on certain services, but if we use GNI, then Ireland's spending may appear normal.

One problem with either type of measure is that they only take account of traded goods and services. Some services, such as the care of a child by its parent, are not measured as a product or income, but if the child is sent to a crèche and this is paid for, this increases GDP. Arguably the child being cared for by the parent is better for society, but not on our most frequently used measure of a country's success. Even more bizarrely an environmental accident can increase the country's GDP because of the economic activity the clean-up operation entails. It may not, however, be a very good measure of the welfare of a country. For this reason the French government has started looking at establishing an improved method of measuring a country's welfare and happiness. It will consider the environment, social cohesion, health and education, as well as traditional economic indicators, to form a view of social progress.

---

The relatively small scale of corporation tax as a revenue belies its importance to the Irish economy. Much of Ireland's economic activity is carried out by foreign firms trading from Ireland. These firms were attracted by low corporation tax rates (now 12.5 per cent, down from 32 per cent for some businesses in the 1990s) for firms that trade internationally. Few of these firms are located there to engage in the

*Figure 6.1*  The National Budget, 2008

(a)  Revenue €42.6 billion

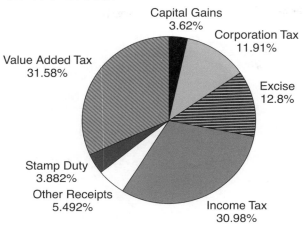

(b)  Expenditure €55.8 billion

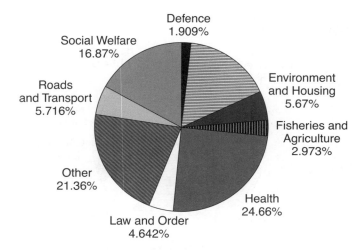

*Note*: Irish government income fell dramatically between 2007 and 2008 with Tax revenue falling by €6.5 billion. but Irish government spending rose by almost €5 billlion. This created a €12.7 billion government deficit in 2008, the first since a small deficit was recorded in 2003.

*Source*: Data from www.finance.gov.ie/documents/exchequerstatements/2010/ analysisenddecspend.pdf and www.finance.gov.ie/documents/exchequerstatements/ 2010/analysisenddectax.pdf, Department of Finance, 2009.

*Figure 6.2*  Ireland's economic trade in 'visible' goods, 2008

(a)  Total imports €67.6 billion

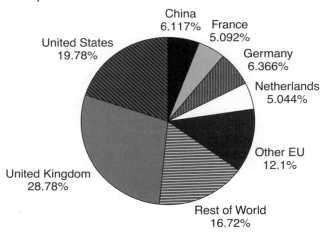

(b)  Total exports €86.4 billion

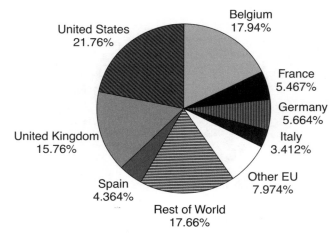

*Source*: Data from Central Statistics Office (www.cso.ie).

local market, but are primarily exporting goods and services manufactured or based in Ireland. As a result the Irish economy is highly globalized. Trade in 'visible' goods or physical merchandise is 75 per cent of Ireland's GDP compared to an OECD average of 40 per cent. Most exports are chemicals and pharmaceuticals, though animal products are also an important component. This export-led growth from US multinationals based in Ireland was to form the basis for the economic boom of the 1990s and early 2000s often styled as the Celtic Tiger.

An important indicator of the health of an economy is the balance of payments (BoP). This is the summary of the outflow of money from people buying goods and services from abroad and the inflow of money from selling good and services abroad. On one definition this will always be zero, because if the USA buys cars from Germany, the Germans buy US dollars in return. But it is more problematic when, as in Ireland's case, the currency is not 'owned' by Ireland. So if Ireland sells the German Euros in return for cars, the Euros are not a specifically Irish asset, so over time a trade deficit, as BoP is sometimes known, indicates that a country is buying consumer goods in return for debt, risking the country's bankruptcy and requiring intervention from external powers such as the International Monetary Fund (IMF). For 'visible' goods, those physical manufactured goods, Ireland has a strong trade surplus (almost €30 billion in 2008). However when we include invisible goods, including the repatriation of profits from Irish-based companies to their parent company outside Ireland, services such as tourism, financial services and others that one cannot 'see', then Ireland has shown deficits since 2004 (almost €10 billion in 2008). The economic crisis, however, has led to a sharp decline in the import of consumer goods, whereas exports remained buoyant, offering hope that Ireland could trade its way out of the crisis.

## The Euro

Ireland was among the first countries to adopt the Euro (€) as its currency when it was introduced for accounting purposes in 1999, and then when it went into circulation on 1 January 2002. Before that Ireland had the Irish pound or punt (IR£). It was pegged to sterling on a (one-for-one) parity basis, but when Ireland joined the European Exchange Rate Mechanism (ERM) in 1978 and the UK stayed out, the link was broken; in 1979 the parity was broken and an exchange rate was established. This also entailed Ireland printing its banknotes itself and minting its own coins, something the UK Royal Mint continued to do up to 1981. Irish coins were also the same size and shape as sterling coins up to 1986. The exchange rate fluctuated greatly (a punt was worth between 74p and £1.10 sterling), causing difficulties for traders with the UK, Ireland's major trading partner, but the punt was generally worth less than the pound.

Ireland's position in the ERM was fraught with difficulty and entailed frequent readjustments. Ireland's increasingly important role as a base for foreign companies based in Europe meant that Ireland had little choice but to join the Euro even though the UK was not doing so. Ireland entered at the rate €1 to 78p. There was none of the nationalistic attachment to the punt that can still be observed in the UK's attachment to sterling. When the Euro was introduced the Irish quickly adapted to the new currency. Within a couple of weeks most shops were just accepting Euros and the Irish pound ceased to be legal tender by 9 February 2002. Unlike in other countries, such as Spain, neither shops nor people continued to refer to prices in the old currency. The Euro has been regarded as a success, though it has been blamed for inflation, as traders may have used the exchange rate to increase prices. Most systematic evidence suggests that it did not increase inflation, but the exchange rate may have led to the perception of price increases because something that had cost IR£1 now cost €1.27.

There have been some problems for Ireland with its membership of the Euro. The Central Bank of Ireland no longer determines interest rate policy, which is now set by the European Central Bank (ECB). As Ireland was alone in the Eurozone (as the collection of countries to have adopted the Euro is called) in experiencing high levels of growth, the Irish government lost its established way of controlling bank lending through interest rate adjustments. Central banks set interest rates at which the banks borrow the currency from the government, and if the government increases them, it increases the costs of borrowing, effectively dampening the demand for money. As the major Eurozone countries, Germany and France, were experiencing low growth, low interest rates suited their economies as a means of stimulating growth. But it meant that the Irish economy was allowed to overheat with low-cost loans increasing Irish indebtedness and property prices.

Membership of the Euro also took away some of the policy options available to deal with the economic crisis that was evident to all by

**Box 6.2   Northern Ireland's economy**

Northern Ireland was once one of the wealthiest places in the world. It was home to the linen industry and later the shipbuilding industry – Belfast was where the Titanic was built. The violence associated with the Troubles meant that many people (particularly middle-class Protestants) left Northern Ireland, and few businesses set up there. But rule by a sectarian government probably did not help the economy and it certainly did little to prevent its slide into becoming one of the poorest parts of the UK. By the 1970s overseas competition led to a sharp contraction in shipbuilding and other heavy industrial activity in Northern Ireland.

Although there is still some shipbuilding and a small aircraft industry, today Northern Ireland is one of the poorer regions in the UK, though its unemployment rate (6.5 per cent in 2009) is lower than the UK average. This is in part due to Northern Ireland's dependence on public sector employment. Nearly a third of those working are employed directly by the state. A report on the Northern Ireland economy (Varney, 2007) found that the UK taxpayer subsidized the public sector in Northern Ireland by £7bn (€9bn) in that year. It was estimated that two-thirds of the economy is accounted for by public sector activity. Northern Ireland's political leaders negotiated additional investment from the British government in return for agreeing to re-enter power-sharing in 2006.

It achieved a mini-boom in part piggybacking on the increased wealth in the South. But the collapse of the Republic's economy led to a major fall in economic activity in Northern Ireland. The cutbacks proposed by the new government in the UK in 2010 may have a severe impact on Northern Ireland's economy.

2008. Ireland had lost some of its competitiveness though high wage increases in the 2000s, but politically reducing wages is difficult. Devaluing the currency simultaneously reduces the purchasing power of that currency and the wages (increasing international competitiveness) and decreases the costs of exports. Instead the Euro steadily gained in value to the US dollar, Japanese yen and sterling, making Irish exports to these important markets more expensive. In 2010 a Euro was worth $1.30, ¥110 and 85 pence sterling. That said, membership of the Euro probably means the ECB and the EU are forced to assist Ireland's recovery. And without membership there may have been a serious run on the currency that could have led Ireland to default on its debt.

## The Celtic Tiger and its causes

While much has been written about the Celtic Tiger, very often this merely charts the phenomenon by providing statistics on growth, employment or trade balances. When economists talk about explanations there is a discussion about whether Ireland was an example of convergence to the European norm. In other words, did Ireland's extraordinary growth occur just because Ireland was catching up, or is Ireland an example of a 'regional' rather than a more stable 'national' economy, which when it started to grow could grow very quickly because it could draw on inward migration to stimulate further growth? If Ireland was just catching up, it still begs the question: why did it catch up in the 1990s and not thirty years earlier or thirty years later? And if Ireland is a regional economy, this explains the rate of growth but not its timing.

When we try to answer the question of why Ireland boomed when it did, we can look for the proximate cause and any underlying or prior causes. It seems obvious that the proximate cause of much of Ireland's growth was the high level of foreign direct investment (FDI) that came into the country from the late 1980s. These were primarily, but not exclusively, US companies and most were in either the pharmaceutical or IT sectors. One estimate has it that 40 per cent of all FDI from the USA in the electronics sector between 1988 and 1995 came to Ireland. So what attracted them to Ireland? Finding the reason these businesses located in Ireland is not the only question. International companies had been attracted to locate in Ireland from the 1960s – Digital had manufactured microcomputers in Ireland from 1971 – in a policy characterized as 'industrialisation by invitation'. We also need to ask why their presence from the early 1990s was associated with growth in the general economy.

The conception if not birth of the economic boom which did much to lift the living standards of the Irish from below average European levels to above average levels can probably be dated to 1987. In this year fiscal policy – how the government spends its money and to what extent – changed radically as a new government cut back government spending (contrary to its election promises). This led to an increased confidence in the credibility of government policy. When there is little trust that a government might not raise taxes in the future this uncertainty deters investment. At the same time the government successfully managed the wage demands of workers, limiting them on the condition that personal taxes would be reduced.

This meant that the actual money in a worker's pocket would rise without the employer having to pay more. The inclusion of employers and trade unions in the policy-making process seemed to reduce tensions, and industrial disputes became much rarer.

If this industrial situation was welcome to potential investors, the Irish government changed its industrial policy to try to attract less and less labour-intensive 'screwdriver' industries and shift to high technology sectors such as pharmaceuticals, software development, computers and processors. That these industries formed the basis for a long US economic upturn also helped. The arrival of these industries and reduced tax rates generated sufficient economic activity that the government finances were in a much healthier state, and with the aid of European Structural Funds, the government started to invest money in Ireland's poor infrastructure. This investment also trickled down into the economy. EU membership became more important from the late 1980s with the creation in Europe of a single market, making Ireland a part of the largest, wealthiest market in the world. This, and Ireland's membership of the European Monetary System (EMS) and later the single currency – which removed the risks of currency fluctuations – reduced the disadvantages of locating in Ireland.

Ireland's location, physically and culturally far from the heart of Europe, had traditionally been a disadvantage. Cheaper air travel, in part due to the deregulation of the airline industry, and the lightness of the high-value goods that Ireland was producing, meant that Ireland was no longer geographically as isolated. The demographics also helped. Ireland had a young population that was relatively well educated and, importantly, could speak English. That it was culturally closer to the USA than Europe (see Box 8.2, p. 194), and the social and cultural links that Ireland had to the USA may have made it attractive for some Irish Americans to locate their businesses in Ireland. The emerging peace in Northern Ireland added to the feel-good factor surrounding the country. Ireland's brand was a powerful signal of vitality.

However if FDI helped kickstart the economic boom, it was not its main engine. The multinationals did not boost employment greatly. Unemployment remained high until the late 1990s and FDI could only explain a small proportion of the new jobs created. One difference in this wave of foreign investment was that the businesses had more links to the broader Irish economy. The cohort that had benefited from the expansion in the education system was in place. Irish people had been employed at higher levels of management and in research and development (R&D). Some left jobs in multinationals to set up companies supplying the multinational, while others saw the opportunity to start up companies developing ideas they had while employed there. The optimism in the economy sustained more growth associated with immigration and the expansion of the banking, financial and construction sectors. Ireland also benefited

**Illustration 6.1   Sunset on the Celtic Tiger? The Anglo Building at Irish Financial Services Centre, Dublin**

The IFSC was started in the late 1980s as a tax haven to attract banking, insurance, wealth management and trading firms to set up in Ireland. These were offered a corporation tax rate of 10 per cent and a lax regulatory regime. The Centre comprises 15 hectares of land in the north inner city, and now houses over 400 companies including half the world's top 50 banks, some of which have their formal European headquarters there. Often this merely means a small office located there for legal purposes. As well as being a business centre, it has become a fashionable residential and retail district. The photo shows the planned headquarters of Anglo-Irish Bank. It was abandoned following the nationalization of the bank. This bank's reckless lending led directly to the IMF/ EU intervention in late 2010.

from agglomeration, where a significant number of companies in similar areas are clustered together they can feed off each other to stimulate further growth. Though FDI was a driver of the growth, it was the confluence of all these factors (EU membership, education, social partnership and so on) that helped start and sustain the economic boom. But we should not discount the fact that Ireland was also lucky that these happened to come together at the same time as a sustained international boom. Ireland may not be as lucky again.

An often overlooked observation of the Celtic Tiger is that it is not really Celtic or Irish at all. Much of the innovation comes from US companies basing themselves in Ireland, with Ireland almost becoming a trading outpost for the USA in Europe. If we look at the biggest companies trading in Ireland in recent years, names like Microsoft, Dell, Google, Intel and Pfizer appear. It was estimated that Dell contributed four per cent of Irish GDP in 2005. The profits these companies make, though taxed at Ireland's low corporation tax rate on trading profits, are then sent back to the USA. This is why GNP or GNI are better measures of Irish performance than GDP (see Box 6.1). Potentially more damning is the idea that the Tiger is not only not Irish but is not real, that it was in fact a Paper Tiger. O'Hearn (1998) argued that not only is much of the economy based on foreign companies basing themselves here, but that those companies actually use accounting practices to maximize the amount that is 'produced' in Ireland to minimize the tax liability in other countries with higher corporation tax. So, for example, a computer firm with operations throughout the globe might produce a PC in Ireland that ultimately trades at €100. If the components are made in China, costing €40, and the research costs from the USA are €50, then the Irish operation produces €10. But if the company says that the research costs were just €20 and the cost of parts was just €20, then Irish productivity is €60 – and then 60 per cent of profits are to be paid in the low-tax Irish regime. If transfer pricing, as this practice is called, is common, then it is possible that some of the growth was purely illusory. So when Ireland could claim that it was the largest exporter of software in the world, the claim may not have been true. The problem was that Irish policy makers came to believe all their own propaganda. However the argument that the Celtic Tiger was illusory cannot be squared with the obvious growth in employment and standards of living. If it was mere accounting sleight of hand, jobs would not have been a spin-off. As it happened, the numbers employed in Ireland doubled from about one million to about two million between 1995 and 2005.

**Why did the Tiger fail? Can it be revived?**

Another more significant problem for the Irish economy was its obsession with property. On some measures construction and property accounted for a quarter of Irish economic activity in 2006 – the peak of the housing bubble. House prices rose dramatically from the early 1990s, doubling between 1995 and 2000 and doubling again between 2000 and 2006, a fact that policy makers, curiously, thought was a good development. Some of the above-inflation house price growth could be explained by the larger numbers of people living in Ireland, the smaller sizes of households, and the improved economy (see Figure 6.3). More of the growth is down to what economists call 'animal instincts', irrational behaviour arising from people copying other people's strategies (Akerlof and Shiller, 2009). Some people had made a great deal of money buying houses, and this drove up demand among people speculating that the price rises would continue. Even though Ireland was building more houses than at any time in its history, which according to classical economic theory should have reduced prices by fulfilling demand, the insatiable demand for property continued unabated. Rather than signal that the market had almost reached saturation point, the booming construction industry only seemed to excite further interest.

Associated with the increased house prices was that ordinary people, especially the young, were spending more and more of their incomes on their home. This led to demands for salary increases to enable their standard of living to be maintained or improved. The increases in wages reduced Ireland's competiveness. At the same time existing home owners, heartened by the increase in the paper value of their houses, borrowed heavily and Irish spending on consumer goods jumped. The government, though claiming to be concerned about uncontrolled house prices, did nothing to dampen expectations that the rises would continue indefinitely. It put no restrictions on banks, all of which seemed to ignore their own research and lent more and more to home buyers, speculators and developers. The government had an interest in maintaining the strong growth because it had become dependent on the stamp duty on house transactions. The economy was becoming dominated by property, but an economy is based on people selling houses to each other with money borrowed from the world's money markets is not sustainable.

The strategy of attracting foreign investment was not augmented by any other strategies to maintain the economy and stimulate Irish

153

*Figure 6.3*  House prices and property investment as a percentage of GDP

(a)  House prices

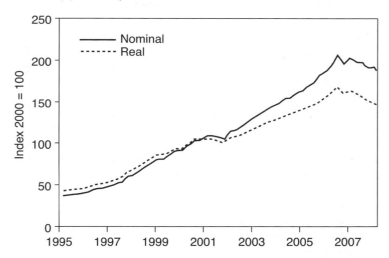

(b)  Housing investment

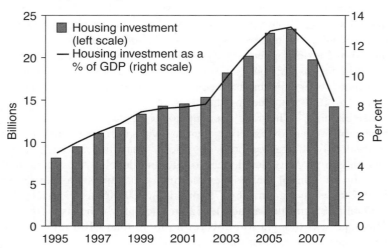

*Source*: Data from *OECD Economic Survey*, no. 17, *Ireland, 2009*.

entrepreneurship. Though there were agencies set up to do these, and there are some successful Irish companies, such as Ryanair, Élan and SmurfitKappa, much of the recent spectacular growth in Irish indigenous business was in construction and property, or banks whose paper growth was spurred by property loans. These in turn became some of the more spectacular business failures by 2009. In fact, of the top 500 companies in Europe, measured by market capitalization in 2009, only four were Irish-based. An illustration of the absence of entrepreneurs is the choice of entrepreneur to front the TV show *The Apprentice,* where would-be business people compete for the right to work as an assistant to a well-known entrepreneur. In the UK it is Sir Alan Sugar who became famous manufacturing personal computers. In Ireland the front man is Bill Cullen, who made most of his money because he had the sole right to import and sell Renault cars in Ireland. Even when Ireland produces indigenous business successes, there seems to be a reluctance to grow the business, with owners often happier to cash in by selling their business to larger international companies, often with few linkages to Ireland.

The proximate cause of the crash in the Irish economy was the international credit crunch from 2007 which forced banks to stop lending and seek repayments of their loans. This was caused by the bursting of the US housing bubble which in turn was caused in large part by lax lending to people without the resources to pay back their loans (the so-called 'sub-primes'). These loans, often 100 per cent of the value of the house, were given on the assumption that property prices would continue to rise indefinitely, something that historical data show never happens. When many borrowers defaulted on their sub-prime loans, this put banks under pressure and led to the realization that property prices had been over-valued; then property prices collapsed, further increasing the pressure on banks to reduce the so-called bad loans. The same phenomenon took place in Ireland, where banks had been extremely generous with mortgage lending for continuously increasing property prices. They had also lent huge amounts to property developers to buy and develop sites in Ireland and abroad. One of the most extraordinary examples was developer Seán Dunne paying almost €379 million in 2005 for a seven-acre site in Dublin (€54 million an acre), €326 million of which was borrowed. This land was thought to be worth no more than €100 million five years later, and even that may overvalue it.

These sub-prime loans put Irish banks under huge financial pressures, and in late 2008 the fears of their imminent collapse caused the

Irish government to offer them a facility to guarantee their debts to investors. While this stopped the immediate threat to the banks, one of the biggest, Anglo-Irish Bank, failed and had to be nationalized in 2009. This added to the problems the Irish economy faced. There was the banking crisis, a subsequent crisis in the government finances, and a recession in the real economy. The crisis also had an impact on Ireland's national reputation, and perhaps most importantly, on the social fabric as unemployment and emigration rose. The crisis in government finances caused fears that Ireland might default on its rapidly rising debt. From the early 2000s Irish governments had made large spending commitments with increased welfare payments, free medical treatment for the elderly and increased pay for public sector workers, but much of the revenue on which these commitments depended was from one-off taxes on house sales. When the property market collapsed, this revenue stream dried up, leaving the government with a current budget deficit for the first time in 16 years. It cut public sector pay and increased taxes in an attempt to shore up the deficit, but this put further pressure on the real economy as it took money out of people's pockets. Figure 6.4 shows that household debt excluding mortgages more than doubled between 2001 and 2007. If one is meant to 'save for a rainy day', the Irish were borrowing heavily when it was sunny. Meanwhile Irish wages were high compared to the productivity of the labour force when we use the more accurate GNP measure.

Throughout the world governments sought strategies to kick-start their economies. Many started to pump money into the economy with infrastructural investment. Ireland's large debt meant that it could not do this, and if anything it was forced to take money out of the economy by raising taxes in a series of 'hair-shirt' budgets. The instability in the banking sector meant that governments in Europe found themselves investing money in the unstable but systemically important banks. Other banks were allowed to go bust. Because Ireland had already given the Irish banks' bondholders – those who lent the banks money – and depositors a guarantee of their investments, Ireland was left with no choice but to protect the banks. The Fianna Fáil-led government set up an agency called Nama, which bought from the banks the property development loans they had made. The government argued it was essential to give the banks enough money to lend to businesses and kick-start the economy. Critics of the scheme argue that it is an expensive and roundabout way of putting money into the economy that could double the national debt without punishing the banks for their mistakes.

*Figure 6.4*  Indicators of decline

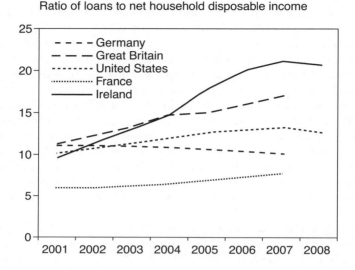

Ratio of loans to net household disposable income

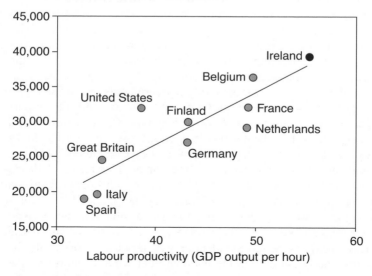

Wage rate of the private sector

*Source*: Data from *OECD Economic Outlook*, no. 85, June 2009.

In fact it is not clear that either the Bank Guarantee Scheme or the Nama legislation did anything to put money into the economy. While they may have protected the banks from collapse, it was at great expense to the taxpayer. One problem with the policies that many economists seemed to agree on was that agreeing to pay back bondholders (those on international money markets that had lent large amounts to banks), effectively forced the full or part nationalization of the most highly indebted banks. It also took huge amounts of money out of the economy at a time when it might have been useful to pump money into it. The money spent on saving Anglo-Irish Bank was already €26 billion by 2010, which dwarfed the money that the government saved in controversial expenditure cuts. This was despite very high unemployment rates, especially among young men in rural areas. Unlike in Greece, however, there were few public demonstrations or strikes. Some complained that the Irish were too passive in the face of policies they felt were designed to bail out bankers and property developers. Other felt the Irish reacted rationally to the realization that its economy and public sector needed to be restructured. Because of these decisions the Irish budget deficit (the difference between how much we spend and how much we earn) is the largest in the Eurozone. However it is also perceived that the Irish government's action to reduce government expenditure was timely and decisive. This has probably meant that Ireland's reputation in money markets was higher than the other so-called PIGS (Portugal, Italy, Greece and Spain) for a time. But there are fears that the uncertainty of the final cost of the bank bailouts has reduced confidence in the Irish economy, and the cost to Ireland of borrowing to fill its large budget deficit continued rising through 2010. Despite the ideas of Keynesians – those who believe that governments can and should regulate the economy by withdrawing and injecting money in good times and bad respectively – confidence is often as important a factor as anything else in driving the economy (see Farmer, 2010). In 1987 the Irish government took a great deal of money out of circulation in an economy that was in recession. It did, however, give people the confidence that someone was dealing with the economy's problems and led to economic growth.

In 2009 the OECD predicted that Ireland would suffer a long-term reduction in standard of living, and in late 2010 the IMF and EU intervened to support Ireland when the markets refused to lend the country or its banks any money. Is it likely that Ireland could revert to being one of the poorer countries in Europe again? It is usual that a country, once wealthy, stays wealthy – but there are exceptions, such as Argentina. To avoid emulating Argentina, Ireland probably needs to adapt to a new economic strategy. It also needs to address some underlying problems: high inflation during the boom means Ireland is one of the most expensive places in the world to live and do business. The cost of living is among the highest in the Eurozone and as a result wages expectations are high. But rents are also high, as are transport and energy costs. The Irish, who now expect to work in high quality jobs and expect a high standard of living, may see and act on opportunities in Ireland. When the Digital computer plant closed in Galway in 1990, many of its employees stayed in Ireland setting up their own businesses, and its closure was not the catastrophe that had been predicted. The danger is that people might leave Ireland if there is a lack of confidence in the political response to the crisis, and the resumption high levels of emigration is of concern to Ireland's ability to recover.

There is also the danger that what was characterized as a 'bail out' for Ireland might sink the economy. In fact it is a loan that enables Ireland to repay maturing high-risk and high-yield bonds in Irish banks, bought when those banks were engaged in idiotic lending. These were purchased by many careless European pension funds and banks. Those debts were then assumed by the Irish taxpayer as a result of a monumentally crass bank-guarantee scheme introduced by the Irish government in late 2008. Many felt that the punitive terms of the loan were designed to dissuade the Spanish from seeking aid. However, it also seemed to make an Irish recovery less likely.

Despite the recent fall in Ireland's reputation and living standards, there is little doubt that the Irish are better off now than twenty years ago and that much of the early boom was real if overblown. Ireland is in danger of deciding that it was *all* an illusion and assuming that all the policies that helped it achieve growth were flawed. What we saw in Ireland is a blueprint for how to achieve growth and how not to manage that growth. Ireland adopted a successful strategy of attracting foreign investment to grow the economy and bring in jobs. The problem was that it assumed that this strategy would continue to work indefinitely. It also failed to see that much of the subsequent growth was related to a property bubble which was to burst with horrendous consequences for Ireland. Ireland needs to adopt a new strategy for growth that is suitable for an already wealthy country.

# 7

# Culture and Lifestyle

One of the key aspects that distinguishes Ireland from the rest of Europe is its culture. It maintained a traditional or folk culture long after many others had lost theirs through modernization. Irish culture is also increasingly popular outside Ireland, probably at the same time as it is undergoing the same forces of change within Ireland that other countries saw much earlier. For many, culture means the arts. But culture can also be thought of as the behavioural norms of a people – it is what people do, how they act and what they expect of others. The popular arts make up a good deal of what people do and how they act – people sing, dance and tell stories, and they consume culture by reading literature, listening to music and watching drama on TV, in cinema or the theatre. But people do more than just what we might mean by the arts. It includes the sports people play, the food they eat, who, where and how they meet and socialize – their lifestyle.

One aspect of Irish culture is the desire by some to emphasize what they are not. The Irish like to think of themselves as distinct from the British (or more specifically the English) in all ways. Certain phrases common in English are not used in Ireland partly because of the association with England – so, for example, few people say 'mate' for friend. Irish nationalist politicians have tried to distinguish between a Gaelic or Celtic culture and modern English culture. Celtic or Gaelic culture according to their accounts, is pre-modern, that is, non-rational, spiritual and, uninterested in 'unchristian materialism'. Irish nationalists romanticized the Irish peasant and then developed folk traditions in the form of a high art for the new state. In fact there has been no popular resistance to modernization, and despite the rhetoric, Irish culture is deeply entwined with that of Britain. This chapter will identify some features of what might be described as an Irish culture.

These range from the arts (music, cinema and literature) to what the Irish spend their leisure time doing (talking, drinking, playing and watching sports). The chapter also looks at symbols of 'Irishness', such as the Irish language and the Catholic religion, and concludes by asking what the Irish culture might be now and if it is distinguishable from any other western culture.

## The arts

During the Protestant Ascendancy in the eighteenth century, while Dublin could not quite rank with Vienna, Paris or London as a cultural centre, it was an important regional city that could expect to experience among the best that European culture could offer. It was here that the first performance of Handel's *Messiah* was given. But the high arts are expensive and so there is no opera house in Dublin and only a small number of theatres. The arts are often a window through which we view a society, and the mirror which allows a country to reflect on itself. Political and social debates take place through the artistic medium as well as in overt ways. Works of art tend to portray a society in a way that the artists wish to express. Sometimes this is tendentious, an attempt to create an idealized or stereotypical version of the country and its people. Art in Ireland is frequently political in its aims or themes. Nationalist writers in the late nineteenth and early twentieth centuries commonly idealized the poor Gaelic peasant as thoughtful and spiritual in an attempt to motivate the general population, comfortable in its Britishness, to recover aspects of the Gaelic culture. Musicians, poets, playwrights and painters were also important in attempts to develop an identity and raise consciousness. Popular arts, such as the theatre and later television and cinema, are of political importance because they can reach people in subtle ways that formal political debate cannot; artists and the new state attempted to control and foster certain images of the country or groups within the country and censor those that were not helpful. Thus one of the first acts of the new state was to set up a censorship board, which in time would ban many of the finest novels in modern literature and films in modern cinema.

It is equally clear that the British in Ireland used art to make political statements. Many of the successful Irish painters usually travelled to London to find commissions and many of these had an imperial quality that celebrated British influence in Ireland. A cultural revival in the late nineteenth century attempted to provoke political nationalism in the population. Artists presented the heroic Gaelic peasant or the beautiful girl as the representation of Ireland. Sir John Lavery, a famous portrait painter in London society, gave Ireland an iconic image in his portrait of his American-born wife, which went on to adorn Irish bank notes for most of the twentieth century (see Illustration 7.1). Francis Bacon, one of the more important modernist painters in the twentieth century, was also Irish-born, but rejected by London society. Whether one regards him as Irish, British, or British-Irish raises questions about what it means to be Irish. More recently, Louis le Brocquy's work has been used by the Irish Industrial Development Authority (IDA) as part of its attempts to market Ireland as a destination for foreign capital. Another prominent Irish artist, Robert Ballagh, often uses his visual art as a means to communicate his political views.

**Illustration 7.1   An old Irish £10 note depicting Lady Lavery**

The portrait of Hazel Lavery was on every Irish banknote in some form from 1928 until the introduction of the Euro. She is shown with the harp, a symbol of Ireland, and herself is presented as Kathleen ní Houlihan, a mythical melancholy Irish figure who is dispossessed from her land. Kathleen ní Houlihan is frequently used by writers and artists as an image of Ireland, or the nation's personification – the Irish equivalent of the UK's John Bull or USA's Uncle Sam.

## Literature

It is in literature that Ireland can claim to have made the most important contribution to world culture. The Irish literary tradition is an oral one where story-telling took place in people's homes. Probably for this reason the short story was a common form for the literate Irish, which continues to this day. Seán Ó Faoláin and Frank O'Connor are, with William Trevor, who is still writing, among the best in the Irish short story tradition. Ó Faoláin was one of the more erudite critics of Irish society and his stories chart the emergence of modern Ireland. Trevor's *Ballroom of Romance* (1972) examined the limiting world of Irish rural life. The Irish have also made significant contributions to literature in the form of the novel. Jonathan Swift's *Gulliver's Travels* (1726), a political satire on human nature and parody of the travelogues popular at the time, is an important book in the history of literature and one of the first novels to be written, a form that only became dominant from the nineteenth century. Many of Ireland's first novelists and novels came from the Ascendancy; for instance, Maria Edgeworth's *Castle Rackrent* (1801) is written from the perspective of or at least about the Big House – the landlord's house. *Castle Rackrent* is often thought to be the first regional novel written in English – though of course nearly all novels are set somewhere and might be considered regional. But at times we might differentiate between Irish writers and writers from Ireland, where Irish writers are thought to cover subjects specific to Ireland. But of course any of these subjects is generally a route to deal with themes that are universal. One of those subjects, Irish nationalism, though present, plays a smaller role in Irish prose fiction. It is unclear, for instance, what some of the modernist works of James Joyce are about, except perhaps an experiment with language and a parody on earlier Irish writers such as Yeats. Although his later work is not very readable, his early autobiographical novel *A Portrait of the Artist as a Young Man* (1916) recounts the troubled youth of Joyce's alter ego Stephen Dædalus as he struggled with the oppressive nature of his family, the church and the state. With *Ulysses* (1922) Joyce confirmed his place as one of the most important writers in modern literature. In it Joyce attempts to write as people actually think, not in clear prose, but in snippets, short phrases and single words. Another avant-garde writer from Ireland who also rejected the country was Samuel Beckett, a middle-class Protestant who rejected the potentially comfortable life of a Trinity academic to live in Paris, a city which accepted his genius. Flann O'Brien's *At Swim-Two-Birds* (1939) seems more obviously Irish but is also experimental in form and, like Joyce and Beckett, full of parody and wit. That wit can also be seen in the very different prose of Brendan Behan, especially in his autobiographical novel *Borstal Boy* (1958) and in J. P. Dunleavy's semi-autobiographical *The Ginger Man* (1955), also set in Dublin.

A very different type of literature emerged from Irish-speaking parts of Ireland. Thanks in part to an English scholar, Robin Flower, a number of books written in Irish about life on the western seaboard at the start of the twentieth century were translated into English. These books, by Muiris Ó Súilleabháin, Peig Sayers and Tomás Ó Criomhthain among others, portray a very different world to those written about Dublin at the time. In fact it is reasonable to suggest that the two literatures represent different countries.

In the 1960s new writers emerged who tended to write about an Ireland that was different from the one most commonly seen. The rural Ireland of the realist novels *The Country Girls* (1960) by Edna O'Brien and *The Dark* (1965) by John McGahern reflected at the time a shocking new, modernizing Ireland, one more concerned with physical pain and elusive pleasures of rural Ireland than with Irish nationalism. The last 40 years have seen a flowering of Irish literature, with Irish novelists appearing regularly on major international prize shortlists and in literary magazines. Another difference is that most of these writers remain based in Ireland, and their influence on each other perhaps goes some way to explaining why more writers have emerged. Contemporary writers such as John Banvillle, Roddy Doyle, Anne Enright, Colum McCann, Joseph O'Neill and Colm Tóibín explore universal themes in their fiction, sometimes but not always set in Ireland. For instance O'Neill's *Netherland* (2008) and McCann's *Let the Great World Spin* (2009) are both set in New York and are generally described as post-9/11 novels, while Tóibín's *Brooklyn* (2009) follows the journey to America of a young Irish emigrant and the forces that pull her home. Here it is harder to talk of an Irish tradition because the writers do not always deal with Ireland or Irish subjects, but one can see that Irish writers are among the most important working in the English language today. Frank McCourt, whose *Angela's Ashes* (1996) is a horrific yet humorous account of childhood poverty in Limerick, popularized the childhood memoir. Some complain that Irish writers set their novels in the 1950s and 1960s with 'grittily realistic, slightly depressing descriptions of events that aren't very interesting' (Julian Gough in *The Guardian*, 11 February, 2010).

That complaint cannot be made of Irish writers also prominent in the genre of popular fiction known as 'chick lit' such as Celia Ahern and Marian Keyes. These tend to be romantic books in which women are 'empowered' through their work and avid consumerism, but a man usually emerges to show the women that they weren't really that 'empowered' after all.

However, other literary forms, such as poetry and plays, were often more important than prose in Ireland. Poetry was once hugely influential in Ireland and poets were of high standing in Gaelic society. They were retained by chieftains to write poems in their praise to influence public opinion, making them akin to an early public relations consultant. Poetry and poets remained important figures in Ireland; W. B. Yeats was both a major figure in world literature and an important commentator on Irish independence. Seamus Heaney, who won a Nobel Prize for literature, is probably the best-known Irish writer alive today. Heaney's poetry is not the Gaelic mysticism of Yeats, but reflects the realities of the rural north of Ireland in the tradition of Patrick Kavanagh.

*Theatre and Film*

In other areas, particularly the theatre, which was more freely available to a mass public than literature because it did not demand wealth or education in the audience, there is a political impact and often purpose in much of the work. The Irish had long been portrayed in English theatre as stupid. The 'stage Irishman' was the village idiot, who could barely speak English and frequently committed malapropisms. It was a mechanism used to introduce comedy, but it had a highly political impact on the English audience. If the Irish were this stupid, how could they be expected to run their own country? Many Irish plays in the nineteenth and early twentieth centuries were overtly political, dealing with subjects such as the 1798 United Irishmen rising but intended for global audiences. Oscar Wilde and George Bernard Shaw wrote some of the most popular and important plays of their time, such as *The Importance of Being Earnest* (1895) and *Pygmalion* (1912), but they travelled to England and only Shaw wrote about subjects that might be considered Irish, for instance in *John Bull's Other Island* (1905). W. B. Yeats and Lady Gregory were keen to create a genuinely Irish theatre for Irish audiences and set up the Abbey Theatre for this purpose. It invented a supposedly ancient Irish theatre by dramatizing Gaelic myth and legend. But it also premiered J. M. Synge's *Playboy of the Western World* (1907), which caused riotous protests by nationalists for its portrayal of the rural west as venal and credulous. Equally Seán O'Casey's *The Plough and the Stars* (1926) treated the 1916 rising in less than heroic terms. An exile in Europe, Samuel Beckett, challenged audiences with his modernist *Waiting for Godot* (1953), which was more influenced by and influential in continental European culture. Rural theatre flourished from this time, depending largely on amateur productions, but it gave opportunities to John B. Keane and Brian Friel whose plays *Sive* (1959) and *Philadelphia, Here I Come* (1964) were important expressions of the realities of rural life. While the Abbey is Ireland's national theatre, it has depended on reproductions of its early plays. The Gate Theatre in Dublin, The Druid in Galway and Field Day in Derry are more likely to produce performances of modern Irish playwrights such as Tom Murphy, Frank McGuinness, Martin McDonagh, Enda Walsh and Conor McPherson. Many of these writers have seen their plays turned into successful films, such as John B. Keane's *The Field* (1965, 1990), while others have started to make films, for instance Martin McDonagh's *In Bruges* (2007) .

The wide access to audiences that film has makes it a more potent medium of communication. Though some films were made in Ireland at the birth of the industry, such as *The Lad from Old Ireland* (1910) and *Irish Destiny* (1926), no indigenous film industry developed in Ireland. The small size and relative poverty of the country and the fact that English was the vernacular meant that the Irish tended to view cinema from the USA and the UK – when the censor allowed it. Also because Ireland did not have a domestic television station until the 1960s there were few means for people to get the technical expertise to make a film. Most films with an Irish theme were made by Irish-American directors for a US audience. *The Quiet Man* (1952), *Darby O'Gill and the Little People* (1959) and later *Far and Away* (1992) presented an image of Ireland unlike anything the Irish might have recognized – in some cases deliberately so. These tended to romanticize Ireland as a place stuck in time. Even the more serious documentaries such as *Man of Aran* (1934) and *Mise Éire* (1959) were nationalist and romantic in tone. From the 1970s an indigenous Irish film industry emerged, with the aid of tax breaks and a publicly funded film board. The new Irish cinema, rather than romanticizing Ireland, tends to deal with problems within society in a way that Hollywood rejects and for that reason Irish cinema is not particularly commercially successful outside Ireland, though the films *My Left*

*Foot* (1989) and *The Crying Game* (1992) enjoyed international critical and commercial success. But many other Irish films dealt with themes that, if not exclusively Irish, benefited from an understanding of Ireland. Themes such as the pressures of conformity and rigid structures in Irish society are common in Irish films such as *Lamb* (1985), *The Field* (1990), *Breakfast on Pluto* (2005) and *Garage* (2007). Others, such as *Michael Collins* (1996) and *The Wind That Shakes the Barley* (2007) are nationalist films set around the Irish civil war. The conflict in Northern Ireland has also inspired many films: *In the Name of the Father* (1994), *Resurrection Man* (1997) and *Hunger* (2008) are among the better ones. Dealing with subjects such as the hunger strikes in the early 1980s (when a number of IRA prisoners starved themselves to death in a dispute about their status as political prisoners), Bloody Sunday (when British paratroopers shot dead 13 people peaceably protesting in Derry), loyalist murder squads, and the miscarriages of justice suffered by some Irish people in Britain at the height of the Troubles, there were naturally accusations that some of these films were biased against Britain and romanticized terrorism.

The Irish economy is also dealt with on film. *Eat the Peach* (1986), *The Commitments* (1991) and *Intermission* (2003) are black comedies that deal with, among other issues, poverty in Ireland. Dublin's criminal gangs are featured in films such as *The General* (1998), *Ordinary Decent Criminal* (1999), *Veronica Guerin* (2002) and the black comedy *In Bruges* (2007). Irish films have also provided opportunities for Irish actors who have become internationally famous, such as Liam Neeson, Daniel Day-Lewis, Gabriel Byrne, Colin Farrell and Saoirse Ronan. The tax breaks that have helped the developing Irish film industry have also led to Ireland being used as a location for many films set elsewhere. The epic *Braveheart* (1995) about the Scottish nationalist leader William Wallace was filmed in Ireland using the Irish army as extras.

Ireland also makes a large number of television programmes, again mainly directed at a domestic audience. Soap operas such as *The Riordans*, *Glenroe* (both set in rural Ireland), *Fair City* (set in Dublin) and *Ros na Rún*, an Irish language soap set in the west of Ireland, are or were popular. The first Irish television station (Telefís Éireann) was set up in 1963, partly in reaction to fears of the exposure of Irish people to non-Irish programmes. But the new television station became a driver of modernization; *The Late Late Show* (which is over by 11 p.m.), hosted by Gay Byrne for over thirty years, dealt with

**Box 7.1   Is there an Irish national character?**

For some culture is 'the collective programming of the mind that distinguishes one group or category from another' (Geert Hofstede, www.geert-hofstede.com). This implies that different nationalities have different characteristics. If Germans are well-organized and cold, the English polite to the point of paralysis, the Scots mean and dour, and Texans brash and vulgar, what are the traits or national characteristics of the Irish? Indeed can we use such cultural stereotypes? And how can they come about?

Psychologists measure personality on an OCEAN scale: Openness (as opposed to closed-mindedness or lack of curiosity), Conscientiousness (versus laziness and unreliability), Extraversion (versus inhibition), Agreeableness (versus aggression and rudeness) and Neuroticism (versus emotional stability). Personality is transmitted both culturally, through socialisztion, and genetically in our mental make-up. Whichever is stronger, one might expect that different countries have their own national characteristics. Some argue that national characteristics have a 'kernel of truth', and our own experiences tend to bear these out. But if we examine how the Irish are portrayed in the arts, media or in political discussions, they are at the same time introverted and extroverted (the shy and retiring pure Irish girl versus the gregarious and sociable rogue with the gift of the gab). We see the closed-minded, dark and brooding character, the honest and conscientious helpful stranger and the lazy drunk. The Irish can be shown as both generous and mean-spirited (begrudgers); both clever ('cute hoor') and backward (stage Irishman). How can the typical Irish person be all of these? In fact research has shown that there is little or no basis for national stereotypes. Given that national characteristics are often contradictory, we might instead look to the motives of those proposing them.

issues of sexuality and morality that had rarely if ever been discussed in public, leading one politician to comment, without irony, that 'there was no sex in Ireland before television'. The small size of the Irish market also meant that the Irish station had little money to make its own programmes and so bought many of its programmes from the UK and USA. There are now four terrestrial channels (RTÉ 1 and RTÉ 2), all but one of which (TV3) are state-run, including an Irish language station, TG4. The state-run channels are funded by payment of a licence fee for owning a television, although they also rely on advertising revenue. All tend to depend heavily on imported US and British programmes and even those that are domestically produced are copies of successful programmes shown elsewhere.

Ireland's small size and proximity to Britain mean that many successful TV personalities tend to leave for the UK if opportunities arise there. Éamon Andrews started a long line of broadcasters who have gone to Britain becoming household names, including Terry Wogan, Graham Norton and Dara Ó Briain. Ireland has some of the world's most successful comedians from Dave Allen in the 1970s to Seán Hughes, Dylan Moran, Tommy Tiernan and David O'Doherty more recently (all winners of the Edinburgh Fringe comedy award). Despite this, Ireland has never matched the quality of British TV sitcoms. Only *Father Ted*, a surreal comedy set around three dysfunctional Catholic priests on an island off the west of Ireland, has been successful and it was made by the British Channel 4 having been rejected as an idea by RTÉ, the state broadcaster.

The Irish watch on average three hours of television a day, which though quite high is less that the over three and a half hours watched by the British daily and almost five hours in the USA. Unlike virtually anywhere else in the world, factual TV including news, current affairs and documentaries is the most popular genre, though Ireland is not immune to soap operas, fatuous reality TV and celebrity-obsessed talk shows. The most popular programme is the British soap opera, *Coronation Street*. Other forms of entertainment and communication are increasingly important in people's lives. So more and more people, especially children, are using video games and the internet as a form of entertainment. Broadband penetration, at 60 per cent, is lower than in most European countries (close to 90 per cent in the Nordic states), but in 2007 the Irish still managed to spend over six hours a week on the web – it has almost certainly risen since then. Political parties have used the internet to circumvent the ban on political broadcast advertising. Irish people are voracious consumers of social networking internet sites such as Bebo and Facebook. The Irish, like most other Europeans, have complete mobile phone penetration – there are 117 phone subscriptions for every 100 people in the county. And the Irish talk more on their mobile phones than other Europeans except the French – about 230 minutes a month. Access to a wide variety of communications media including large numbers of TV channels via satellite, may have reduced what some call 'social capital', the social glue that binds us together. When just one or two channels were available, television programmes could be experiences shared by a large part of the community, and these types of experiences might bind the society together. With more access to suit everyone's individual tastes, people within a geographically defined community may have less in common, making society less cohesive.

## Music

Another area of the arts that has popular engagement is music. Unlike in most other European countries, folk music is still popular, though this popularity may be waning. Again the importance of politics can be seen, so where elites normally sponsor high art such as classical European music, the Irish state was keen to assert an Irish tradition and so promoted traditional forms. It chose the harp as a symbol of Irishness – this was how Irish melodies had been played in fashionable circles. But it is not easy to define Irish traditional music, nor does Irish music possess one feature common to all forms. Music served different purposes and so is different in nature. There are jigs and reels for dancing, folk songs (to tell stories), keens (for grieving), and *sean nós* (unaccompanied singing which sounds like flamenco). Instruments such as the *uilleann* pipes, fiddle and *bodhrán* (handheld drum) are associated with Irish music. Irish dancing is closely associated with the music and is still practised by many people. The nature of Irish dancing was strictly controlled by the increasingly powerful Church after the famine, which disallowed the use of the arms that had been common in some forms of Irish dance. Shows such as *Riverdance* have popularized it globally and reintroduced the free movement of the arms. This popularity and the fact that the music introduced influences from other musical cultures perhaps made it less acceptable among traditionalists in Ireland. But Irish music has been the subject of continuous change and experiment. The composer, Seán Ó Riada, while working in the classical European music form, was much more influenced by traditional Irish music, as is obvious from his music for the film *Mise Éire*. Ó Riada himself influenced and supported younger musicians such as Paddy Moloney who went on to form The Chieftains, one of the music groups that has pushed the boundaries of traditional Irish music by fusing it with other forms, in a way that many traditionalists find offensive. Other musicians such as The Dubliners and The Clancy Brothers became popular during the folk revival in the USA and the UK in the 1960s. Indeed it is argued that Irish folk music brought to the USA by Irish (and especially Scots Irish) immigrants became country music which in turn influenced the invention of rock music, when fused with blues. The country style is still remarkably popular in the northern

**Illustration 7.2    U2 playing Madison Square Gardens**

U2 has been at the forefront of rock music for over two decades, having been described as 'the biggest band in the world' consistently since their release of *The Joshua Tree* in 1987. As well as their music, Bono's forays into politics have been notable. He has been particularly active in anti-war campaigns and the campaign for the West to write off the debt third world countries owe. His high profile gives him access to world leaders, and U2 were the only non-US band to play for Barack Obama's inaugauration concert.

parts of Ireland. More modern exponents of traditional Irish music, Planxty, Clannad, Moving Hearts, Altan and Kíla have continued the tradition of developing new musical styles. The success of artists such as Enya who have traded on the 'spiritual and Celtic' quality of their music shows the global interest in this form.

Though the main popular music form in the 1960s was the 'show-band', which covered the popular songs emerging from the USA and the UK, apart from Van Morrison, whose extraordinary *Astral Weeks* (1968) is regarded as one of the greatest albums in modern popular music, it was in the 1970s with the emergence of punk-influenced bands like Thin Lizzy and the Boomtown Rats that Irish popular music became better known outside Ireland. Since then Irish music has been dominated by U2's presence (see Illustration 7.2). Other musicians such as Sineád O'Connor, The Pogues and The Cranberries have made a mark but none have the longevity or commercial success that U2 has had. It might be argued that apart from Van Morrison, no Irish popular musicians have been influential in music in the way that Bob Dylan, The Beatles, The Sex Pistols, Nirvana or Radiohead have been. Since the late 1980s U2 has adapted to new musical styles, but usually copying trends in modern music rather than setting them. The most popular Irish musicians, such as The Villagers, Damian Rice and Snow Patrol, tend to offer rock ballads that could have been released two decades earlier. Ireland has also produced boy bands that have been commercially successful if musically bland – of these Boyzone and Westlife are the most successful.

## The Irish language and Irish English

Irish or Gaelic is one of the Celtic languages associated with Wales, Scotland, Cornwall in south-west England, the Isle of Man and Brittany in north-west France. Irish and Scottish Gaelic are very similar. The origins of the languages are unclear. It is probable the Celtic language that was to become Gaelic arrived with Celtic trade and immigration over 5,000 years ago. Fourth century Ogham stones – an ancient writing system – show that it was the written language used in Ireland then. Scandinavian, Latin, French and English have influenced Irish, so for instance an Irish word for boy, *garsún*, derives from the French *garçon*, probably brought by the Anglo-Normans. The Anglo-Normans brought French and English, and it was English that started to be spoken in the cities by both the immigrants and native Gaels.

The defeat in 1601 of Irish and Spanish forces in the Battle of Kinsale and the Cromwellian Plantations of the 1640s and 1650s displaced large numbers of Irish speakers to the west of the country. The beginning of the nineteenth century brought a rapid decline in the language that was associated with poverty. The Great Famine from 1845 affected Gaelic speakers most, and as over a million people died and more emigrated, the use of the language was in serious decline. Despite the independent state's stated intention to effect a revival of the language, there are fewer than 50,000 native speakers left, mainly from the *Gaeltacht* areas on the west coast in Kerry, South

Connemara and Donegal. Census results show, however, that many more claim to be able to speak Irish, and there are an increasing number of Gaelscoileanna, Irish-speaking schools, being set up in urban centres. One might now hear Irish being spoken in universities.

The major policy instrument of successive Irish governments to effect a revival in the use of the language has been the forced teaching of Irish throughout schooling. It is compulsory for students to take Irish until they leave school at 17 or 18. Despite this, Irish has continued to decline and a recent policy of translating all official documents seems more directed at employing fluent Irish speakers rather than promoting the language.

If Irish has not survived and looks unlikely to be revived, it has left an imprint on the way English is spoken in Ireland (and elsewhere). Hiberno-English or Irish English differs from the English spoken in England not just in the way words are pronounced – so the Irish accent means *tube* is pronounced *choob* – but also in the structure of speech (the way words are ordered) and the use of different vocabulary. Many first- generation English speakers in Ireland used a word order derived from Irish and literal translations of some words that gave the English spoken in Ireland an unusual quality. The Irish form sentences that would be regarded as ungrammatical outside Ireland, but most Irish people would not realise this. For instance, *I'm after washing the kitchen* means *I've (just) cleaned the kitchen*. Some emotions and states are described as being worn, thus *I have a terrible thirst on me*. To describe what one does habitually, the verb 'to do' was frequently used, so *I do be learning the English* would mean *I study English*. This form is less common now. The absence of a word for yes or no in Irish meant that Irish speakers of English could be wordy and perhaps accused of not giving a straight answer.

In addition many words absorbed into the English spoken in Ireland (and sometimes beyond) are derived from Irish. So Irish words such as *amadán* (omadAWN – fool) and *flathuleach* (flaHOOlock – generous, show off) are commonly used with English in Ireland. Other words, such as smithereens or galore, are derived from Irish (*smiodar* – to fragment; *go leor* – plenty). The Irish pronunciation of English words has also added new words, so *eejit* (a fool) is derived from the Irish pronunciation of idiot. Many other words seem to be used exclusively in Ireland, but are of indeterminate origin, such as *wojus,* meaning terrible or awful, and some words mean something different in Ireland to their normal English use, so *bold* in Ireland is usually used as a synonym for naughty.

Still there are differences in the use of language throughout the country. The English spoken in Northern Ireland differs significantly from that in the south. Words and phrases used in some parts of Ireland might be meaningless in another part. For instance, the word *tackie* means trainer or sports shoe in Limerick, but nowhere else (except, oddly, in South Africa).

## Sports

Like nearly all societies, sport is an important activity for many, especially men, either because they play sports or because they follow sports that others play. More so than in most countries, sport also plays an important unifying role in Irish people's identity, for instance, when Ireland plays in the football (or as it is called in Ireland, soccer) World Cup, or as is also common, in separating Irish people along class, geographic county or cultural lines. Even in sport, which is often thought to rise above politics, the influence of politics is very much in evidence.

Ireland is unusual in that the largest sporting organization and most popular sports are native games that are only played in Ireland (or by Irish people abroad). Gaelic football and hurling are both popular, though Gaelic football is played throughout Ireland whereas hurling, which required good quality land to play on, is played in pockets mainly in the south of the country. Gaelic football is a sport not unlike Australian rules football except that the ball is round. Hurling is played with a stick (hurley) and small leather ball (*sliotar*). One of the fastest field sports in the world, it requires remarkable skill, which makes it difficult to follow for the casual spectator. The Gaelic Athletic Association (GAA) was set up in 1884 as part of the general trend of cultural revival. It was also a reaction to the snobbishness of the English sports where refusal to play on Sundays prevented the working classes from participating. While the GAA revived hurling, native forms of football had been wiped out as people used the English association football (soccer). The GAA essentially invented Gaelic football to give those interested in football a 'Gaelic' alternative. Closely connected both to Irish nationalism and the Catholic Church, the GAA's sports are organized at parish and county level. The remarkable speed with which they became the most popular sports in Ireland gave some democratic credence to the cultural revivalists.

Gaelic games are popular throughout rural Ireland, and are essentially classless in rural areas. The GAA has an estimated 300,000 members and accounts for over half of attendances at sporting events in Ireland. Because of its association with Irish nationalism and cultural politics in urban areas, particularly Dublin and Cork, the now small Protestant population maintained their own sports, rugby, cricket and hockey. Many of these sports are now played by the middle classes, and indeed rugby, is no longer the preserve of a middle-class elite having increased its popularity greatly since 2000. As a sporting nation the Irish had become used to their role as valiant losers. However in rugby at club level, Munster and later Leinster have won European championships, and the national team, which is all-island, won the Six Nations Grand Slam in 2009. Much of its popularity has come at the expense of Gaelic games. That the GAA has allowed rugby and football to be played at its main stadium, Croke Park, suspending a rule which banned the playing of 'foreign sports' on GAA grounds, has reduced the sectarian image from which the GAA has sometimes suffered.

Football is mainly organized in urban areas and on the east coast. Where it is popular in towns on the west, such as Sligo, this is thought to be because of a tradition left over from the British garrison based there. The Football Association of Ireland (FAI) governs the game in

*Table 7.1*    Ireland's main sporting events

| Event | Sport | Venue | Times |
|-------|-------|-------|-------|
| Six Nations Championship | Rugby | Lansdowne Road, Dublin | Each spring |
| All Ireland Hurling and Football Championships | Gaelic football and Hurling | Croke Park and various venues throughout Ireland | Each summer, finals take place in September |
| Punchestown Festival | National Hunt horse racing | Co. Kildare | March |
| The Irish Derby | Horse racing | The Curragh, Co. Kildare | July |
| The Dublin Horse Show | Equestrian | Royal Dublin Society | August |
| The Irish Open | Golf | Various | July |

the Republic, whereas the Irish Football Association governs it in Northern Ireland. It is the only major sport that has two separate national teams based on the border, which causes some problems as many people in the North naturally support the Republic of Ireland team (see Box 7.2). Though the FAI-organized game is played mainly by working-class people, many middle-class people play it in informal or non-aligned recreational leagues. In fact it is the most popular sport in terms of player numbers. Some of the few truly nation-unifying moments come when the Irish team qualifies for the World Cup, when all people from all backgrounds tend to support the Irish team and this is highly visible on the streets which are festooned with flags and bunting. Over half the people in the country watch matches like these. Ireland's first success as a soccer nation came when a former English player, Jack Charlton, took over as manager. Unfortunately Ireland qualifies only irregularly and controversially failed to qualify for the 2010 World Cup; in 2002 it divided the nation when the team's best player walked out, refusing to play for the rest of the tournament, prompting the then Taoiseach to intervene and offer his conciliation skills, which had been tested in the Northern Ireland peace process, to seek a resolution to the dispute.

An unusual aspect of football in Ireland is its organizational weakness despite its national side's popularity. Few people support the domestic league, but many more follow the fortunes of English football teams, particularly Manchester United and Liverpool. Pubs show English football matches live – in fact sport in Ireland tends to be associated with drinking. The Irish TV programme that shows reports of English football matches is among the most popular. Many people travel to England to attend these games, but rarely travel to see their local club play.

The sport one chooses to play and follow is often dictated by one's class and more specifically the school one attends. Schools in Ireland tend to promote certain sports over others and part of the strength of the GAA stems from the fact that many Catholic schools promote Gaelic games to the exclusion of others, particularly soccer. However sporting success in the international arena in particular does act as a unifier across social class and is frequently, after the weather, the safest topic of conversation.

The other most popular sports in Ireland include swimming and tennis, but horse racing (which is essentially a spectator sport) and golf (which many people play) play a bigger role in society. It is estimated that there are 350,000 members of golf clubs in Ireland and

**Box 7.2   Sport in Northern Ireland**

If we can see sports a means of weakening class cleavages or divisions in the Republic of Ireland, the reverse is true in Northern Ireland. The existence of a nationalist sporting organization (the GAA) makes it difficult for unionists to play the sport that most Catholics play. Their difficulty with Gaelic games was made more troublesome as there was a ban on members playing English sports lifted only in 1971 and a ban on those working for British security forces, removed in 2000. The use of GAA grounds for commemorations of the hunger strikes further deepens divisions, though the GAA organization in the south has not sanctioned this. In Northern Ireland, Gaelic football is popular, and outside Belfast and Antrim, hurling is uncommon.

In urban areas soccer is popular among both Catholic and Protestant working classes. This causes some degree of tension, though virtually all the teams in the local (Northern) Irish League are Protestant. One team, Derry City, left the league and joined the southern-based League of Ireland, and another, Belfast Celtic, left the League following rioting at one match, only to be dissolved later. It is appropriate that the team's ground was sold to developers to become a shopping centre, shopping being Northern Ireland's other favoured pastime. The tension between Protestants and Catholics is also played out in Scottish football, where the two groups support Glasgow Rangers and Glasgow Celtic respectively. Many people travel from Belfast for their derby games, which are hate-filled and often violent.

Football in Ireland is partitioned, so there is a Northern Ireland team which has competed in World Cups, most recently in 1982 when they beat the hosts Spain and topped their group. Despite this few nationalists supported the Northern Irish team, and when Catholics play for Northern Ireland they can be subject to abuse from Protestant fans. An excellent play by Marie Jones, *A Night in November,* looks at the difficult relationship Northern Irish people have with their sporting traditions.

Middle-class Protestants, like their counterparts in the south, tend to play rugby, hockey and cricket, all of which are organized on a all-island basis, giving them more contact with people in the south. Rugby is also increasingly popular among middle-class Catholics.

the country has hosted major international golf events, such as the Ryder Cup. It also has some of the best players in the world, like Pádraig Harrington and Rory McIlroy. Golf clubs are middle-class and male-dominated and are thought to be an important venue for business, thus perpetuating class divisions. Horse racing, on the

**Illustration 7.3   Mulligan's Pub, Dublin**

The Irish pub is many people's first experience of Irish culture. There are, however, very few original Irish pubs left like this one. Many are a pastiche of what we think an Irish pub should be.

other hand, can legitimately claim to bring together all sections of society. Irish horses, jockeys and trainers are among the best in the world. Vincent O'Brien, for instance, is thought to be horse racing's greatest trainer ever. Watching horses run around a field might be considered dull were it not for the gambling that takes place around it, and the Irish, on courses, in betting shops visible in every village and town and online, gamble on sports more than most people in the world.

## The Irish pub and Irish drinking

One stereotype about Ireland that the Irish have used to create a global industry is their propensity to drink. On the back of this, Irish-themed pubs have opened the world over. Though the Irish have quite a high rate of abstention – 22 per cent of adults never take alcohol, probably for religious reasons – this stereotype, like many others, has some truth to it. Measuring alcohol consumption is notoriously difficult and surveys which ask people suffer from a societal expectations bias – so people under-report their consumption to accord with what society expect of them. The more reliable way is to look at the amount of alcohol sold in a country, but as many Irish buy their alcohol in Northern Ireland this may under-report also.

Europeans are the heaviest drinkers in the world but alcohol consumption as measured has fallen from a high of 17 litres of pure alcohol consumed per annum to about 11 litres today. In Ireland the amount more than doubled between 1970 (7 litres) and 2000 (14.5 litres). The predominately beer-drinking Irish have high rates of binge drinking and heavy drinking, especially among the young. Youth drinking is comparatively high and public drunkenness is culturally acceptable, though drinking during the day is not.

Some of the changes in Irish drinking habits may have to do with changes in Irish pubs. The pub in Ireland is an important part of the social fabric, and attempts to limit access to pubs often fall foul of the pub trade's significant political lobby – though it failed in its opposition to a ban on smoking in pubs. Pubs in Ireland have increased in size and are more likely to be corporate-owned. These businesses have spent large amounts of money updating pubs to whatever theme is fashionable at the time. As a result Irish pubs are not very personal and not particularly pretty – few have been preserved in the way that can be seen in rural English villages. Nor do they offer good food or drink – so the monopoly of Diageo (owners of Guinness) means that very few bars serve anything other than mass-produced chemically-laden beers available anywhere else in the world. Guinness itself, once notoriously hard to find a good pint of, is now so standardized that it tastes the same virtually anywhere in Europe.

Emigration is the main reason why Irish pubs can be found abroad. Emigrant communities need places to gather and meet – and especially where that emigrant community is predominantly young and male a pub was a natural choice. It acted as a sort of informal community centre, where people would go on arriving in a new town looking for work or accommodation. Non-Irish started to frequent these bars, often for the Irish music that was offered. Irish pubs may have become popular because drunkenness is reasonably acceptable, and people stand around, so groups tend to merge. Part of the attraction of the Irish pub culture, then, may be that it is more sociable than most pub cultures in the world.

## Religion in Ireland and the decline of the Catholic Church

More so than in any other country, religion has formed part of the identity of what it means to be part of Irish society. As such it is much more than the belief in a supernatural being and one's relationship to that. The comedian Dara Ó Briain probably put it well in describing himself as an atheist but 'ethnically Catholic': 'I don't believe in God, but I do still hate Rangers' (the protestant Scottish football team). Irish people's religion is cultural rather than spiritual – it defines the sense of belonging to the society. It was said of the original Northern Irish parliament that it was a Protestant parliament for a Protestant people. The same could be said of the Irish state: that it was a Catholic state for a Catholic people. Protestants were welcome but only as long as they signed up to a concept of Irishness that included Catholicism. They had to realize that they could never really be Irish. Catholicism was extraordinarily important to the social fabric and guided how many people, even non-Catholics, behaved and were permitted to behave.

The success of Christianity in Ireland was initially uncertain, and it had to compete with other pre-existing supernatural belief systems. Christian missionaries seem to have failed to get the Irish to reject these and instead the church in Ireland adapted to pagan beliefs, so Gaelic festivals such as *Samhain* (Halloween) became Christianized. The traditional version of Catholicism, as opposed to the more European version celebrated by some, still venerated holy wells and sacred bushes – a tradition probably pre-dating Christianity. By the late nineteenth century the church had significant institutional power and was accepted by the British government as a restraining force on Irish nationalism. The Church played its hand carefully and became associated with nationalism when it could see that independence was becoming inevitable. After independence the Church set about exercising that power to the exclusion of other points of view, pervading public life in its control of schools and hospitals. In the 1950s a future Labour leader was among the queue of Irish politicians wishing to tell their electorate that they were Catholic first and Irish second (Patterson, 2006: 161). When Irish bishops objected to legislation, then the legislation fell. The 1937 constitution, while not establishing the Roman Catholic Church as the state church, gave it a special position and the nature of the constitution itself, its rights and fundamental laws, were said to be based on Catholic social teaching at the time. In 1972 the Irish and British governments covered up the suspected involvement of a Catholic priest in a bombing that killed nine people.

Irish Catholicism is perhaps less private and less self-reflective than religious faith for others elsewhere. The Irish are not likely to read the Bible at home or think about or debate their faith. It is something that involves going to Mass on Sundays and having most of the major ceremonies in one's life celebrated in a church. Many people's houses are still replete with religious memorabilia, such as fonts for holy water, crucifixes, statues and pictures of saints. Traditionally, when people spoke, religion was often invoked, so it was common – and still is among certain sections of the community – to hear people say, 'I'll say a prayer for you'. Even prayers, such as the rosary, involved public recital rather than private reflection. Much of the religion was about self-sacrifice – where the self-sacrifice and piety of the person was widely advertised, literally in the case of some of the prayers frequently published by people in local papers. It affected people's behaviour deeply. Very few people had sex before or outside marriage. Women were expected to and did dress in appropriately modest attire. Irish people's morality was that which the Catholic Church said it would be. Irish television and radio still plays bells each day at midday and six o'clock to call Catholics to prayer. If the Irish church had a great deal of power, however, it was probably only because the vast majority of people looked to religious leaders for guidance on questions of morality. When the Pope visited Ireland in 1979, literally millions of people turned out to see and hear him – Catholic Ireland might have seemed at the pinnacle of its powers. 95 per cent of the population was Catholic and weekly church attendance of those was about 90 per cent.

Since the 1990s Irish Catholicism has undergone individualization and secularization (Inglis, 1998). Individualization in the sense that people no longer look to the institution to form their views on questions of morality, and secularization in the sense that religion does not influence public decision making and behaviour. There has been an obvious decline in religious observance – the percentage of people describing themselves as Catholic is still high at 87 per cent, but weekly mass attendance of those Catholics has fallen to 56 per cent. Those who do attend are from a declining cohort – born before 1960 and living in rural areas. The Archbishop of Dublin, Diarmuid Martin, said in 2006 that in parts of Dublin church attendance was as low as one per cent. As we saw in Chapter 3, Irish people's behaviour and attitudes have become less determined by Catholic teaching. The Church is no longer held in fear and awe as it once was. Many put this down to the scandals that afflicted the church – these initially related to sexual relations some clergy had with women, which naturally reduced their authority to instruct others on their sexual behaviour. Later more brutal revelations emerged of the rape and beatings inflicted on children by Roman Catholic clergy and the attempts to cover these up by the Roman Catholic hierarchy. However it is probably a fallacy to think that these *caused* the decline of the Church's influence. Many people had known about these allegations for many years but had done nothing; the difference was that in the 1990s and 2000s, the media, public figures and ordinary people were willing to voice their criticisms.

The changes had probably started well before the Pope came to Ireland in 1979. The decline might be connected to urbanization and the improved educational opportunities for the Irish. The conventions of Irish rural life meant that families were large (one needed sons to work on the farm) but only the eldest son would inherit the farm. The other sons were forced to emigrate or, if they could afford it, perhaps join the priesthood. The eldest son often deferred marriage until he had control of the farm. In this context sexual relations that risked pregnancy might have spelled economic disaster. The growth of manufacturing in urban areas offered men more opportunities, and living in more anonymous urban areas there was reduced societal pressure to conform. At the same time educational opportunities had expanded, which enabled, and even if the church controlled the education system, may have encouraged people to question the Church's authority. In 1962 a survey of Catholics in Dublin showed that although 88 per cent agreed that the Church was the greatest force for good in the country, 83 per cent of the survey respondents with high levels of education *disagreed* with this statement. A liberal intelligentsia developed in 1960s Dublin which openly questioned the authority of the Church, and a new generation of politicians was emerging, which was more willing to ignore the Church. So by the 1980s it was possible for legislation opposed by the Church to be proposed and passed by Irish governments. The Catholic Church is still amazingly strong in a European context, but its monolithic power has faded. The divorce referendum was passed in the mid-1990s by only the slimmest majority. But the reaction of different religious orders to public criticism of them in the light of a report into their treatment of children in their care showed the religious orders to be an interest group with no moral authority.

## Unrestrained consumerism?

If the Catholic Church no longer commands Irish people's devotion, what does? As we saw in the last chapter, much of the latter part of the economic boom was driven by a demand for consumer goods funded by borrowing on house price appreciation. The Irish became obsessed with house prices, and property supplements in newspapers became popular with all, not just those buying or selling houses. Second homes in Spain became normal. Shopping trips to New York were no longer the preserve of the fabulously wealthy and even serious newspapers were full of advice on where to get bargains and how to avoid paying customs duty on your return. The arrival of new shopping centres with ever more expensive shops was commented on by the same papers. Irish streets have become indistinguishable from ones in British cities. Food became a lifestyle, not a mean of survival. The traditionally plain Irish food – meat and two veg – was replaced by celebrity-endorsed recipes from anywhere other than Ireland. Those traits that many had attributed to the Irish were not easy to discern. But references of folklorists to the importance of kinship and family, community over economic concerns, superstition and myth, and the link to the soil, may only be a romanticization of poverty and peasantry. This probably suited many political leaders unable to deliver their vision.

In fact the new political class shows itself to be materialist, having awarded itself massive pay increases and subsidies since the 1990s. Their willingness to use taxpayers' money to feed extravagant lifestyles shows that Ireland had come some way from the simple frugality promised by Éamon de Valera two generations earlier. The almost childlike obsession with the trappings of wealth that Charles Haughey displayed – he bought racehorses, an island and a mansion – rarely drew rebuke from ordinary people, possibly because they aspired to such wealth themselves. The Irish embraced consumerism with a zeal that would make the most ardent capitalist proud, but that would certainly have shocked de Valera. In 2007 the departing German ambassador to Ireland noted that the Irish had become 'coarse' in their obsession with collecting the trappings of wealth. One of the things he noted was that some people always had cars that were no more than two years old. The Irish people became conspicuous consumers – where lavish spending on goods is primarily for the purpose of displaying one's wealth.

# 8

# Ireland and the World

Ireland is a country that is more open to and engaged with the outside world than most others. We have seen that despite the attempts of early policy makers to create a self-sufficient state, Ireland's small size and limited natural resources meant that the Irish economy depended on its contact with Britain. So despite independence, the Irish economy was effectively a region of Britain. Ireland's almost complete dependence on Britain has eased in the last thirty years as the EU and the USA have become important markets for Irish goods and sources for investment. But the Irish have had an impact well beyond the economic sphere. The Irish, more than most in western Europe, were and are willing to travel for employment opportunities. This has created a population that was, again despite the efforts of policy makers, open to outside influences, particularly from the main destination countries, the UK and USA.

So Ireland is a very globalized place. One index of globalization, the A.T. Kearney/*Foreign Policy* Globalization Index 2007, measured in terms of FDI, numbers of foreign-born people working in the country, external trade as a percentage of GDP, political engagement in selected international organizations, foreign aid, tourism, telephone traffic and internet connectivity, put Ireland as the fifth most globalized country in the world. Small countries are usually more globalized than big ones on these measures because small countries are more dependent on trade, but the high inward and outward migration and Ireland's commitment to international organizations are also significant.

Ireland's major interests with the outside world are determined by its openness. In the EU, and the World Trade Organization (WTO) it seeks to secure free trade, except in relation to the agricultural sector where it is protectionist. Ireland's experience as a colony rather than a colonizer is unusual in developed countries and it sometimes claims to be a defender of the rights of small, poor nations. But Ireland's small size means that it is not a very important country in those organizations to which it belongs, and unlike, say, the UK, France or Germany, Ireland could not force its way by virtue of its political importance. Furthermore its small army means that Ireland effectively relies on other countries for its security. Despite this Ireland has a formal policy of military neutrality, though as we shall see, this is a flexible concept as practised in Ireland. Ireland's neutrality means it is actively involved in peace-keeping duties and with the achievement of relative peace in Northern Ireland, the country sees itself as having a role in conflict resolution. When it tries to achieve its foreign policy ends it is often through moral pressure and by being part of a coalition.

Though Ireland's most important political relationship is with the EU, other relationships with the rest of the world are of more cultural or economic importance. Ireland's long history of emigration means that Ireland has left its mark on other countries such as the USA, Canada, New Zealand, Australia and of course Britain. Northern Ireland has been very important in many ways, and though most Irish people have tended to ignore Northern Ireland as a place (few people from the south are regular visitors, and many have never been), it has had a major impact on foreign policy decisions. This chapter will examine Ireland's neutrality; the impact of the EU on Irish society and politics will also be discussed, with reference to the apparent reduction in support for the EU (or its continued integration). A third important relationship is that with the USA. Like many other countries in the world, Ireland feels it has a special relationship with the USA, and it can claim to have benefited economically from that relationship through investment by US companies. This chapter will look at the debate as to whether Ireland is culturally closer to Boston than Berlin, and will argue that in fact Ireland is probably closer to Birmingham.

## Emigration

It is estimated that between 1800 and 2000 over eight million people emigrated from Ireland. Given its size, this is a remarkable figure, and for its size it has had the most emigration of any European country. Before the mass emigration of the eighteenth and nineteenth centuries there had been some emigration to continental Europe which led to the setting up of Irish colleges in Paris, Leuven, Salamanca and Rome. These were mainly intended as colleges where Irish Catholics could receive an education. Even where Ireland's emigration rate to particular countries was low, Irish emigrants have made a mark. Only five per cent of Irish emigrants went to Australia, but the Irish made up about a quarter of the initial plantation there. Only a small number of emigrants went to South America, but their social status was such that they became military and political leaders in Argentina and Chile. Ireland was producing so many priests in the

**Illustration 8.1    Food distribution programme in Ethiopia, 2008**

Ireland has a long tradition of involvement in Africa, first trying to 'save their souls' and later save their lives. The Irish were among the most enthusiastic missionairies in Africa, and Irish Catholics right up to the 1970s were encouraged to give money to save 'black babies'. More recently Irish-based charities such as Concern, Trócaire, Gorta and Goal are active in development and emergency relief in Africa. Irish celebrities such as Bono and Bob Geldof are also prominent in the debt relief campaigns and Geldof was the driving force behind Band Aid and Live Aid in the 1980s. Ireland's foreign aid budget is quite high although it was one of the first items to be cut when the Irish budgetary crisis hit. In 2008 a severe drought and rising food costs resulted in a massive food crisis in Ethiopia. The photo shows an Ethiopian Government Food distribution programme in Bedessa.

1950s that half ended up on missions to Africa, attempting to convert people to Catholicism. The schools set up by Irish priests and nuns in Africa would have brought an experience of Irish culture there as well.

In the late eighteenth century many non-conformist Ulster Scots left Ireland for the USA in order to escape religious persecution. However most of Ireland's emigration was economic by people who had little prospect of surviving in an economically depressed Ireland, and it is in the United Kingdom and the United States of America that the Irish have been most noticeable. Ireland's proximity to the UK made it the simplest place to travel to. Liverpool and Glasgow were among the most Irish-influenced cities in Britain, but London, Manchester and Coventry also had large-scale Irish immigration. Most Irish tended to work in construction – men initially building canals, then roads, and women in domestic service (maids) or nurses – and lived in concentrated areas, such as Kilburn, which became Irish ghettos. For much of the time Irish immigrants in Britain would have been regarded with suspicion. This was fed by the stereotype that the Irish were lazy drunks, propagated in the theatre in the nineteenth and early twentieth centuries (and some feel today), and by anti-Catholic sentiment. The IRA bombings in England, particularly in the 1970s, would have also contributed to this suspicion of the Irish.

Since the 1990s the relationship has improved markedly. The peace in Northern Ireland removed some of the tainted associations with terrorism. Cheaper travel between Ireland and the UK means that many more Britons have visited Ireland rather than relying on media reports of the place. The economic boom changed the direction of migration, with some English of Irish extraction moving to Ireland. Much of the recent Irish emigration to Britain tends to be among the middle classes working in the City, London's financial district, and so the Irish are no longer likely to be the people taking the more menial jobs. Many of the most accomplished people in Britain claim Irish descent including former Prime Minister Tony Blair, musician Morrissey, *The Wire* actor Dominic West and comedian Paul Merton. About six million Britons (mainly Scottish and English) could claim Irish citizenship through having at least one Irish grandparent, and there are almost 700,000 Irish-born people living in Britain. Despite this, the Irish community in Britain is now less easily identified as a separate ethnic group, and there is no label for a Briton of Irish descent – Irish Briton – such as there is Irish American in the United States.

The first Irish emigration to the USA was primarily by Scots-Irish in the eighteenth century. These were often Presbyterians escaping the religious persecution of non-conformist Protestants by the Anglicans (Episcopalians) in Ireland. They settled in rural areas, often in the southern states of the USA. They assimilated into US society easily, not retaining a strong separate Irish identity. Many of the earliest US presidents were of Ulster-Scots extraction, and for some it was important – James Buchanan reportedly said, 'My Ulster blood is a priceless heritage'. Ulster Scots made up the majority of Irish immigrants in the USA until the Famine. When Irish Catholics started to migrate to the USA, particularly from the 1820s, they settled in the industrial cities in the north-eastern states of Boston, New York and Philadelphia. They worked in factories and in construction, but also started to enter the police force and fire departments. Because the major cleavage in the USA at the time was race, the Irish on arriving in the USA (unlike in Britain) went up the social scale 'becoming white', though as Illustration 8.2 shows, they encountered some of the racism now reserved for blacks. For this reason Irish America is often associated with racism. By the time of the Great Famine and the upsurge in Irish migration to the USA, Irish Catholics had established tight political and social networks from which they excluded other ethnic groups. The scale of the immigration from Ireland (accounting for about a third of all immigration to the USA between 1820 and 1860) meant that the Irish could become a significant political lobby, and it was to the USA that Irish nationalists tended to travel in order to raise funds and to lobby a usually reluctant US administration to take action. Remittances from emigrants (the 'letters from America') also played an important role in the Irish economy. The willingness of the USA to accept dual identities also meant that the Irish in America could be both Irish and American without any conflict. Emigration to the USA has continued but on a much smaller scale, partly due to restrictions placed on immigration by the US government. Despite this, the keen awareness of their Irishness held by many of the children and grandchildren of Irish emigrants means that Irish America remains a very powerful lobby group.

That sense of Irishness that emigrants have can be seen from the memoirs of the descendents of Irish immigrants. Books such as John Gregory Dunne's *Harp* (1989), John Healy's *The Grass Arena* (1988), Pete Hamill's *A Drinking Life* (1994), or *All Souls* (2000) and *Easter Rising* (2006) by Michael Patrick MacDonald give some idea

**Illustration 8.2   The portrayal of Irish immigrants in the USA**

Irish Catholics in the USA were regarded by many in the waspish US society as inferior and depicted with simian facial features. The bigotry they encountered, however, was never as virulent, violent and extreme as that seen towards blacks. The Irish successfully 'rehabilitated' themselves, 'becoming white' (Ignatiev, 1995) as some have put it, and in doing so often adopted a racism and bigotry themselves that can be detected in many Irish-American communities in contemporary US society.

of what it was like to grow up Irish abroad. Healy's book shows some of the problems those of Irish descent have where they might regard themselves as Irish in Britain, but dubbed 'Plastic Paddies' – fake Irish – in Ireland. More so than in the USA, the Irish in Britain tend to have assimilated fully into British society, and probably because of their proximity to Ireland, tend to have less idealized views of Ireland and a more nuanced sense of the causes of the conflict in Northern Ireland.

## Ireland, Northern Ireland and the world

The issue of Northern Ireland and the relationship with Britain is at the forefront of every aspect of Ireland's foreign policy. The partition of Ireland was sorely felt by the revolutionary leaders of the new Irish state and Ireland acted to assert itself through membership of international organizations like the League of Nations and later the United Nations (UN). Ireland left the British Commonwealth in an attempt to assert the county's separation from Britain. Attempts to raise the issue of Ireland's partition within international organizations were usually ignored as most countries regarded it as an internal matter for Britain and even those US administrations (such as that of John F. Kennedy) with a instinctive sympathy for the Irish cause were cognizant of the more strategically important relationship with the UK. When the Troubles (see Box 2.5, p. 63) broke out in the early 1970s and there were genuine fears for the safety of the Catholic population in Northern Ireland, Irish attempts to raise the issue internationally once again failed to lead to anything more than sympathetic noises. Thus Ireland's policy regarding Northern Ireland, which was to claim the whole island as being part of the state of Ireland and to seek to end partition, failed. The antagonism of the two parts of the island to each other was never going to work as policy if ending partition was the goal, and the more cordial, if formal, relationship of the 1960s sparked off suspicion in the more extreme parts of the unionist community that led to the outbreak of the Troubles. British governments had allowed Northern Ireland to be run by the Unionist governments without interference since its inception, and though there was a more sympathetic attitude to unification in the Labour party (which tended to have the support of the large Irish immigrant population) the outbreak of the Troubles then refocused British attention on Northern Ireland from being a political issue to a security issue. Misguided British suspicion of Irish state complicity in protecting the IRA – the Irish state was more virulently anti-IRA than even the British government was – meant that Irish attempts to influence British policy in Northern Ireland were ignored. The Irish government engaged senior US politicians to pressurize the British to allow Dublin be involved and have an input into any solution to the problem (see Box 8.1), and this eventually paid off. Now Ireland has some input into the government of Northern Ireland, through the North South Ministerial Council (see Box 4.2, p. 103) and Ireland has dropped its constitutional claims to Northern Ireland's territory, though there is no sense that the Northern Ireland question is settled and that it would not happily be revisited by Irish nationalists in the future if union were more likely then. Ireland maintains close relations with the UK and the Taoiseach and British prime minister still meet regularly. Ireland also has a close relationship with Britain in Europe as the two countries share many interests in common.

---

**Box 8.1    Irish America and the Northern Ireland peace process**

Irish Americans have had a major influence on politics in the USA – not least by providing some of the more prominent politicians that country has. John F. Kennedy is the president with most obvious Irish roots, but all US presidents can and do claim some Irish roots, even Barack Obama who has roots in Co. Offaly. Even the 'machine style' of politics may have been imported by Irish immigrants to the USA, who used politics and the patronage that comes with it to control the Democratic Party in many cities, such as New York, Boston and Chicago.

From the late 1970s the Irish government sought to involve Irish-American politicians in the Northern Irish situation. There were concerns that most Irish Americans had a green-tinted idealized vision of what was happening there and that as a result Sinn Féin and the Provisional IRA were receiving publicity and financial support. The government lobbied the 'Four Horsemen' of Irish-American politics, including Senator Ted Kennedy and the then Speaker Tip O'Neill.

Their involvement allowed Irish politicians access to the highest political office in the USA, and by the time the peace process had started, US presidents, in particular Bill Clinton, were used to push the process forward. Clinton's visits were important symbolic events and his appointment of Senator George Mitchell as a special envoy was important for the signing of the Good Friday or Belfast Agreement. More important than either of these was the fact that the US government was seen as an impartial third party, something that the Irish and British governments were not, and that the US government was sufficiently powerful to reassure Irish nationalists that it could ensure that the British government could not renege on its side of the bargain.

Amidst the torturously slow implementation of the GFA, with unionists and nationalists refusing to move first on a number of issues, such as disarmament of the IRA or the devolution of police powers, the threats and entreaties of US presidents helped to unblock the way. In the aftermath of the September 11 attacks in New York and elsewhere, pressure from the US government to dissociate itself from terrorism in any way and Sinn Féin's reliance on money raised in the USA led to Sinn Féin and the IRA moving to decommission their weaponry faster than they might otherwise have done.

The other major bilateral relationship Ireland has is with the USA. Ireland's interests with regard to the USA revolve around Northern Ireland and economic factors. The USA was the one large country which tended to sympathize with the Irish nationalist position and to which the UK government would listen. Thus it played an important role pressurizing the British to engage in the peace process and acted as an 'honest broker' in the peace talks. Economically Ireland has received a great deal of inward investment from the USA and, as we saw in Chapter 6, the USA is one of Ireland's major trading partners. Obviously the relationship is somewhat skewed as Ireland is of limited importance to the USA given its size. But because of Irish immigration and the resultant cultural ties Ireland probably gets more attention in the USA than similar-sized countries with limited strategic importance. Ireland's reliance on US investment means that Ireland needs to protect that relationship. When the Obama administration targeted offshore tax loopholes, one of the countries mentioned as potential targets was Ireland with its low corporation tax and possible transfer pricing (see Chapter 6). Ireland successfully lobbied to ensure that it was not included in the targeted countries. Ireland's relationship with the USA had one odd feature, despite the apparent closeness of the two countries: Ireland never joined NATO (North Atlantic Treaty Organization), the western hemisphere's military alliance during the Cold War.

## Ireland's neutrality

While some might question whether a country the size of Ireland can have a foreign policy, Ireland is quite certain that it does and the Irish people are very attached to that policy. Ireland is a neutral state, and so during the Cold War was not aligned with either NATO or the Warsaw Pact countries. The policy of neutrality emerged at the outbreak of World War II, when Ireland was forced to make a choice. The British hoped that Ireland would join the Allies, not because of anything the Irish army could have offered, but because it wanted access to Irish naval ports. Ireland's proximity to the UK would have (again) made it a useful base to force Britain into a multi-front war. Had Ireland indicated any support for Germany, this would have given Britain good cause to invade Ireland. Had Ireland supported the Allies, it would probably not have added much to the Allied war effort, but exposed Ireland to German attack. Had the Germans attacked, the Irish were secure in the knowledge that the British would invade to prevent this. The then Taoiseach, Éamon de Valera, chose to assert Ireland's independence and took the most practical course open to Ireland by remaining neutral. Though this was criticized heavily in Britain, it was popular in Ireland, and there were few dissenting voices, although de Valera's decision to commiserate with the German ambassador on the death of Hitler was probably taking the appearance of neutrality too far.

Neutrality, however, was more illusory than real, as during the war the Irish actively assisted in sending volunteers from Ireland both into the British army (more people from the south than the north fought in the British army during the war) and to work in factories in the UK supplying the war effort. German soldiers captured on Irish soil were detained in military camps for the duration of the war, whereas British and US soldiers were returned to their countries. The policy probably made an end to the partition of the country less likely, as it further alienated unionists from the government in the south.

The subsequent decision to not align itself with NATO against the Soviet bloc countries in the early 1950s came not because Ireland was neutral about communism – the country was virulently anti-communist – but because the British were members of NATO. It meant that Ireland became a link between the Soviet Union and Cuba, as the Soviet airline Aeroflot planes stopped and refuelled at Shannon Airport. However, during the Cuban missile crisis these were searched for military materials. Ireland was always closer to the USA and offered to come to a bilateral arrangement with it, but the USA refused, not seeing any advantage to this. Ireland, however, piggy-backed on the Atlantic alliance, safe in the knowledge that any attack on it would provoke a reaction by Britain and the USA. The neutrality policy became very popular and one of the defining aspects of the Irish state. It struck a chord with many that this small post-colonial state was not part of a larger military machine, and throughout the 1960s the left-leaning Minister for Foreign Affairs, Frank Aiken, established a foreign policy in the UN in which the country was seen to stand up for the rights of small nations. Ireland was an early opponent of apartheid and sought to use its position as a neutral country to be an acceptable peacekeeper in conflict zones.

Ireland's policy is one of military non-alignment rather than non-involvement. Few if any consider, as say the Swiss might, that membership of the EU is incompatible with neutrality. However one of the most controversial aspects of EU membership for the Irish is

**Illustration 8.3   Irish peacekeeping troops in Congo, 1960**

Ireland has a long, and for it, proud tradition of engagement with UN
peace missions, initially in the Middle East and Africa but subsequently
throughout the world. Decisions as to Ireland's participation in UN or UN-
mandated missions are made by the government on a case-by-case basis,
using the 'triple lock' system. Irish military personnel have contributed to
over 50 peacekeeping operations, including in Central America, Russia,
Georgia, the former Yugoslavia, Cambodia, Lebanon, Iran, Iraq,
Afghanistan, Kuwait, Angola, Namibia, Western Sahara, Cote d'Ivoire,
Liberia and Timor-Leste. Irish participation in Congo in 1960 introduced a
word to Irish English, when Irish UN soldiers were killed by forces from
the Baluba tribe. Since then in Ireland to 'go balubas' means to go crazy.

the increasing foreign policy and military competence taken on by
Brussels. In fact neutrality is invoked when it suits Ireland, or more
specifically Irish governments. So for domestic political reasons,
Ireland said its neutrality meant it could not agree a common EEC
position on the Falklands/Malvinas war between Argentina and the
UK in the early 1980s. Ireland joined the NATO-led Partnership for
Peace and is a member of the European Defence Agency, designed to
bolster Europe's military capabilities, and of the Nordic EU Battle
Group. Ireland's policy criterion for military involvement is based on

a 'triple lock' of i) UN Security Council resolution, ii) resolution of the Dáil, and iii) government support. The Iraq war shows that Security Council resolutions can be somewhat vague and of dubious legality. There is also some disagreement about what participation in war might mean. In the aftermath of the 11 September 2001 attacks on New York, Ireland took no formal position on the invasion of Iraq, the legality of which was in some doubt. An anti-war demonstration in February 2003 was attended by over 100,000 people in Dublin, making it among the largest protest marches in recent Irish history. Ireland allowed US planes to stop on route to Iraq to refuel, and there were allegations that these flights were used for 'extraordinary rendition' – the illegal detention and transfer – of prisoners. The government tended to ignore these allegations as the USA is seen as an important economic, political and cultural ally.

---

**Box 8.2   Boston or Berlin? Ireland's international identity**

A speech by a senior Irish politician, Mary Harney, in 2000 asked the question whether Ireland was culturally closer to Boston or Berlin. The question she was asking was whether Ireland is culturally closer to continental Europe or the USA. Though the cities were chosen for their alliteration, it was perhaps a choice that would have biased the responses of Irish people. Most people in Ireland are naturally closer to Boston insofar as it has a large Irish population there and many would have relatives there, whereas the Irish connection with Berlin is minimal. Had she asked whether we were closer to Boulder or Birmingham, the British city would have been chosen.

The question was rhetorical and set to make her point that Europe is a less homogeneous place than the USA, and that Ireland was in economic terms the beneficiary of Ireland's close relationship with the USA. She also wished to make the point that the Irish economic model, despite the allusion to corporatism and social partnership, is a US one. But the speech sparked off a wider debate about Ireland's cultural identity. Ireland, unlike the UK, always saw itself as close to European traditions, and for many Europe is a place that offered a way of escaping from Britain's shadow. The idea that Ireland is not under strong Anglo-American influence is often fuelled by a snobbish attitude to, especially, American culture. But this elite attachment to Europe is not underscored by the behaviour of the general population who are suspicious of the European Union and avid consumers of British and American culture. One might also question to what extent German, French, Dutch or Spanish teenagers are not equally infatuated with American and British culture.

## The impact of the European Union

According to some estimates, over 70 per cent of Irish laws come directly or indirectly from the EU. Despite this the institutions of the Irish government and policy-making process do not reflect the importance of the EU. The EU has probably had more impact on Ireland than any international actor since the British left Ireland. In most ways this influence has been seen as a positive, liberalizing force which has modernized Ireland in areas where Irish politicians feared to tread. The Irish have been active participants in Europe and are generally seen as 'good Europeans', though in 2001 and 2008 the Irish voters rejected EU treaties in referendums, causing something of a crisis within the EU and to some extent marginalizing Ireland. Those votes probably had more to do with disaffection with Ireland's government than with the EU, but also reflect an underlying unwillingness to proceed with the integration process whereby the EU is taking over more and more competencies for policy making. The EU has not caused any splits within or between Irish political parties, as most of the main parties are broadly supportive of EU membership. Fianna Fáil, however, is a more pragmatic than emotional supporter of EU membership, and when the EU was seen to (rightly as it turned out) criticize Ireland's fiscal policies during the boom, representatives of Fianna Fáil were willing to engage in nationalist rhetoric of a style usually reserved for British Conservative politicians. Sinn Féin is the only representative political party to campaign actively against EU integration.

The European Union started life as an organization for economic co-operation and developed into, among other things, a free trade area. Ireland joined the EEC in 1973 with the UK and Denmark, making it a nine-country group. Ireland could neither enter nor stay out of the EEC on its own and followed the UK in because of its economic dependence on its larger neighbour. Further enlargements have brought the Union to a membership of 27 countries including most of central and eastern Europe, (see Map 8.1) and it has increased both the range of policy areas it covers and the complexity of its institutions. The EU is made up of a number of institutions:

- The *European Council* is the strategic head of the EU. It is the meeting of heads of government and can decide long-term strategy at six-monthly summits. Since 2010 it has had a permanent president, although the choice of a former Belgian prime minister shows that this is not intended to be a powerful office.

- The *European Commission*, based in Brussels, could be styled as the civil service for Europe but it is much more powerful than that. It proposes and ensures that European law is implemented. Ireland provides one of the 27 Commissioners. These are usually senior politicians from the governing party. It is up to the Commission to translate the European Council's strategy into concrete policy proposals.
- The *Council of Ministers* is analogous to a cabinet. It is the decision-making body of the EU, with a six-monthly rotating chair. The ministers for a particular policy area will meet and make decision, usually by consensus, but sometimes (in less contentious areas) by simple majority or qualified majority votes. The weight of a country's vote depends on its size.
- The *European Parliament* is a large and increasingly powerful body. It retains powers of veto over most issues, including the make-up of the Commission. However it still has limited rights of proposal, so depends on policy proposals from the Commission.
- The *European Court of Justice*'s role is to adjudicate on the application of EU law. It has become a particularly important body and has forced the modernization of many Irish state policies.

The large number and increasing complexity of laws developed at EU level in an increasingly broad and diverse range of policy areas puts some pressure on national governments. While the Irish civil service is thought to have adapted well to the need to interpret and implement these directives, the Irish political system has failed to find a mechanism for oversight of and influence on EU law. The advent of Economic and Monetary Union (EMU) and the Euro notably removed monetary policy from Irish hands, but in many other areas the EU effectively makes law, with limited Irish influence. The parliamentary committee system set up to oversee EU law only comes into play after the laws have been implemented, and much of EU law is transposed into Irish law via Statutory Instruments which ministers can decree without recourse to the Oireachtas (parliament). The Department of Foreign Affairs has an official co-ordinating role for EU matters, but EU influence is dealt with through Council of Ministers meetings and regulation by the European Commission. The legislation is effectively agreed and cannot really be rejected by the Irish or any other parliament at this stage, so it tends to be ignored by most parliamentarians. The EU offers a more opaque, less democratic means of policy making, with less accountability for policy. Despite this many regard

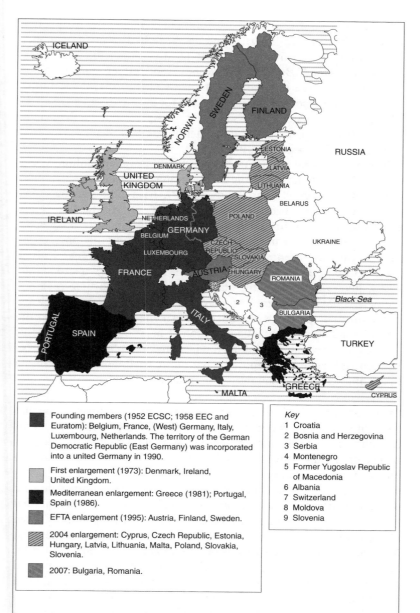

*Map 8.1*   Political map of the European Union

the impact of the EU as almost wholly positive, and the Irish people almost universally feel that Ireland has benefited from EU membership. The Irish are among the most positive about the EU and its impact on Ireland. But the Irish do not want further enlargement or integration. We see that they are the least likely to want the further decision making powers given to the EU for the environment. And the EU has failed to win the hearts of the Irish. Apart from the British, the Irish are the most national-oriented in terms of their identity. Few Irish people feel 'European' (see Figure 8.1).

The major initial impact of membership was on agriculture which brought in a system of subsidies and non-market mechanisms through the Common Agricultural Policy (CAP). Irish farm incomes rose rapidly and farmers became among the most enthusiastic Europeans. CAP still accounts for a large amount of the total EU budget but attempts to reform it usually falter because farming nations, led by France, can veto proposed changes. The position of women in Irish society when Ireland entered the EEC in 1973 was not a strong one. The Catholic outlook of the state and society at the time regarded women as having the roles of wives and mothers. The second wave of feminism in the 1970s, though causing some colourful protests, did not bring about any immediate change of heart in Irish governments – though it probably gradually raised the consciousness of Irish women. The state had imposed a bar on married women working in the public sector, and pay rates were routinely (and legally) lower for women than for men in comparable jobs. On joining the EEC the Treaty of Rome, which guaranteed equal rights for women, came into force in Ireland, allowing legal challenges to these forms of discrimination. Though governments were slow in adjusting to the requirements of membership, it was EEC membership that did most to ensure equality legislation was introduced.

In Chapter 6 we saw that EU membership was important for the development of the Irish economy. Ireland's exposure to international markets forced the modernization of some industries and the closure of others. It was the access to the European single market that allowed the small, open Irish economy to attract inward investment. As the poorest member of the EEC for some time, Ireland benefited from funds designed to develop those regions that lagged behind. It benefited from significant investment that started a drive to improve the still poor Irish infrastructure as well as putting in large amounts of money that helped stimulate the economy at a time when it was realizing its potential. EU membership also exposed Ireland's politi-

*Figure 8.1*   Attitudes to EU membership, 2009

(a)  Is your country's membership of the EU a good thing?
     Percentage saying yes

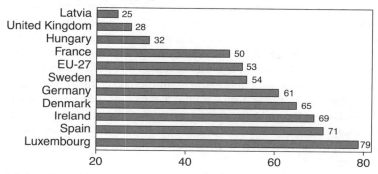

(b)  Has your country benefited from membership of the EU?
     Percentage saying yes

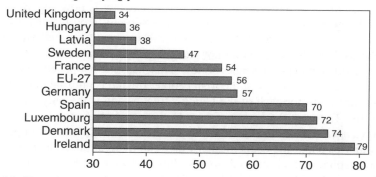

(c)  Should the EU have further decision-making powers about the
     environment? Percentage saying yes

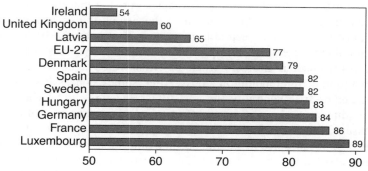

*Source*: Data from Eurobarometer 72, Country Report Ireland.

cal class to alternative policies and methods of policy analysis. The EU Structural Funds led to Ireland starting five-year National Development Plans, which purported to set out a vision for the country. The EU probably imposed stricter environmental policies than the Irish would have introduced on their own. It was also as a result of informal contacts at the European level that Ireland's once fêted 'social partnership' procedure for policy making was introduced. This shifted Irish industrial relations and policy making away from more conflictual Anglo-American methods. Much of Ireland's immigration has come from within the EU, as Europeans availed themselves of the right to live and work throughout Europe. The EU has thus also contributed to the cosmopolitanization of Irish society. Whether Ireland is closer to European or the US in culture is a point of some debate (see Box 8.2).

Though it still retains the façade of a sovereign, independent, democratic state Ireland has ceded control over a large number of policy areas to the European Union, and EU law is now superior to Irish law, so it is possible to appeal some Supreme Court decisions to the European Court of Justice or the European Court of Human Rights. The EU is therefore not part of foreign policy, it is central to Irish domestic politics and policy. This has not happened without debate or the approval of the Irish people. Ireland is unusual in having a referendum for each of the Union's treaties and is the only country of the 27 to put the Lisbon Treaty to the people for approval. There have been none of the tensions that have been seen in other European countries about the deepening of European integration. Ireland was a poor country joining a rich man's club, and as a net receiver of EU funds, Ireland has done well out of Europe.

However in a country which claims to be neutral and one which has a nationalist tradition, it is perhaps surprising that there has not been more sustained opposition than that which the small numbers against the EU have been able to muster. That even the Irish were beginning to reject the 'European dream' should have caused a crisis of confidence in Brussels when the Irish voted against the Nice Treaty in a referendum in 2001. After some 'concessions' were granted on Irish neutrality and a hastily arranged re-run in which the government made more of an effort to sell the treaty, it secured its passage. But in 2008 the Irish again rejected a European treaty, and once more accepted it on the second time of asking. While most people voted in favour of the Lisbon Treaty the second time around there was like the first time, some variation in who voted yes. Older,

*Figure 8.2* Who voted 'yes' to Lisbon II?

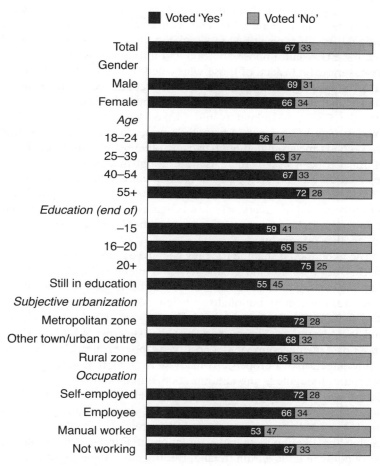

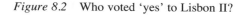

Q11. How did you vote in the referendum on Friday, 2nd October?
Did you vote Yes or No to the Treaty?

% Base: who participated in the referendum in October 2009, DK/REF excluded

*Source*: Data from Richard Sinnott and Johan A. Elkink, 'Attitudes and behaviour in the second referendum on the Treaty of Lisbon', report prepared for the Department of Foreign Affairs, July 2010.

better educated men who live in urban areas are much more likely to support the EU. Students and manual workers are most likely to be against. The coalition that campaigned for a 'no' vote was a bizarre collection of neo-liberals, Marxists, conservative Catholics and Irish nationalists. This meant that few took their concerns, which included that the EU would impose abortion and military conscription on the Irish, seriously. In fact, of those who voted 'no' to the Lisbon Treaty in 2008, most were in favour of Ireland's continued membership of the EU, but if a unifying theme could be found in their opposition, it was the fear that Ireland would further lose control over policy making. The EU seemed to have little patience with Irish indecision the second time around, though had any other peoples in the countries of Europe been asked, there is little doubt that many would have rejected the Lisbon Treaty as the French and Dutch had rejected the Constitutional Treaty. The Irish returned to the polls a year later and dutifully passed the treaty, which was again changed in 2010. No-one in Ireland had the appetite to question whether these changes required yet another referendum.

The likelihood is that the EU may become a more contentious issue in the future as Ireland's benefits from membership become less tangible. Though most see that the EU has been good for Ireland, the Irish are much more nationalistic when asked about how European they feel. As the EU has grown, Ireland's voice has become diluted and the 'centre' of Europe has shifted eastwards. While questions about past membership yield a positive response, questions about the future direction of Europe show the Irish to be more Eurosceptic than is usually thought. In the autumn 2008 Eurobarometer survey, only Latvia was ranked lower than Ireland on satisfaction with the direction Europe was taking. And as Figure 8.2 shows, young people are much less likely to vote in favour of EU treaties than older citizens, raising the likelihood that the direction of Europe may become a party political issue within Ireland. But Ireland's domestic situation is so uncertain that we cannot know whether the EU will be seen as a saviour or a villain in the coming decade.

# Conclusion

In the decade that will see the hundredth anniversary of the 1916 rising and the War of Independence, there will be a great deal of focus on how Ireland has performed in the previous century. At the start of this decade there was much despondency in Ireland about the country's prospects. That the then-Taoiseach, Brian Cowen, was ridiculed on Jay Leno's popular US chat show for his drinking habits added to the national embarrassment. Even the weather seemed to reflect the inundation of the country's morale. Looking back on the century since 1916, one could make arguments both that Ireland's performance was a success and a failure. Ireland went from being a colony to independence, achieving remarkable peace and democratic stability. It went from being one of the poorest countries in western Europe in the 1980s to one of the richest. It matured from being a clerically-dominated country to one where the Church is just another actor, and one, moreover, with little credibility. On the other hand we could say that Ireland started the last century as a reasonably developed place in one of the richest countries in the world and imposed poverty, clerical dominance and cultural hegemony on itself. It managed to waste the opportunity presented by its wealth by failing to understand why it came about. There is little social or even physical infrastructure to show for the wealth generated in the 1990s and 2000s. Even when the Church is at its weakest point, there is no appetite for the state to remove from the Church its stranglehold over the education of Irish children, even though the Catholic Church was shown to have had no respect for some among those children and instead systematically engaged in their abuse.

At a time when Ireland has to make a decision about its future, there is little agreement about how the country should seek a way out of its financial crisis. Political parties tread carefully for fear of upsetting any constituency that might cost them electorally. The often lauded 'social partnership' process collapsed as soon as pressure was put on it. Still political leaders seemed more interested in getting *any* agreement with social actors such as unions and employers rather than doing the right thing.

The changing fortunes of the Irish state and its people are a result of the political decisions that have been made. We saw in Chapter 6 that it is possible to trace the upturn in the economy to the decisions to open it up. Equally the failure to think beyond this model of development that was lauded around the world was down to short-term electoral thinking as political leaders were unwilling to dampen an over-heating economy. Nor did the Irish political establishment think that it needed a next stage of development. If a company discovers a successful new strategy, others will soon follow, and if that company does not develop new products or strategies then there is a good chance that company will go bankrupt. The same thing happened to Ireland. It thought it could rely on exports by foreign companies investing in the country. But Ireland needed to adapt to its new situation as a rich country and it should have been investing its own money and building up its own wealth. Instead the Irish sold houses to each other in transactions that transferred wealth from the young to the old.

The state lacked the ability to engage in strategic thinking. Even the National Development Plans had the appearance of a shopping list of electoral goodies rather than a serious attempt to plan for the country's future. There was no attempt to design the physical layout of the country and the legacy of the Celtic Tiger is an urban sprawl of nondescript housing estates and retail parks. The policy of decentralization of the bureaucratic system outside Dublin foundered because of the attempts to gain local electoral benefits. Nor could the state engage in original thinking. The political system tended to produce similar men and women who were necessarily obsessed with re-election. The bureaucratic system tended to produce intellectually capable but risk-averse men and women, who despite independence still looked to Britain for guidance on policy whenever new issues arose. In all major directions that Ireland took, it was reacting to events and the decisions taken reflected the triumph of politics over any other considerations.

Ireland risks talking itself down in the same way as it talked itself up. The situation in Ireland is a good deal better than in most other countries, and despite the downturn Ireland remains one of the wealthier countries in Europe. The social system, as we saw in Chapter 3, is still remarkably cohesive and stable, as is the political and democratic system studied in Chapters 4 and 5. As bankrupt as the Church is, it provided a moral compass for people to live their lives by, and it is not obvious that anything has replaced it except, as we saw in Chapter 7, an avid consumerism. Ireland embraced materialism with the devotion with which earlier generations idolized the Virgin Mary. Culturally it is now closer to Britain than it has ever been in its history. Almost a century after independence it is clear that Ireland is a region more than a sovereign state, and this openness has been to its benefit in the era of globalization. The Irish are a more tolerant people than they were and Ireland is a more interesting and pleasant place to live than it was. But it cannot stand still. If Ireland is going to take a new direction, that shift will come from politics. Many complain that Ireland no longer produces strong leaders in the way that the USA could produce a Roosevelt, Kennedy or Obama. This they blame on the political system – its institutional architecture and political culture.

At the start of this decade many books were published calling for a new republic or a second republic, all certain that the notional 'first' republic had failed its people in some way (see, for instance, O'Toole, 2011). Many of these are leftist aspirants irritated that their favoured policies have not been adopted, but there is also a strong and plausible sense that those running the state did so for themselves. The feeling is that a small elite was closely connected and designed policies to serve itself rather than its people. There is a sense that Ireland could be on the cusp of some radical changes.

Whether or not it is, we will have to wait and see.

# Recommended Reading

There are not as many books written about Ireland as about larger countries such as the USA, Germany, France, Spain or the UK. But Irish publishers have become more active in recent years, which mean that more and more books on Ireland are published every year. Below I give a selection of readings that the reader might choose to follow up for more detailed study (so as not to clutter the text with references and make the book more readable, bibliographic references are not included). These came from a variety of sources. Irish data mainly came from Central Statistics Office publications. Specific publications like the annual Statistical Abstract are particularly useful and freely available online. Comparative data come from the Eurostat, UN and OECD databases. Some others come from World Values Survey and the World Health Organization Many of the books listed below are also sources for much of the information contained in the text.

## 1 The Historical Context

A good introduction, though a bit outdated, that covers the whole span of Irish history is *The Oxford Illustrated History of Ireland* edited by R.F. Foster (1989). Foster (1988) also has a detailed general history concentrating on the period from 1600 to 1972. Lee (1989) has an excellent history of Ireland in the twentieth century, but Patterson's (2006) *Ireland since 1939* is an excellent and readable history of the modern period including up to the turn of the century. For a social and cultural history, Brown (2004) is excellent. For very readable versions of modern Irish politics especially in Fianna Fáil, see Collins (2001) and Leahy (2009).

## 2 Land and Peoples

There are many works on the Irish landscape and environment aimed at the general reader. Among the best is de Butléir's *Ireland's Wild Countryside* (1993). Woodcock (1994) has a geological history of Ireland. Bartley and Kitchen (2007) have a geographer's take on contemporary Ireland, though it might be too heavy on data for some readers. Dudley Edwards (2005) has *An*

*Atlas of Irish History* which also tells much about modern Ireland. Graham (1997) contains many interesting essays on Ireland's cultural geography. For an essay on 'Being Irish' see O'Kelly (2004). Language is discussed in essays in Britain (2007). McGarry and O'Leary (1995) provide perhaps the best overview of the Northern Ireland conflict. Shirlow and Murtagh (2006) have a study of segregation in Belfast which shows the urban geography of the Northern Ireland conflict.

## 3   The Changing Society

The best single book that looks at Irish society in some detail from the perspective of a sociologist is Sara O'Sullivan's (2005) edited volume *Contemporary Ireland*. It has chapters on a host of the issues discussed in this chapter. Inglis (1998) has an excellent if slightly outdated book on the position of the church in Ireland, as does Fuller (2002). Bruce Arnold (2009) has a terrific book on the way Irish authorities colluded with the church to imprison and abuse children. There are also some good autobiographical accounts of this. One of the first was Paddy Doyle's *The God Squad* (1988). There are many recent books outlining the attitudes of the Irish to social issues. These include Lyons (2008), Hilliard and Nic Giolla Phádraig (2007) and Garry, Hardiman and Payne (2006). Fahey, Russell and Whelan (2007) is an edited volume which looks at the impact of the Celtic Tiger, and as such may already be out of date. Goldthorpe and Whelan (1992) and Nolan, O'Connell and Whelan (2000) are earlier, similar volumes that together can be used to track changes in the economy and society. Heath, Breen and Whelan (1999) do something similar but compare the north and south of Ireland. For a discussion of crime in Ireland, the best book is O'Mahony (2002). The journalist Fintan O'Toole (2009) is always worth reading for his analysis of Irish society – *The Lie of the Land* (1997) has a good selection of his work.

## 4   Government and Policy Making

The standard text on Irish politics is Coakley and Gallagher's (2009) excellent *Politics in the Republic of Ireland*. It does not cover or compare Northern Ireland's politics, which Adshead and Tonge (2009) do in a single volume. Those interested in the structures of government and the public sector would do well to consult O'Toole and Dooney (2009), *Irish Government Today*. Byrne and McCutcheon (2009) provide an excellent and extensive introduction to the legal system in Ireland. A more basic introduction is Doolan (2007). There are not many recent discussion of the constitution. Litton (1988) and Farrell (1988) provide the best discussions for the general reader, and Morgan (2001) has a provocative take on the role of the judiciary.

## 5   Politics and Civil Society

There are a number of books on Irish political parties and elections. Collins (2001) and Leahy (2009) provide exciting descriptions of Fianna Fáil in power. Fine Gael is given a similar treatment by Rafter (2009). There is one major study of Irish voters by Marsh *et al.* (2008). After each election the *How Ireland Voted* series (Gallagher and Marsh 2003, 2008) provide in-depth yet accessible discussion of every aspect of the election. Fewer works are available on interest groups or surprisingly, social partnership. Hardiman's (1988) work is excellent if difficult and out-of-date. Allen (2000) is a tendentious but important critique of social partnership. There are some good essays on this in Adshead, Kirby and Millar (2008). There have been some popular books on the economic collapse including O'Toole (2009), Cooper (2009) and Ross (2009). These look at the relationship between banks, builders and Ireland's political elite and were best sellers in Ireland.

## 6   The Economy

Despite the Celtic Tiger being the subject of global interest, few works actually discuss the causes and consequences of the phenomenon in an accessible way. O'Hagan and Newman (2005) is the standard text on the Irish economy. Leddin and Walsh (2003) is a textbook for Irish economics students and contains a useful perspective on the Irish economy. Barry (1999) and Gray (1997) both attempt to explain the changes in the Irish economy but neither is very accessible, nor do they provide cogent explanations. O'Sullivan and Miller (2010) try to take positives from the economic miracle. A work that looks at Ireland's economic and political future is Burke and Lyons (2011). An excellent historical account of Ireland's economic development is found in Garvin (2004). Kirby (2010) has written a critique of the Irish economic system from a left wing perspective.

## 7   Culture and Lifestyle

Field Day is a publishing company that published works on literary criticism and culture in Ireland, and its works have been very influential. The best single book on Irish culture is Cleary and Connolly's (2005) *Companion to Modern Irish Culture*, although modern is taken to be less than 200 years old! The best known, but dense book on Irish literature is Kiberd (1995). The *Oxford Companion to Irish Literature,* edited by Welch (1996), is a general purpose reference. Irish dance is explored in Brennan (2004) and Irish traditional music is given an airing in *The Spire and Other Essays in Irish Culture* (Arnold, 2003).

Arnold (1969, 2003) has a general history of Irish art and essays on Irish culture. There are few serious examinations of Irish sport; Bairner (2005) is an exception. Irish cinema and how Ireland is represented in cinema is discussed in Pettitt (2000). The same is done for documentary film by O'Brien (2004).

# 8   Ireland and the World

Perhaps not surprisingly, very little has been written about Ireland's foreign relations in the formal sense. O'Sullivan (2006) and Crotty and Schmitt (2002) are exceptions. But there are works, some of them scholarly, on Ireland's relationship with the UK (Arthur 2000), the Americas (Byrne *et al.*, 2008), the EU (Laffan and O'Mahony, 2009) and the Middle East (O'Sullivan and Miller 2010). The relationship with the UN is explored in Kennedy and McMahon (2005). There are many more works on specific aspects of these relationships, many of which are merely sentimental. On the evolution of opinion of and on the Irish in America see Ignatiev (1995).

# Online Resources

Though many in rural Ireland complain about the problems of getting a decent broadband connection, Ireland and the Irish use the internet a great deal and there are a huge number of resources on Ireland available on the web. In addition I maintain an up-to-date list of links at http://webpages.dcu.ie/~omalle/ including links to popular Irish blogs.

## History

UCC history resources http://multitext.ucc.ie/
UCD archives http://www.ucd.ie/archives/
Trinity Library catalogue http://www.tcd.ie/Library/
National Archives http://www.nationalarchives.ie/
The National Library http://www.nli.ie

## Land and people

Geological Survey of Ireland: http://www.gsi.ie/
Heritage Ireland: http://www.heritageireland.ie/en/
An Taisce, the national trust: http://www.antaisce.org/
On Irish travellers: http://www.travellersrest.org/Travellers.htm

## Government and politics

The Irish State: http://www.gov.ie/
The Irish Constitution: http://www.constitution.ie/
The Dáil and Seanad: http://www.oireachtas.ie/parliament/
Politics discussion forum: http://www.politics.ie/
How the Irish voting system works:
   http://www.citizensassembly.bc.ca/flash/bc-stv-full.
A blog that aims to investigate corruption and malpractice in Ireland is
   http://thestory.ie/
A blog on the political system and policy is at www.politicalreform.ie
Irish election results are available at http://electionsireland.org/

## Economy and society

Ireland's national broadcaster, RTÉ: http://www.rte.ie/
The bestselling broadsheet, *Irish Independent:* http://www.independent.ie/
The *Irish Times:* http://www.irishtimes.com/
Central Statistics Office: www.cso.ie
Social research unit, ESRI: www.esri.ie
Social Science data archive: http://issda.ucd.ie/index.html
Tasc is a left-wing think tank that comments on social issues:
    http://www.tascnet.ie/
The National Economic and Social Council also publishes research on social
    and economic issues: http://www.nesc.ie/
Nama: http://www.nama.ie/
Nama explained: http://www.irishtimes.com/focus/2009/nama-explained/index.pdf
A property website that includes research on prices: www.daft.ie
A blog on the Irish economy: http://www.irisheconomy.ie/

## Sports, arts and culture

Gaelic games: http://www.gaa.ie/
Rugby:http://www.irishrugby.ie/
Football or soccer: http://www.fai.ie/
The National Theatre, the Abbey:- http://www.abbeytheatre.ie/
Irish traditional music and dance: http://comhaltas.ie/
National Library of Ireland: http://www.nli.ie
National Concert Hall: http://www.nch.ie/
Irish-English resource centre including accents: http://www.uni-due.de/IERC/
Irish culture and folklore including texts of some out-of-print books:
    http://www.libraryireland.com/
Irish Film Institute: http://www.irishfilm.ie/
Irish language: http://www.uni-due.de/DI/

# Bibliography

Adshead, Maura, Peadar Kirby and Michelle Millar (2008) *Contesting the State: lessons from the Irish case* (Manchester: Manchester University Press).

Adshead, Maura and Jon Tonge (2009) *Politics in Ireland: convergence and divergence in a two-polity island* (Basingstoke: Palgrave Macmillan).

Akerlof, George A. and Robert Shiller (2009) *Animal Instincts: how human psychology drives the economy, and why it matters for global capitalism* (Princeton: Princeton University Press).

Allen, Kieran (2000) *The Celtic Tiger: the myth of social partnership* (Manchester: Manchester University Press).

Andrews, Todd (1979) *Dublin Made Me* (Cork: Mercier Press).

Arnold, Bruce (1969) *A Concise History of Irish Art* (London: Thames & Hudson).

Arnold, Bruce (2003) *The Spire and Other Essays in Irish Culture* (Dublin: Liffey Press).

Arnold, Bruce (2009) *The Irish Gulag: how the state betrayed its innocent children* (Dublin: Gill & Macmillan).

Arthur, Paul (2000) *Special Relationships: Britain, Ireland and the Northern Ireland problem* (Belfast: Blackstaff Press).

Bairner, Alan (2005) *Sport and the Irish: histories, identities, issues* (Dublin: UCD Press).

Barry, Frank (ed.) (1999) *Understanding Ireland's Economic Growth* (Basingstoke: Palgrave).

Bartley, Brendan and Rob Kitchin (2007) *Understanding Contemporary Ireland* (London: Pluto).

Beckett, J.C. (1981) *The Making of Modern Ireland 1603–1923* (London: Faber & Faber).

Benoit, Kenneth and Laver, Michael (2005) 'Mapping the Irish policy space: voter and party spaces in preferential elections', *Economic and Social Review*, 36 (2) pp. 83–108.

Boyd, Andrew (1969) *Holy War in Belfast* (Tralee: Anvil Books).

Brennan, Helen (2004) *The Story of Irish Dance* (Dingle: Brandon Books).

Britain, David (ed.) (2007) *Language in the British Isles* (Cambridge: Cambridge University Press).

Brooks, David (2000) *Bobos in Paradise: the new upper class and how they got there* (New York: Simon & Schuster).

Brown, Terence (2004) *Ireland: A Social and Cultural History 1922–2002* (London: HarperCollins).

Burke, Ed and Ronan Lyons (eds) (2011) *Ireland after the Celtic Tiger: perspectives from the next generation* (Dublin: Blackhall).

Byrne, James P., Philip Coleman and Jason King (eds) (2008) *Ireland and the Americas: Culture, Politics and History* (Santa Barbara: ABC-CLIO).

Byrne, Raymond and Paul McCutcheon with Clare Bruton and Gerard Coffey (2009) *Byrne and McCutcheon on the Irish Legal System* (Dublin: Bloomsbury Professional).

Chubb, Basil (1992) *The Government and Politics of Ireland*, 3rd edn (London: Longman).

Cleary, Joe and Claire Connolly (eds) (2005) *The Cambridge Companion to Modern Irish Culture* (Cambridge: Cambridge University Press).

Coakley, John and Michael Gallagher (eds) (2010) *Politics in the Republic of Ireland*, 5th edn (Abingdon: Routledge).

Collins, Michael (1922) *The Path to Freedom* (Dublin: Talbot Press)

Collins, Stephen (2001) *Ireland: the power game – Ireland under Fianna Fáil* (Dublin: O'Brien Press).

Constitution Review Group (1996) *Report of the Constitution Review Group* (Dublin: Stationary Office).

Cooper, Matt (2009) *Who Really Runs Ireland? The story of the elite who led Ireland from bust to boom ... and back again* (Dublin: Penguin Ireland).

Corcoran, Mary (2004) 'The political preferences and value orientations of Irish journalists', *Irish Journal of Sociology*, Vol.13, No, 2, pp 23–42.

Crotty, William and David E. Schmitt (2002) *Ireland on the World Stage* (Harlow: Longman).

Davies, Norman (1999) *The Isles: a history* (London: Macmillan).

Dawkins, Richard (1997) 'Three herring gull chicks . . . the reason juries don't work' in *The Observer* (London), Sunday November 16.

de Butléir, Éamonn (1993) *Ireland's Wild Countryside* (Dublin & London: RTÉ & Tiger Books).

Doolan, Brian (2007) *Principles of Irish Law,* 7th edn (Dublin: Gill & Macmillan).

Doyle, Paddy (1988) *The God Squad* (Dublin: Raven Arts Press).

Dudley Edwards, Ruth (with Bridget Hourican) (2005) *An Atlas of Irish History,* 3rd edn (London: Routledge).

Duffy, Patrick J., David Edwards, and Elizabeth FitzPatrick (eds) (2001) *Gaelic Ireland, c. 1250–c.1650: land, lordship and settlement* (Dublin: Four Courts Press).

Eagleton, Terry (1999) *The Truth about the Irish* (Dublin: New Island Books).

Esping-Andersen, Gøsta (1990) *Three Worlds of Welfare Capitalism* (Oxford: Polity Press).

Fahey, Tony, Helen Russell and Christopher T. Whelan (eds) (2007) *Best of Times? The social impact of the Celtic Tiger* (Dublin: IPA).

Farmer, Roger E.A. (2010) *How the Economy Works: Confidence, Crashes, and Self-Fulfilling Prophecies* (New York: Oxford University Press).

Farrell, Brian (ed.) (1988) *De Valera's Constitution and Ours* (Thomas Davis Lectures) (Dublin: Gill & Macmillan).

Fitzpatrick, David (1989) *The Two Irelands, 1912–1939* (Oxford: Oxford University Press).

Foster, R.F. (1988) *Modern Ireland 1600–1972* (London: Allen Lane).

Foster, R.F. (ed.) (1989) *The Oxford Illustrated History of Ireland* (Oxford: Oxford University Press).

Foster, R.F. (2001) *The Irish Story: telling tales and making it up in Ireland* (London: Allen Lane).

Fuller, Louise (2002) *Irish Catholicism since 1950: the undoing of a culture* (Dublin: Gill & Macmillan).

Gallagher, Michael (1987) 'Does Ireland need a new electoral system?', *Irish Political Studies*, Vol 2, No. 1, pp. 27–48.

Gallagher, Michael, Michael Marsh and Paul Mitchell (eds) (2003) *How Ireland Voted 2002* (Basingstoke: Palgrave Macmillan).

Gallagher, Michael and Michael Marsh (eds.) (2008) *How Ireland Voted 2007: the full story of Ireland's general election* (Basingstoke: Palgrave Macmillan).

Garry, John, Niamh Hardiman and Diane Payne (eds) (2006) *Irish Social and Political Attitudes* (Liverpool: Liverpool University Press).

Garry, John (2006) 'Political Alienation' in J. Garry, N. Hardiman and D. Payne (eds.) *Irish Social and Political Attitudes* (Liverpool: Liverpool University Press).

Garvin, Tom (1981) *The Evolution of Irish Nationalist Politics* (Dublin: Gill & Macmillan).

Garvin, Tom (2004) *Preventing the Future: why was Ireland poor for so long?* (Dublin: Gill & Macmillan).

Goldthorpe, John (1987) *Social Mobility and Class Structure in Modern Britain* (Oxford: Clarendon Press).

Goldthorpe, John and Christopher T. Whelan (1992) *The Development of Industrial Society in Ireland* (Oxford: Oxford University Press).

Graham, Brian (ed.) (1997) *In Search of Ireland: a cultural geography* (London: Routledge).

Gray, Alan W. (ed.) (1997) *International Perspectives on the Irish Economy* (Dublin: Indecon).

Hallin, Daniel C. and Paolo Mancini (2004) *Comparing Media Systems: three models of media and politics* (Cambridge: Cambridge University Press).

Hardiman, Niamh (1988) *Pay, Politics and Economic Performance in the Republic of Ireland* (Oxford: Clarendon Press).

Heath, Anthony F., Richard Breen and Christopher T. Whelan (1999) *Ireland North and South: perspectives from social science* (Oxford: Oxford University Press).

Hilliard, Betty and Máire nic Giolla Phádraig (2007) *Changing Ireland in International Comparison* (Dublin: Liffey Press).

Ignatiev, Noel (1995) *How the Irish became White* (London: Routledge).

Inglis, Tom (1998) *Moral Monopoly: the rise and fall of the Catholic Church in modern Ireland* (Dublin: UCD Press).

Kennedy, Michael J. and Deirdre McMahon (eds) (2005) *Obligations and Responsibilities: Ireland and the United Nations, 1955–2005* (Dublin: IPA).

Kiberd, Declan (1995) *Inventing Ireland: the literature of the modern nation* (London: Jonathan Cape).

Kirby, Peadar (2010) *The Celtic Tiger in Collapse: explaining the weaknesses of the Irish Model* (Basingstoke: Palgrave Macmillan).

Laffan, Brigid and Jane O'Mahony (2009) *Ireland and the European Union* (Basingstoke: Palgrave Macmillan).

Leahy, Pat (2009) *Showtime: The Inside Story of Fianna Fáil in Power* (Dublin: Penguin Ireland).

Leddin, Anthony and Brendan Walsh (2003) *The Macroeconomy of the Eurozone: an Irish perspective* (Dublin: Gill & Macmillan).

Lee, J.J. (1989) *Ireland 1912–1985: politics and society* (Cambridge: Cambridge University Press).

Litton, Frank (ed.) (1988) *The Constitution of Ireland, 1937–1987* (Dublin: IPA).

Lyons, Pat (2008) *Public Opinion, Politics and Society in Contemporary Ireland* (Dublin: Irish Academic Press).

Mair, Peter (1992) 'Explaining the absence of class politics in Ireland' in J.H. Goldthorpe and C.T. Whelan (eds.) *The Development of Industrial Society in Ireland* (Oxford: The British Academy and Oxford University Press).

Marsh, Michael et al. (2008) *The Irish Voter: the nature of electoral competition in the Republic of Ireland* (Manchester: Manchester University Press).

McCartney, Donal (1986) 'The founding of the Gaelic League', in Liam de Paor (ed.) *Milestones in Irish History* (Cork: Mercier Press).

McGarry, John and Brendan O'Leary (1995) *Explaining Northern Ireland* (Oxford: Blackwell).

McWilliams, David (2006) *The Pope's Children: Ireland's new elite* (Dublin: Gill & Macmillan).

Miller, Kerby (2008) *Ireland and Irish America: culture, class, and transatlantic migration* (Dublin: Field Day).

Miller, Rory (ed.) (2008) *Ireland and the Middle East: trade, society and peace* (Dublin: Irish Academic Press).

Moody, T.W. (2001) 'Fenianism, Home Rule and the Land War: 1850–91' in T.W. Moody and F.X. Martin (eds), *The Course of Irish History* (Dublin: Mercier Press).

Morgan, David Gwynn (2001) *A Judgement Too Far? Judicial activism and the constitution* (Cork: Cork University Press).

Munck, Ronaldo (2006) 'Social class and inequality', in Sara O'Sullivan (ed.) *Contemporary Ireland: a sociological map* (Dublin: UCD Press).

Murray, C.H. (1990) *The Civil Service Observed* (Dublin: IPA).

Newton, Ken and Jan W. van Deth (2005) *Foundations of Comparative Politics: democracies of the modern world* (Cambridge: Cambridge University Press).

Nolan, Brian, Philip J. O'Connell and Christopher T. Whelan (eds) (2000) *Bust to Boom? The Irish experience of growth and inequality* (Dublin: IPA).

O'Brien, Harvey (2004) *The Real Ireland: the evolution of Ireland in documentary film* (Manchester: Manchester University Press).

Ó Corráin, Donnchadh (1989) 'Prehistoric and early Christian Ireland', in R.F. Foster (ed.) *The Oxford History of Ireland* (Oxford: Oxford University Press).

O'Hagan, John and Carol Newman (eds) (2005) *The Economy of Ireland: national and sectoral policy issues* (Dublin: Gill & Macmillan).

O'Hearn, Denis (1998) *Inside the Celtic Tiger: the Irish economy and the Asian model* (London: Pluto Press).

O'Kelly, Ciarán (2004) 'Being Irish', *Government and Opposition*, vol. 39 no.3, pp. 504–520.

O'Mahoney, Paul (2002) *Criminal Justice in Ireland* (Dublin IPA).

O'Sullivan, Michael J. (2006) *Ireland and the Global Question* (Cork: Cork University Press).

O'Sullivan, Michael J. and Rory Miller (eds) (2010) *What Did We Do Right? Global perspectives on Ireland's miracle* (Dublin: Blackhall).

O'Sullivan, Sara (ed.) (2005) *Contemporary Ireland: a sociological map* (Dublin UCD Press).

O'Toole, Fintan (1995) *Meanwhile Back at the Ranch: the politics of Irish beef* (London: Vintage).

O'Toole, Fintan (1997) *The Lie of the Land: Irish identities* (London: Verso).

O'Toole, Fintan (2009) *Ship of Fools: how stupidity and corruption sank the Celtic Tiger* (London: Faber & Faber).

O'Toole, Fintan (2011) *Enough is Enough: how to build a new republic* (London: Faber & Faber).

O'Toole, John and Seán Dooney (2009) *Irish Government Today*, 3rd edn (Dublin: Gill & Macmillan).

Patterson, Henry (2006) *Ireland since 1939: the persistence of conflict* (Dublin: Penguin Ireland).

Pettitt, Lance (2000) *Screening Ireland: film and television representation* (Manchester: Manchester University Press).

Rafter, Kevin (2009) *Fine Gael: party at the crossroads* (Dublin: New Island).

Raven, John. and Whelan, Christopher T. (1976) 'Irish adults' perceptions of their civic institutions' in J. Raven, C.T. Whelan, P.A. Pfretzschner and D.M. Borock (eds), *Political Culture in Ireland* (Dublin: IPA).

Richter, Michael (1986) 'The Norman Invasion' in Liam de Paor (ed.) *Milestones in Irish History* (Cork: Mercier Press).

Ross, Shane (2009) *The Bankers: how the banks brought Ireland to its knees* (Dublin: Penguin Ireland).

Saunders, Peter (1990) *Social Class and Stratification* (London: Routledge).

Shirlow, Pete and Brendan Murtagh (2006) *Belfast: segregation, violence and the city* (London: Pluto Press).

Sinnott, Richard and Fiachra Kennedy (2006) 'Irish social and political cleavages', in Garry, John, Niamh Hardiman and Diane Payne (eds) *Irish Social and Political Attitudes* (Liverpool: Liverpool University Press).

Szirmai, Adam (2005) *The Dynamics of Socio-Economic Development: an introduction* (Cambridge: Cambridge University Press).

Vallely, Fintan (ed.) (1999) *The Companion to Irish Traditional Music* (Cork: Cork University Press).

Varney, Sir David (2007) *Review of Tax Policy in Northern Ireland* (London: HM Stationery Office).

Welch, Robert (ed.) (1996) *The Oxford Companion to Irish Literature* (Oxford: Oxford University Press).

Whelan, C. T and Layte, R (2007) 'Opportunities for All in the New Ireland?' in *The Best of Times? The Social Impact of the Celtic Tiger* (Dublin: Institute of Public Administration).

Woodcock, Nigel (1994) *Geology and Environment in Britain and Ireland* (London: UCL Press).

# Index

*Note*: page numbers in *italics* indicate the subject of a box.